ABOUT THIS PUBLICATION

FOR SERVICE ASSISTANCE

Customer Service Department
704.898.0770

North Carolina General Statues is published by The Muliti-Media Group of Greater Charlotte in Charlotte, North Carolina. Copyright 2015 by the Multi-Media Group of Greater Charlotte. This book or parts thereof may not be reproduced in any form, stored in a retrieval system, or transmitted in any form by any means—electronic, mechanical, photocopy, recording or otherwise—without prior written permission of the publisher, except as provided by United States of America copyright law.

The records required by U.S. Code 2257(a) through (c) and the pertinent regulations 28 C.F.R. Cli. 1, Part 75 with respect to this publication and all materials associated with such records are maintained by The Multi-Media Group of Greater Charlotte, Publisher and available for review by Attorney General.

www.visionbooks.org

Copyright © 2015 by MMGGC
All rights reserved!

TID: 5031678
ISBN (10) digit: 1502598345
ISBN (13) digit: 978-1502598349

123-4-56789-01234-Paperback
123-4-56789-01234-Hardback

First Edition

090520140547

Printed in the United States of America

2015 EDITION

North Carolina Criminal Law And Procedure-Pamphlet # 20

Printed In conjunction with the Administration of the Courts

North Carolina Criminal Law and Procedure
Pamphlet Reference Guide

Chapters	Pamphlet
Chapter 1 Civil Procedure	1
Chapter 1 Civil Procedure (Continue)	2
Chapter 1A Rules of Civil Procedure	2
Chapter 1B Contribution.	2
Chapter 1C Enforcement of Judgments.	2
Chapter 1D Punitive Damages.	2
Chapter 1E Eastern Band of Cherokee Indians.	2
Chapter 1F North Carolina Uniform Interstate Depositions and Discovery Act.	2
Chapter 2 - Clerk of Superior Court [Repealed and Transferred.]	3
Chapter 3 - Commissioners of Affidavits and Deeds [Repealed.]	3
Chapter 4 - Common Law	3
Chapter 5 - Contempt [Repealed.]	3
Chapter 5A - Contempt	3
Chapter 6 - Liability for Court Costs	3
Chapter 7 - Courts [Repealed and Transferred.]	3
Chapter 7A – Judicial Department	3
Chapter 7A – Continuation (Judicial Department)	4
Chapter 7A – Continuation (Judicial Department)	5
Chapter 7B - Juvenile Code	5
Chapter 8 - Evidence	6
Chapter 8A - Interpreters for Deaf Persons [Recodified.]	6
Chapter 8B - Interpreters for Deaf Persons	6
Chapter 8C - Evidence Code	6
Chapter 9 - Jurors	6
Chapter 10 - Notaries [Repealed.]	6
Chapter 10A - Notaries [Recodified.]	6
Chapter 10B - Notaries	6
Chapter 11 - Oaths	6
Chapter 12 - Statutory Construction	6
Chapter 13 - Citizenship Restored	6
Chapter 14 - Criminal Law	7
Chapter 14 –Criminal Law (Continuation)	8
Chapter 15 - Criminal Procedure	9
Chapter 15A - Criminal Procedure Act (Continuation)	10
Chapter 15A - Criminal Procedure Act (Continuation)	11
Chapter 15B - Victims Compensation	11
Chapter 15C - Address Confidentiality Program	11
Chapter 16 - Gaming Contracts and Futures	11
Chapter 17 - Habeas Corpus	11

Chapter 17A - Law-Enforcement Officers [Recodified.]	11
Chapter 17B - North Carolina Criminal Justice Education and Training System [Recodified.] Chapter 17C - North Carolina Criminal Justice Education and Training Standards Commission	11
	11
Chapter 17D - North Carolina Justice Academy	11
Chapter 17E - North Carolina Sheriffs' Education and Training Standards Commission	11
Chapter 18 - Regulation of Intoxicating Liquors [Repealed.]	12
Chapter 18A - Regulation of Intoxicating Liquors [Repealed.]	12
Chapter 18B - Regulation of Alcoholic Beverages	12
Chapter 18C - North Carolina State Lottery	12
Chapter 19 - Offenses against Public Morals	12
Chapter 19A - Protection of Animals	12
Chapter 20 - Motor Vehicles	13
Chapter 20 - Motor Vehicles (Continuation)	14
Chapter 20 - Motor Vehicles (Continuation)	15
Chapter 20 - Motor Vehicles (Continuation)	16
Chapter 21 - Bills of Lading	17
Chapter 22 - Contracts Requiring Writing	17
Chapter 22A - Signatures	17
Chapter 22B - Contracts Against Public Policy	17
Chapter 22C - Payments to Subcontractors	17
Chapter 23 - Debtor and Creditor	17
Chapter 24 – Interest	17
Chapter 25 – Uniform Commercial Code	18
Chapter 25 – Uniform Commercial Code (Continuation)	19
Chapter 25A – Retail Installment Sales Act	20
Chapter 25B - Credit	20
Chapter 25C - Sales of Artwork	20
Chapter 26 - Suretyship	20
Chapter 27 - Warehouse Receipts [Repealed.]	20
Chapter 28 - Administration [Repealed.]	20
Chapter 28A - Administration of Decedents' Estates	20
Chapter 28B - Estates of Absentees in Military Service	20
Chapter 28C - Estates of Missing Persons	20
Chapter 29 - Intestate Succession	21
Chapter 30 - Surviving Spouses	21
Chapter 31 - Wills	21
Chapter 31A - Acts Barring Property Rights	21
Chapter 31B - Renunciation of Property and Renunciation of Fiduciary Powers Act	21
Chapter 31C - Uniform Disposition of Community Property Rights at Death Act	21
Chapter 32 - Fiduciaries	21
Chapter 32A - Powers of Attorney	21
Chapter 33 - Guardian and Ward [Repealed and Recodified.]	21

Chapter 33A - North Carolina Uniform Transfers to Minors Act	21
Chapter 33B - North Carolina Uniform Custodial Trust Act	21
Chapter 34 - Veterans' Guardianship Act	22
Chapter 35 - Sterilization Procedures	22
Chapter 35A - Incompetency and Guardianship	22
Chapter 36 - Trusts and Trustees [Repealed.]	22
Chapter 36A - Trusts and Trustees	22
Chapter 36B - Uniform Management of Institutional Funds Act [Repealed.]	22
Chapter 36C - North Carolina Uniform Trust Code	22
Chapter 36D - North Carolina Community Third Party Trusts, Pooled Trusts	23
Chapter 36E - Uniform Prudent Management of Institutional Funds Act	23
Chapter 37 - Allocation of Principal and Income [Repealed.]	23
Chapter 37A - Uniform Principal and Income Act	23
Chapter 38 - Boundaries	23
Chapter 38A - Landowner Liability	23
Chapter 38B - Trespasser Responsibility	23
Chapter 39 - Conveyances	23
Chapter 39A - Transfer Fee Covenants Prohibited	23
Chapter 40 - Eminent Domain [Repealed.]	23
Chapter 40A - Eminent Domain	23
Chapter 41 - Estates	23
Chapter 41A - State Fair Housing Act	23
Chapter 42 - Landlord and Tenant	23
Chapter 42A - Vacation Rental Act	23
Chapter 43 - Land Registration	23
Chapter 44 - Liens	24
Chapter 44A - Statutory Liens and Charges	24
Chapter 45 - Mortgages and Deeds of Trust	24
Chapter 45A - Good Funds Settlement Act	24
Chapter 46 - Partition	24
Chapter 47 - Probate and Registration	25
Chapter 47A - Unit Ownership	25
Chapter 47B - Real Property Marketable Title Act	25
Chapter 47C - North Carolina Condominium Act	25
Chapter 47D - Notice of Settlement Act [Expired.]	25
Chapter 47E - Residential Property Disclosure Act	25
Chapter 47F - North Carolina Planned Community Act	25
Chapter 47G - Option to Purchase Contracts	25
Chapter 47H - Contracts for Deed	25
Chapter 48 - Adoptions +	26
Chapter 48A - Minors	26
Chapter 49 - Bastardy	26
Chapter 49A - Rights of Children	26
Chapter 50 - Divorce and Alimony	26

Chapter 50A - Uniform Child-Custody Jurisdiction and Enforcement Act	26
Chapter 50B - Domestic Violence	26
Chapter 50C - Civil No-Contact Orders	26
Chapter 51 - Marriage	26
Chapter 52 - Powers and Liabilities of Married Persons	27
Chapter 52A - Uniform Reciprocal Enforcement of Support Act [Repealed.]	27
Chapter 52B - Uniform Premarital Agreement Act	27
Chapter 52C - Uniform Interstate Family Support Act	27
Chapter 53 - Banks	27
Chapter 53A - Business Development Corporations and North Carolina Capital Resource Corporations	28
Chapter 53B - Financial Privacy Act	28
Chapter 54 - Cooperative Organizations	28
Chapter 54A - Capital Stock Savings and Loan Associations [Repealed.]	28
Chapter 54B - Savings and Loan Associations	29
Chapter 54C - Savings Banks	29
Chapter 55 - North Carolina Business Corporation Act	30
Chapter 55A - North Carolina Nonprofit Corporation Act	31
Chapter 55B - Professional Corporation Act	31
Chapter 55C - Foreign Trade Zones	31
Chapter 55D - Filings, Names, and Registered Agents for Corporations, Nonprofit Corporations, and Partnerships	31
Chapter 56 - Electric, Telegraph and Power Companies [Repealed.]	31
Chapter 57 - Hospital, Medical and Dental Service Corporations [Recodified.]	31
Chapter 57A - Health Maintenance Organization Act [Recodified.]	31
Chapter 57B - Health Maintenance Organization Act [Recodified.]	31
Chapter 57C - North Carolina Limited Liability Company Act.	31
Chapter 58 - Insurance.	32
Chapter 58 - Insurance (Continuation)	33
Chapter 58 - Insurance (Continuation)	34
Chapter 58 - Insurance (Continuation)	35
Chapter 58 - Insurance (Continuation)	36
Chapter 58 - Insurance (Continuation)	37
Chapter 58 - Insurance (Continuation)	38
Chapter 58A - North Carolina Health Insurance Trust Commission [Recodified.]	38
Chapter 59 - Partnership.	39
Chapter 59B - Uniform Unincorporated Nonprofit Association Act.	39
Chapter 60 - Railroads and Other Carriers [Repealed and Transferred.]	39
Chapter 61 - Religious Societies	39

Chapter 62 - Public Utilities	39
Chapter 62 - Public Utilities (Continuation)	40
Chapter 62A - Public Safety Telephone Service And Wireless Telephone Service	40
Chapter 63 - Aeronautics	40
Chapter 63A - North Carolina Global TransPark Authority	40
Chapter 64 - Aliens	40
Chapter 65 – Cemeteries	40
Chapter 66 - Commerce and Business	41
Chapter 67 - Dogs	41
Chapter 68 - Fences and Stock Law	41
Chapter 69 - Fire Protection	41
Chapter 70 - Indian Antiquities, Archaeological Resources and Unmarked Human Skeletal Remains Protection	42
Chapter 71 - Indians [Repealed.]	42
Chapter 71A - Indians	42
Chapter 72 - Inns, Hotels and Restaurants	42
Chapter 73 - Mills	42
Chapter 74 - Mines and Quarries	42
Chapter 74A - Company Police [Repealed.]	42
Chapter 74B - Private Protective Services Act [Repealed.]	42
Chapter 74C - Private Protective Services	42
Chapter 74D - Alarm Systems	42
Chapter 74E - Company Police Act	42
Chapter 74F - Locksmith Licensing Act	42
Chapter 74G - Campus Police Act	42
Chapter 75 - Monopolies, Trusts and Consumer Protection	42
Chapter 75A - Boating and Water Safety	43
Chapter 75B - Discrimination in Business	43
Chapter 75C - Motion Picture Fair Competition Act	43
Chapter 75D - Racketeer Influenced and Corrupt Organizations	43
Chapter 75E - Unlawful Activities in Connection With Certain Corporate Transactions	43
Chapter 76 - Navigation	43
Chapter 76A - Navigation and Pilotage Commissions	43
Chapter 77 - Rivers, Creeks, and Coastal Waters	43
Chapter 78 - Securities Law [Repealed.]	43
Chapter 78A - North Carolina Securities Act	43
Chapter 78B - Tender Offer Disclosure Act [Repealed.]	43
Chapter 78C - Investment Advisers	43
Chapter 78D - Commodities Act	43
Chapter 79 - Strays [Repealed.]	43
Chapter 80 - Trademarks, Brands, etc.	44
Chapter 81 - Weights and Measures [Recodified.]	44
Chapter 81A - Weights and Measures Act of 1975.	44
Chapter 82 - Wrecks [Repealed.]	44

Chapter 83 - Architects [Recodified.]	44
Chapter 83A - Architects	44
Chapter 84 - Attorneys-at-Law	44
Chapter 84A - Foreign Legal Consultants	44
Chapter 85 - Auctions and Auctioneers [Repealed.]	44
Chapter 85A - Bail Bondsmen and Runners [Recodified.]	44
Chapter 85B - Auctions and Auctioneers	44
Chapter 85C - Bail Bondsmen and Runners [Recodified.]	44
Chapter 86 - Barbers [Recodified.]	44
Chapter 86A - Barbers	44
Chapter 87 - Contractors	44
Chapter 88 - Cosmetic Art [Repealed.]	44
Chapter 88A - Electrolysis Practice Act	44
Chapter 88B - Cosmetic Art	45
Chapter 89 - Engineering and Land Surveying [Recodified.]	45
Chapter 89A - Landscape Architects	45
Chapter 89B - Foresters	45
Chapter 89C - Engineering and Land Surveying	45
Chapter 89D - Landscape Contractors	45
Chapter 89E - Geologists Licensing Act	45
Chapter 89F - North Carolina Soil Scientist Licensing Act	45
Chapter 89G - Irrigation Contractors	45
Chapter 90 - Medicine and Allied Occupations	45
Chapter 90 - Medicine and Allied Occupations (Continuation)	46
Chapter 90 - Medicine and Allied Occupations (Continuation)	47
Chapter 90 - Medicine and Allied Occupations (Continuation)	48
Chapter 90A - Sanitarians and Water and Wastewater Treatment Facility Operators	48
Chapter 90B - Social Worker Certification and Licensure Act	48
Chapter 90C - North Carolina Recreational Therapy Licensure Act	48
Chapter 90D - Interpreters and Transliterators	48
Chapter 91 - Pawnbrokers [Repealed.]	48
Chapter 91A - Pawnbrokers Modernization Act of 1989	48
Chapter 92 - Photographers [Deleted.]	48
Chapter 93 - Certified Public Accountants	48
Chapter 93A - Real Estate License Law	49
Chapter 93B - Occupational Licensing Boards	49
Chapter 93C - Watchmakers [Repealed.]	49
Chapter 93D - North Carolina State Hearing Aid Dealers and Fitters Board.	49
Chapter 93E - North Carolina Appraisers Act	49
Chapter 94 - Apprenticeship	49
Chapter 95 - Department of Labor and Labor Regulations	49
Chapter 95 - Department of Labor and Labor Regulations (Continuation)	50
Chapter 96 - Employment Security	50
Chapter 97 - Workers' Compensation Act	50

Chapter	Page
Chapter 97 - Workers' Compensation Act (Continuation)	51
Chapter 98 - Burnt and Lost Records	51
Chapter 99 - Libel and Slander	51
Chapter 99A - Civil Remedies for Criminal Actions	51
Chapter 99B - Products Liability	51
Chapter 99C - Actions Relating to Winter Sports Safety and Accidents	51
Chapter 99D - Civil Rights	51
Chapter 99E - Special Liability Provisions	51
Chapter 100 - Monuments, Memorials and Parks	51
Chapter 101 - Names of Persons	51
Chapter 102 - Official Survey Base	51
Chapter 103 - Sundays, Holidays and Special Days	51
Chapter 104 - United States Lands	51
Chapter 104A - Degrees of Kinship	51
Chapter 104B - Hurricanes or Other Acts of Nature	51
Chapter 104C - Atomic Energy, Radioactivity and Ionizing Radiation [Repealed and Recodified.]	51
Chapter 104D - Southern States Energy Compact	51
Chapter 104E - North Carolina Radiation Protection Act	51
Chapter 104F - Southeast Interstate Low-Level Radioactive Waste Management Compact [Repealed]	51
Chapter 104G - North Carolina Low-Level Radioactive Waste Management Authority Act of 1987 [Repealed]	51
Chapter 105 - Taxation	51
Chapter 105 - Taxation (Continuation)	52
Chapter 105 - Taxation (Continuation)	53
Chapter 105 - Taxation (Continuation)	54
Chapter 105A - Setoff Debt Collection Act	55
Chapter 105B - Defaulted Student Loan Recovery Act	55
Chapter 106 - Agriculture	55
Chapter 106 - Agriculture (Continue)	56
Chapter 106 - Agriculture (Continue)	57
Chapter 107 - Agricultural Development Districts [Repealed.]	57
Chapter 108 - Social Services [Repealed and Recodified.]	57
Chapter 108A - Social Services	57
Chapter 108B - Community Action Programs	58
Chapter 108C Medicaid and Health Choice Provider Requirements.	58
Chapter 108D Medicaid Managed Care for Behavioral Health Services.	58
Chapter 109 - Bonds [Recodified.]	58
Chapter 110 - Child Welfare	58
Chapter 111 - Aid to the Blind	58
Chapter 112 - Confederate Homes and Pensions [Repealed.]	58
Chapter 113 - Conservation and Development	58

Chapter 113 - Conservation and Development (Continuation)	59
Chapter 113A - Pollution Control and Environment	59
Chapter 113A - Pollution Control and Environment (Continuation)	60
Chapter 113B - North Carolina Energy Policy Act of 1975	60
Chapter 114 - Department of Justice	60
Chapter 115 - Elementary and Secondary Education [Repealed.]	60
Chapter 115A - Community Colleges, Technical Institutes, and Industrial Education Centers [Repealed.]	60
Chapter 115B - Tuition and Fee Waivers	60
Chapter 115C - Elementary and Secondary Education	60
Chapter 115C - Elementary and Secondary Education (Continuation)	61
Chapter 115C - Elementary and Secondary Education (Continuation)	62
Chapter 115C - Elementary and Secondary Education (Continuation)	63
Chapter 115D - Community Colleges	63
Chapter 115E - Private Educational Facilities Finance Act [Recodified]	63
Chapter 116 - Higher Education	63
Chapter 116 - Higher Education (Continuation)	63
Chapter 116A - Escheats and Abandoned Property [Repealed.]	64
Chapter 116B - Escheats and Abandoned Property	64
Chapter 116C - Continuum of Education Programs	64
Chapter 116D - Higher Education Bonds	64
Chapter 117 - Electrification	64
Chapter 118 - Firemen's and Rescue Squad Workers' Relief and Pension Funds [Recodified.]	64
Chapter 118A - Firemen's Death Benefit Act [Repealed.]	64
Chapter 118B - Members of a Rescue Squad Death Benefit Act [Repealed.]	64
Chapter 119 - Gasoline and Oil Inspection and Regulation	64
Chapter 120 - General Assembly	65
Chapter 120 - General Assembly (Continuation)	66
Chapter 120 - General Assembly (Continuation)	67
Chapter 120C - Lobbying	67
Chapter 121 - Archives and History	67
Chapter 122 - Hospitals for the Mentally Disordered [Repealed.]	67
Chapter 122A - North Carolina Housing Finance Agency	67
Chapter 122B - North Carolina Agricultural Facilities Finance Act [Repealed.]	67
Chapter 122C - Mental Health, Developmental Disabilities, and Substance Abuse Act of 1985	67
Chapter 122C - Mental Health, Developmental Disabilities, and Substance Abuse Act of 1985 (Continuation)	68

Chapter 122D - North Carolina Agricultural Finance Act	68
Chapter 122E - North Carolina Housing Trust and Oil Overcharge Act	68
Chapter 123 - Impeachment	69
Chapter 123A - Industrial Development [Repealed.]	69
Chapter 124 - Internal Improvements	69
Chapter 125 - Libraries	69
Chapter 126 - State Personnel System	69
Chapter 127 - Militia [Repealed.]	69
Chapter 127A - Militia	69
Chapter 127B - Military Affairs	69
Chapter 127C - Advisory Commission on Military Affairs	69
Chapter 128 - Offices and Public Officers	69
Chapter 128 - Offices and Public Officers (Continuation)	70
Chapter 129 - Public Buildings and Grounds	70
Chapter 130 - Public Health [Repealed.]	70
Chapter 130A - Public Health	70
Chapter 130A - Public Health (Continuation)	71
Chapter 130A - Public Health (Continuation)	72
Chapter 130B - Hazardous Waste Management Commission [Repealed.]	72
Chapter 131 - Public Hospitals [Repealed.]	72
Chapter 131A - Health Care Facilities Finance Act	72
Chapter 131B - Licensing of Ambulatory Surgical Facilities [Repealed.]	72
Chapter 131C - Charitable Solicitation Licensure Act [Repealed.]	72
Chapter 131D - Inspection and Licensing of Facilities	72
Chapter 131E - Health Care Facilities and Services	72
Chapter 131E - Health Care Facilities and Services (Continuation)	73
Chapter 131F - Solicitation of Contributions	73
Chapter 132 - Public Records	73
Chapter 133 - Public Works	74
Chapter 134 - Youth Development [Recodified.]	74
Chapter 134A - Youth Services [Repealed.]	74
Chapter 135 - Retirement System for Teachers and State Employees; Social Security; Health Insurance Program for Children	74
Chapter 135 - Retirement System for Teachers and State Employees; Social Security; Health Insurance Program for Children	75
Chapter 136 - Transportation	75
Chapter 136 - Transportation (Continuation)	76
Chapter 137 - Rural Rehabilitation [Repealed.]	76
Chapter 138 - Salaries, Fees and Allowances	76
Chapter 138A - State Government Ethics Act	76

Chapter 139 - Soil and Water Conservation Districts	76
Chapter 140 - State Art Museum; Symphony and Art Societies	76
Chapter 140A - State Awards System	76
Chapter 141 - State Boundaries	76
Chapter 142 - State Debt	76
Chapter 143 - State Departments, Institutions, and Commissions	77
Chapter 143 - State Departments, Institutions, and Commissions (Continuation)	78
Chapter 143 - State Departments, Institutions, and Commissions (Continuation)	79
Chapter 143 - State Departments, Institutions, and Commissions (Continuation)	80
Chapter 143A - State Government Reorganization	80
Chapter 143B - Executive Organization Act of 1973	80
Chapter 143B - Executive Organization Act of 1973 (Continuation)	81
Chapter 143B - Executive Organization Act of 1973 (Continuation)	82
Chapter 143C - State Budget Act	83
Chapter 143D - The State Governmental Accountability and Internal Control Act	83
Chapter 144 - State Flag, Official Governmental Flags, Motto, and Colors	83
Chapter 145 - State Symbols and Other Official Adoptions.	83
Chapter 146 - State Lands	83
Chapter 147 - State Officers	83
Chapter 148 - State Prison System	84
Chapter 149 - State Song and Toast	84
Chapter 150 - Uniform Revocation of Licenses [Repealed.]	84
Chapter 150A - Administrative Procedure Act [Recodified.]	84
Chapter 150B - Administrative Procedure Act	84
Chapter 151 - Constables [Repealed.]	84
Chapter 152 - Coroners	84
Chapter 152A - County Medical Examiner [Repealed.]	84
Chapter 152A - County Medical Examiner [Repealed.] (Continuation)	85
Chapter 153 - Counties and County Commissioners [Repealed.]	85
Chapter 153A - Counties	85
Chapter 153B - Mountain Resources Planning Act	85
Chapter 153C - Uwharrie Regional Resources Act	85
Chapter 154 - County Surveyor [Repealed.]	85
Chapter 155 - County Treasurer [Repealed.]	85
Chapter 156 - Drainage	85

Chapter 156 – Drainage (Continuation)	86
Chapter 157 - Housing Authorities and Projects	86
Chapter 157A - Historic Properties Commissions [Transferred.]	86
Chapter 158 - Local Development	86
Chapter 159 - Local Government Finance	86
Chapter 159 - Local Government Finance (Continuation)	87
Chapter 159A - Pollution Abatement and Industrial Facilities Financing Act [Unconstitutional.]	87
Chapter 159B - Joint Municipal Electric Power and Energy Act	87
Chapter 159C - Industrial and Pollution Control Facilities Financing Act	87
Chapter 159D - The North Carolina Capital Facilities Financing Act	87
Chapter 159E - Registered Public Obligations Act	87
Chapter 159F - North Carolina Energy Development Authority [Repealed.]	87
Chapter 159G - Water Infrastructure	87
Chapter 159H - [Reserved.]	87
Chapter 159I - Solid Waste Management Loan Program and Local Government Special Obligation Bonds	87
Chapter 160 - Municipal Corporations [Repealed And Transferred.]	87
Chapter 160A - Cities and Towns	88
Chapter 160A - Cities and Towns (Continuation)	89
Chapter 160B - Consolidated City-County Act	89
Chapter 160C - Baseball Park Districts [Repealed.]	90
Chapter 161 - Register of Deeds	90
Chapter 162 - Sheriff	90
Chapter 162A - Water and Sewer Systems	90
Chapter 162B Continuity of Local Government in Emergency.	90
Chapter 163 Elections and Election Laws.	90
Chapter 163 Elections and Election Laws. (Continuation)	91
Chapter 164 Concerning the General Statutes of North Carolina.	92
Chapter 165 Veterans.	92
Chapter 166 Civil Preparedness Agencies [Repealed.]	92
Chapter 166A North Carolina Emergency Management Act.	92
Chapter 167 State Civil Air Patrol [Repealed.]	92
Chapter 168 Persons with Disabilities.	92
Chapter 168A Persons With Disabilities Protection Act.	92

Chapter 25A.

Retail Installment Sales Act.

§ 25A-1. Scope of act.

This Chapter applies only to consumer credit sales as hereinafter defined, except that G.S. 25A-37, referral sales, applies to all sales of goods or services as provided therein. This Chapter does not apply to a bona fide direct loan transaction in which a lender makes a direct loan to a borrower, and such lender is not regularly engaged, directly or indirectly, in the sale of goods or the furnishing of services as defined in this Chapter.

Except for G.S. 25A-37, referral sales, those sales defined in G.S. 25A-2(b), and those sales with amounts financed in excess of twenty-five thousand dollars ($25,000) under G.S. 25A-2(a)(5), this Chapter does not apply to any party or transaction that is not also subject to the provisions of the Consumer Credit Protection Act (Federal Truth-in-Lending Act). (1971, c. 796, s. 1; 1983, c. 686, s. 1; 2005-338, s. 1.)

§ 25A-2. "Consumer credit sale" defined.

(a) Except as provided in subsection (c) of this section, a "consumer credit sale" is a sale of goods or services in which

(1) The seller is one who in the ordinary course of business regularly extends or arranges for the extension of consumer credit, or offers to extend or arrange for the extension of such credit,

(2) The buyer is a natural person,

(3) The goods or services are purchased primarily for a personal, family, household or agricultural purpose,

(4) Either the debt representing the price of the goods or services is payable in installments or a finance charge is imposed, and

(5) The amount financed does not exceed seventy-five thousand dollars ($75,000) or, in the case of a debt secured by real property or a manufactured home as defined in G.S. 143-145(7), regardless of the amount financed.

(b) "Sale" includes but is not limited to any contract in the form of a bailment or lease if the bailee or lessee contracts to pay as compensation for use a sum substantially equivalent to or in excess of the aggregate value of the goods and services involved, and it is agreed that the bailee or lessee will become, or for no other or for a nominal consideration, has the option to become, the owner of the goods and services upon full compliance with his obligations under such contract.

The term also includes a contract in the form of a terminable bailment or lease of goods or services in which the bailee or lessee can renew the bailment or lease contract periodically by making the payment or payments specified in the contract if:

(1) The contract obligates the bailor or lessor to transfer ownership of the property to the bailee or lessee for no other or a nominal consideration (no more than ten percent (10%) of the cash price of the property at the time the bailor or lessor initially enters into the contract with the bailee or lessee) upon the making of a specified number of payments by the bailee or lessee; and

(2) The dollar total of the specified number of payments necessary to exercise the purchase option is more than ten percent (10%) in excess of the aggregate value of the property and services involved. For the purposes of this subsection, the value of goods shall be the average cash retail value of the goods. The value of services shall be the average retail value, if any, of such services, as determined by substantial cash sales of such services. If a contract is found to be a sale under this subsection, these values shall be used to determine the amount financed for purposes of G.S. 25A-15.

(c) A sale in which the seller allows the buyer to purchase goods or services pursuant to a credit card issued by someone other than a seller that is engaged in part or entirely in the business of selling goods or services or similar arrangement is not a consumer credit sale. A sale in which the seller allows the buyer to purchase goods or services pursuant to a credit card issued by the seller, a subsidiary or a parent corporation of the seller, a principal supplier of the seller or any corporation having shareholders in common with the seller holding over twenty-five percent (25%) of the voting stock in each corporation is a consumer credit sale within the terms of this Chapter.

(d) For the purposes of this Chapter, a consumer credit sale shall be deemed to have been made in this State, and therefore subject to the provisions of this Chapter, if the seller offers or agrees in this State to sell to a buyer who is a resident of this State, or if such buyer accepts or makes the offer in this State to buy, regardless of the situs of the contract as specified therein.

Any solicitation or communication to sell, oral or written, originating outside of this State, but forwarded to and received in this State by a buyer who is a resident of this State, shall be deemed to be an offer or agreement to sell in this State.

Any solicitation or communication to buy, oral or written, originating within this State, from a buyer who is a resident of this State, but forwarded to and received by a retail seller outside of this State, shall be deemed to be an acceptance or offer to buy in this State.

(e) If an advertisement for a terminable bailment or lease defined as a sale in subsection (b) above states the amount of any payment, the advertisement must also clearly and conspicuously state the following items, as applicable:

(1) A statement that the transaction advertised is a lease;

(2) The total amount of periodic payments necessary to acquire ownership or a statement that the consumer has the option to purchase the property and at what time;

(3) That the consumer acquires no ownership rights if either the property is not leased for the term required for ownership to transfer or the terms of purchase are not otherwise satisfied.

If an advertisement for a terminable bailment or lease defined as a sale in subsection (b) above refers to the right to acquire ownership, the advertisement must clearly and conspicuously state whether or not the consumer may terminate the lease at any time without penalty and that the consumer acquires no ownership rights if either the property is not leased for the term required for ownership to transfer or the terms of purchase are not otherwise satisfied.

No one shall advertise in connection with any terminable bailment or lease defined as a sale in subsection (b) above the ownership option as a means of deceiving any lessee into believing that he is purchasing the item of personal property. (1971, c. 796, s. 1; 1979, c. 706, s. 1; 1981, c. 970, s. 2; 1983, c. 686, ss. 2, 3; 1987, c. 282, s. 5; 1991, c. 602, s. 1; 2005-338, s. 2.)

§ 25A-3. "Payable in installments" defined.

A debt is "payable in installments" when the buyer is required or permitted by agreement to make payment in more than four installments, excluding a down payment, and whether or not a finance charge is imposed by the seller. (1971, c. 796, s. 1.)

§ 25A-4. "Goods" defined.

(a) "Goods" means all things which are moveable at the time of the sale or at the time the buyer takes possession, including goods not in existence at the time the transaction is entered into and goods which are furnished or used at the time of sale or subsequently in modernization, rehabilitation, repair, alteration, improvement or construction on real property so as to become a part thereof whether or not they are severable therefrom. "Goods" also includes merchandise certificates.

(b) "Merchandise certificate" means a writing issued by a seller not redeemable in cash and usable in its face amount in lieu of cash in exchange for goods and services. (1971, c. 796, s. 1.)

§ 25A-5. "Services" defined.

(a) "Services" includes:

(1) Work, labor, and other personal services; and

(2) Privileges with respect to transportation, hotel and restaurant accommodations, education, entertainment, recreation, physical culture, hospital accommodations, funerals and other similar services.

(b) "Services" does not include:

(1) Services for which the cost is by law fixed or approved by or filed with or subject to approval or disapproval by the United States or the State of North Carolina or any agency, instrumentality or subdivision thereof;

(2) Insurance premiums financing covered by G.S. 58-35-1 through G.S. 58-35-95 and 58-3-145; or

(3) Insurance provided by an insurer that is licensed to do business in this State. (1971, c. 796, s. 1.)

§ 25A-6. "Seller" defined.

"Seller" means one regularly engaged in the business of selling goods or services. Unless otherwise provided, "seller" also means and includes an assignee of the seller's right to payment but use of the term does not itself impose on an assignee any obligation of the seller with respect to events occurring before the assignment. (1971, c. 796, s. 1.)

§ 25A-7. "Cash price" defined.

"Cash price" of goods and services means the price at which the goods or services are offered for sale by the seller to cash buyers in the ordinary course of business and may include:

(1) Applicable sales, use, and excise and documentary stamp taxes; and

(2) The cash price of accessories or related services such as installation, delivery, servicing, repairs or alterations. (1971, c. 796, s. 1.)

§ 25A-8. "Finance charge" defined.

(a) "Finance charge" means the sum of all charges payable directly or indirectly by the buyer and imposed by the seller as an incident to the extension of credit, including any of the following types of charges which are applicable:

(1) Interest, time price differential, service, carrying or other similar charge however denominated;

(2) Premium or other charges for any guarantee or insurance protecting the seller against the buyer's default or other credit loss;

(3) Loan fee, finder's fee or similar charge; and

(4) Fee for an appraisal, investigation or credit report.

(b) Finance charge does not include transfer of equity fees, substitution of collateral fees, default or deferment charges, or additional charges for insurance as permitted by G.S. 25A-17 or charges for insurance excluded by Section 226.4(a) of Regulation Z promulgated pursuant to section 105 of the Consumer Credit Protection Act.

(c) With respect to a transaction in which the seller acquires a security interest in real property, finance charge does not include charges excluded by section 226.4(e) of Regulation Z promulgated pursuant to section 105 of the Consumer Credit Protection Act. (1971, c. 796, s. 1.)

§ 25A-9. "Amount financed" defined.

(a) "Amount financed" means the total of the following to the extent that payment is deferred by the seller:

(1) The cash price of the goods or services less the amount of any down payment whether made in cash or property traded in,

(2) The amount actually paid or to be paid by the seller pursuant to an agreement with the buyer to discharge a security interest or lien on property traded in,

(3) Additional charges for insurance described in G.S. 25A-8(b) and charges referred to in G.S. 25A-8(c), and

(4) Official fees as described in G.S. 25A-10, to the extent they are itemized and disclosed to the buyer.

(b) If not included in the cash price, the amount financed includes any applicable sales, use or documentary stamp taxes and any amount actually paid or to be paid by the seller for registration, certificate of title or license fees. (1971, c. 796, s. 1.)

§ 25A-10. "Official fees" defined.

"Official fees" means:

(1) Fees and charges prescribed by law which actually are or will be paid to public officials for determining the existence of or for perfecting, releasing, or satisfying a security interest related to a consumer credit sale; or

(2) Premiums payable for insurance in lieu of perfecting a security interest otherwise required by the seller in connection with a consumer credit sale if the premium does not exceed the fees or charges described in subdivision (1) of this section which would otherwise be payable. (1971, c. 796, s. 1.)

§ 25A-11. "Revolving charge account contract" defined.

"Revolving charge account contract" means an agreement or understanding between a seller and a buyer under which consumer credit sales may be made from time to time, under the terms of which a finance charge or service charge is to be computed in relation to the buyer's unpaid balance from time to time, and under which the buyer has the privilege of paying the balance in full or in installments. This definition shall not affect the meaning of the term "revolving charge account" appearing in G.S. 24-11(a). (1971, c. 796, s. 1.)

§ 25A-12. "Consumer credit installment sale contract" defined.

"Consumer credit installment sale contract" means the agreement between a buyer and a seller in a consumer credit sale other than a sale made pursuant to a revolving charge account. (1971, c. 796, s. 1.)

§ 25A-13. "Consumer Credit Protection Act" defined.

"Consumer Credit Protection Act" means the Consumer Credit Protection Act, an act of Congress of May 29, 1968, as amended (Public Law 90-321; 82 Stat. 146; 15 U.S.C. 1601 et seq.), and regulations and rulings promulgated thereunder. (1971, c. 796, s. 1.)

§ 25A-14. Finance charge rates and service charge for revolving charge account contracts.

(a) The finance-charge rate and either the annual charge or the monthly service charge for a consumer credit sale made under a revolving charge account contract may not exceed the rates and charge provided for revolving credit by G.S. 24-11.

(b) In the event the revolving charge account contract is secured in whole or in part by a security interest in real property, then the finance-charge rate shall not exceed the rate set out in G.S. 25A-15(d).

(c) No default or deferral charge shall be imposed by the seller in connection with a revolving charge-account contract, except as specifically provided for in G.S. 24-11(d1). (1971, c. 796, s. 1; 1983, c. 126, s. 7; 1991, c. 506, s. 7.)

§ 25A-15. Finance charge rates for consumer credit installment sale contracts.

(a) With respect to a consumer credit installment sale contract, a seller may contract for and receive a finance charge not exceeding that permitted by this section. For the purposes of this section, the finance charge rates are the rates that are required to be disclosed by the Consumer Credit Protection Act.

(b) Except as hereinafter provided, the finance charge rate for a consumer credit installment sales contract may not exceed:

(1) Twenty-four percent (24%) per annum where the amount financed is less than one thousand five hundred dollars ($1,500);

(2) Twenty-two percent (22%) per annum where the amount financed is one thousand five hundred dollars ($1,500) or greater, but less than two thousand dollars ($2,000);

(3) Twenty percent (20%) where the amount financed is two thousand ($2,000) or greater, but less than three thousand dollars ($3,000);

(4) Eighteen percent (18%) per annum where the amount financed is three thousand dollars ($3,000) or greater,

except that a minimum finance charge of five dollars ($5.00) may be imposed.

(c) A finance charge rate not to exceed the higher of the rate established in subsection (b) or the rate set forth below may be imposed in a consumer credit installment sale contract repayable in not less than six installments for a self-propelled motor vehicle:

(1) Eighteen percent (18%) per annum for vehicles one and two model years old;

(2) Twenty percent (20%) per annum for vehicles three model years old;

(3) Twenty-two percent (22%) per annum for vehicles four model years old; and

(4) Twenty-nine percent (29%) per annum for vehicles five model years old and older.

A motor vehicle is one model year old on January 1 of the year following the designated year model of the vehicle.

(d) Notwithstanding the provisions of subsections (b) and (c), above, in the event that the amount financed in a consumer credit sale contract is secured in whole or in part by a security interest in real property, the finance charge rate may not exceed sixteen percent (16%) per annum.

(e) A seller may not divide a single credit sale transaction into two or more sales to avoid the limitations as to maximum finance charges imposed by this section.

(f) Notwithstanding the provisions of subsections (b) or (d), the parties to a consumer credit installment sale contract for the sale of a residential manufactured home which is secured by a first lien on that home or on the land on which such home is located may contract in writing for the payment of a finance charge as agreed upon by the parties. Provided, this subsection shall only apply if the parties would have been entitled to so contract by the provisions of section 501 of United States Public Law 96-221, and have complied with the regulations promulgated thereto.

For the purposes of this subsection (f), a "residential manufactured home" means a mobile home as defined in G.S. 143-145(7) which is used as a dwelling. (1971, c. 796, s. 1; 1979, 2nd Sess., c. 1330, ss. 1, 2; 1981, c. 446, ss. 1-3; 1983, c. 126, s. 2.)

§ 25A-16. Transfer of equity.

If a buyer voluntarily transfers his rights in collateral pursuant to applicable law and the seller agrees, the seller may impose a transfer fee not to exceed ten percent (10%) of the unpaid balance of the debt or thirty-five dollars ($35.00), whichever is less. (1971, c. 796, s. 1; 2000-169, s. 31.)

§ 25A-17. Additional charges for insurance.

(a) As to revolving charge account contracts defined in G.S. 25A-11, in addition to the finance charges permitted in G.S. 24-11(a), a seller in a consumer credit sale may contract for and receive additional charges or premiums (i) for insurance written in connection with any consumer credit sale, against loss of or damage to property securing the debt pursuant to G.S. 25A-23, provided a clear, conspicuous and specific statement in writing is furnished by the seller to the buyer setting forth the cost of the insurance if obtained from or through the seller and stating that the buyer may choose the insurer through which the insurance is obtained; (ii) for credit life, credit accident and health, or credit unemployment insurance, written in connection with any consumer credit sale, provided the insurance coverage is not required by the seller and this fact is clearly disclosed to the buyer, and any buyer desiring such insurance coverage gives affirmative indication of such desire after disclosure of the cost of such insurance.

(b) As to revolving charge account contracts defined in G.S. 25A-11, insurance that is required by a seller and is not an additional charge permitted by subsection (a) of this section, shall be included in the finance charge as computed according to G.S. 24-11(a).

(c) As to consumer credit installment sale contracts defined in G.S. 25A-12, in addition to the finance charges permitted in G.S. 25A-15, a seller in a consumer credit sale may contract for and receive additional charges or premiums (i) for insurance written in connection with any consumer credit sale, for loss of or damage to property or against liability arising out of the ownership or use of property, provided a clear, conspicuous and specific statement in writing is furnished by the seller to the buyer setting forth the cost of the insurance if obtained from or through the seller and stating that the buyer may choose the person through which the insurance is to be obtained; (ii) for credit life, credit accident and health, or credit unemployment insurance, written in connection with any consumer credit sale, provided the insurance coverage is not required by the seller and this fact is clearly and conspicuously disclosed in writing to the buyer; and any buyer desiring such insurance coverage gives specific dated and separately signed affirmative written indication of such desire after receiving written disclosure to him of the cost of such insurance. (1971, c. 796, s. 1; 1993, c. 226, s. 15.)

§ 25A-18. Confession of judgment.

A buyer may not authorize any person to confess judgment on a claim arising out of a consumer credit sale. An authorization in violation of this section is void. (1971, c. 796, s. 1.)

§ 25A-19. Acceleration.

With respect to a consumer credit sale, the agreement may not provide for repossession of any goods or acceleration of the time when any part or all of the time balance becomes payable other than for breach by the buyer of any promise or condition clearly set forth in the agreement. (1971, c. 796, s. 1.)

§ 25A-20. Disclaimer of warranty.

With respect to any consumer credit sale, the agreement may not contain any provision limiting, excluding, modifying or in any manner altering the terms of any express warranty given by any seller (excluding assignees) to any buyer and made a part of the basis of the bargain between the original parties. (1971, c. 796, s. 1.)

§ 25A-21. Attorneys' fees.

With respect to a consumer credit sale:

(1) In the event that the seller institutes a suit and prevails in the litigation and obtains a money judgment, the presiding judge shall allow a reasonable attorney's fee to the duly licensed attorney representing the seller in such suit, said attorney's fee to be taxed to the buyer as part of the court costs.

(2) In the event that a seller instituting suit does not prevail in the litigation, the presiding judge shall allow a reasonable attorney's fee to the duly licensed attorney representing the buyer in such suit, said attorney's fee to be taxed to the seller as a part of the court costs. (1971, c. 796, s. 1.)

§ 25A-22. Receipts for payments; return of title documents upon full payment.

(a) When any payment is made under any consumer credit sale transaction, the person receiving such payment shall, if the payment is made in cash, give the buyer a written receipt therefor. If the buyer specifies that the payment is made on one of several obligations, the receipt shall so state.

(b) Upon the payment of all sums for which the buyer is obligated under a consumer credit sale, the seller shall promptly release any security interest in accordance with the terms of G.S. 25-9-513 or G.S. 20-58.4, whichever is applicable. In the event a security interest in real property is involved, the seller shall take such action as is necessary to enable the lien to be discharged of record under the provisions of G.S. 45-37. (1971, c. 796, s. 1; 2000-169, s. 32.)

§ 25A-23. Collateral taken by the seller.

(a) The seller in a consumer credit sale may take a security interest only in the following property of the buyer to secure the debt arising from the sale:

(1) The property sold,

(2) Property previously sold by the seller to the buyer and in which the seller has an existing security interest,

(3) Personal property to which the property sold is installed, if the amount financed is more than three hundred dollars ($300.00),

(4) Real property to which the property sold is affixed, if the amount financed is more than one thousand dollars ($1,000), and

(5) A self-propelled motor vehicle to which repairs are made, if the amount financed exceeds one hundred dollars ($100.00).

(6) Any property which is used for agricultural purposes, if the property sold is to be used in the operation of an agricultural business.

(b) A security interest taken in property other than that permitted in subsection (a) of this section shall be void and not enforceable.

(c) Nothing in this section shall affect any right or liens granted by Chapter 44A of the General Statutes.

(d) The provisions of G.S. 24-11(a), limiting the taking of a security interest in property under an open end credit or similar plan, shall not apply to revolving charge account contracts regulated by this Chapter; provided, however, the application of payments rule set out in G.S. 25A-27 shall apply to such contracts; provided further, that in any action initiated by the seller for the possession of such property, a judgment for the possession thereof shall be restricted to commercial units (as defined in G.S. 25-2-105(6)) for which the cash price was one hundred dollars ($100.00) or more. (1971, c. 796, s. 1; 1977, c. 508; c. 789, s. 1.)

§ 25A-24. Identification of instruments of indebtedness.

With respect to consumer credit sales, each instrument of indebtedness shall be identified on the face of the instrument as a consumer credit document, or otherwise clearly indicate on its face that it arises out of a consumer credit sale, provided, that such designation of an instrument of indebtedness regarding as sale which is not by definition a "consumer credit sale," shall not solely because of such designation cause the transaction to be a consumer credit sale. (1971, c. 796, s. 1.)

§ 25A-25. Preservation of consumers' claims and defenses.

(a) In a consumer credit sale, a buyer may assert against the seller, assignee of the seller, or other holder of the instrument or instruments of indebtedness, any claims or defenses available against the original seller, and the buyer may not waive the right to assert these claims or defenses in connection with a consumer credit sales transaction. Affirmative recovery by the buyer on a claim asserted against an assignee of the seller or other holder of the instrument of indebtedness shall not exceed amounts paid by the buyer under the contract.

(b) Every consumer credit sale contract shall contain the following provision in at least ten-point boldface type:

NOTICE

ANY HOLDER OF THIS CONSUMER CREDIT CONTRACT IS SUBJECT TO ALL CLAIMS AND DEFENSES WHICH THE DEBTOR COULD ASSERT AGAINST THE SELLER OF GOODS OR SERVICES OBTAINED PURSUANT HERETO OR WITH THE PROCEEDS HEREOF. RECOVERY HEREUNDER

BY THE DEBTOR SHALL NOT EXCEED AMOUNTS PAID BY THE DEBTOR HEREUNDER.

(c) Compliance with the requirements of the Federal Trade Commission rule on preservation of consumer claims and defenses is considered full compliance with this act. (1971, c. 796, s. 1; 1977, c. 921.)

§ 25A-26. Substitution of collateral.

Subject to the provisions of G.S. 25A-23, if all involved parties agree, there may be a substitution of collateral under a security instrument in a consumer credit sale. For such substitution, the seller may impose a fee not to exceed ten percent (10%) of the unpaid balance of the debt or fifteen dollars ($15.00), whichever is less. (1971, c. 796, s. 1.)

§ 25A-27. Application of payments.

(a) Where a seller in a consumer credit sale makes a subsequent sale to a buyer and takes a security interest pursuant to G.S. 25A-23 in goods previously purchased by the buyer from the seller, the seller shall make application of payments received, for the purpose of determining the amount of the debt secured by the various security interests, as follows:

(1) The entire amount of all payments made prior to such subsequent purchase shall be deemed to have been applied to the previous purchases, and

(2) Unless otherwise designated by the buyer, the amount of down payment on such subsequent purchase shall be applied to the subsequent purchase, and

(3) All subsequent payments shall be applied first to finance charges and then to principal. The application of payments to principal shall be applied to the various purchases on the basis that the first sums paid in shall be deemed applied to the oldest purchase or obligation assumed to satisfy the original debt secured by the purchase money security interest until payment is received in full and other payments shall be applied accordingly to all other purchases in the order that each obligation is assumed. At the time any original debt would have

been satisfied by subsequent payments, the purchase money security interest in said purchase shall be extinguished.

(b) Where a seller and a buyer agree to consolidate two or more consumer credit installment sale contracts pursuant to G.S. 25A-31, the seller shall apply payments received, for the purpose of determining the amount of the debt secured by the various security interests, as follows:

(1) The entire amount of all payments received prior to the consolidation shall be applied to the respective contracts under which the payments were made, and

(2) All subsequent payments shall be applied first to finance charges and then to principal. The application of payments to principal shall be applied to the various purchases on the basis that the first sums paid in shall be deemed applied to the oldest purchase or obligation assumed to satisfy the original debt secured by the purchase money security interest until payment is received in full and other payments shall be applied accordingly to all other purchases in the order that each obligation is assumed. At the time any original debt would have been satisfied by subsequent payments, the purchase money security interest in said purchase shall be extinguished.

(c) For payments received by a seller on or after October 1, 1988, but before October 1, 1993, a seller may elect to apply the provisions of this section as the section read October 1, 1993, or as the section read September 30, 1993. A seller made this election when the seller determined, and disclosed to the buyer, how payments received on a consumer credit sale would be applied: either on a proportional basis or on a "first in - first out" basis with the payments applied first to finance charges and then to principal in the order that each obligation is assumed.

(d) The exclusive remedy for failure of a seller to apply payments of a buyer as required by subdivision (a)(3) or (b)(2) of this section during the period October 1, 1993, through October 1, 1996, is an order that the seller apply the payments as required by those provisions. (1971, c. 796, s. 1; 1993, c. 370, s. 2; 1993 (Reg. Sess., 1994), c. 745, s. 38.3(a).)

§ 25A-28. Form of consumer credit installment sale contract.

Every consumer credit installment sale contract shall be in writing, dated and signed by the buyer. (1971, c. 796, s. 1.)

§ 25A-29. Default charges.

If any installment is past due for 10 days or more according to the original terms of the consumer credit installment sale contract, a default charge may be made in an amount not to exceed five percent (5%) of the installment past due or six dollars ($6.00), whichever is the lesser. A default charge may be imposed only one time for each default.

If a default charge is deducted from a payment made on the contract and such deduction results in a subsequent default on a subsequent payment, no default charge may be imposed for such default.

If a default charge has been once imposed with respect to a particular default in payment, no default charge shall be imposed with respect to any future payments which would not have been in default except for the previous default.

A default charge for any particular default shall be deemed to have been waived by the seller unless, within 45 days following the default, (i) the charge is collected or (ii) written notice of the charge is sent to the buyer. (1971, c. 796, s. 1.)

§ 25A-30. Deferral charges.

(a)   A seller may, by agreement with the buyer, defer the due date of all or any part of one or more installments under an existing consumer credit installment sale contract.

(b)   Except as provided by subsections (e) and (f) of this section, a deferral agreement must be in writing, dated and signed by the parties.

(c)   A deferral agreement may provide for a deferral charge not to exceed the rate of one and one-half percent (1 1/2%) of each installment for each month from the date which such installment or part thereof would otherwise have been payable to the date when such installment or part thereof is made payable under the deferral agreement.

(d)   If a deferral charge is made pursuant to a deferral agreement, a default charge provided in G.S. 25A-29 may be imposed only if the installment as deferred is not paid when due and no new deferral agreement is entered into with respect to that installment.

(e)   If the deferral agreement extends the due date of only one installment, the agreement need not be in writing.

(f)   A deferral agreement for which no charge is made shall not be subject to subsections (b), (c) or (d) of this section. (1971, c. 796, s. 1.)

§ 25A-31. Consolidation and refinancing.

(a)   A seller and a buyer may agree at any time to refinance an existing consumer credit installment sale contract or to consolidate into a single debt repayable on a single schedule of payments, two or more consumer credit installment sale contracts.

(b)   A refinancing or consolidation agreement must be in writing, dated and signed by the parties.

(c)   The refinancing or consolidation agreement may provide for a finance charge which shall not exceed the rates provided in G.S. 25A-15, with the amount financed being the unpaid time balance of the contract or contracts refinanced or consolidated, less the rebate provided by G.S. 25A-32. In computing the rebate to be credited to the previous time balances for purposes of this section, no prepayment charge shall be imposed. (1971, c. 796, s. 1.)

§ 25A-32. Rebates on prepayment.

Notwithstanding any provision in a consumer credit installment sale contract to the contrary, any buyer may satisfy the debt in full at any time before maturity, and in so satisfying such debt, shall receive a rebate, the amount of which shall be computed under the "rule of 78's," as follows:

"The amount of such rebate shall represent as great a proportion of the finance charge (less a prepayment charge of ten percent (10%) of the unpaid balance, not to exceed twenty-five dollars ($25.00)) as the sum of the periodical time balances after the date of prepayment in full bears to the sum of all the periodical time balances under the schedule of payments in the original contract." No rebate is required if the amount thereof is less than one dollar ($1.00).

If the prepayment is made otherwise than on the due date of an installment, it shall be deemed to have been made on the installment due date nearest in time to the actual date of payment.

If a seller obtains a judgment on a debt arising out of a consumer credit installment sale or the seller repossesses the collateral securing the debt, the seller shall credit the buyer with a rebate as if the payment in full had been made on the date the judgment was obtained or 15 days after the repossession occurred. If the seller obtains a judgment and repossesses the collateral, the seller shall credit the buyer with a rebate as if payment in full had been made on the date of the judgment or 15 days after the repossession, whichever occurs earlier. (1971, c. 796, s. 1.)

§ 25A-32.1. Unearned finance charge credits on prepayment of loans secured by real property and mobile home loans.

(a) Notwithstanding any statutory or contractual provision to the contrary, in a consumer credit installment sale contract with an amount financed of five thousand dollars ($5000.00) or more secured by real estate or by a residential manufactured home as defined in G.S. 143-145(7), any buyer may satisfy the debt in full at any time before maturity, and in so satisfying the debt, shall be credited with all unearned finance charges as computed on the simple interest or actuarial method.

(b) If a seller obtains a judgment on a debt arising out of a consumer credit installment sale described in subsection (a) of this section, or if the seller forecloses or repossesses the collateral securing the debt, the seller shall credit the buyer with all unearned finance charges as computed on the simple interest or actuarial method as if the payment in full had been made on the date the judgment was obtained or 15 days after the foreclosure or repossession occurred, whichever is earlier. If the seller obtains a judgment and repossesses the collateral, the seller shall credit the buyer with all unearned finance charges as if payment in full had been made on the date of the judgment or 15 days after the repossession, whichever occurs earlier. (1991, c. 602, s. 2.)

§ 25A-33. Terms of payments.

A consumer credit installment sale contract shall provide for complete payment of all charges due under the contract, including the amount financed, the finance charge, and additional insurance charges, if any, within a period from the time of the sale of

(1) Forty-two months, if the amount financed is less than one thousand five hundred dollars ($1,500), or

(2) Sixty-four months, if the amount financed is one thousand five hundred dollars ($1,500) or greater, but less than two thousand five hundred dollars ($2,500), or

(3) One hundred and twenty-two months, if the amount financed is two thousand five hundred dollars ($2,500) or greater, but less than five thousand dollars ($5,000), or

(4) One hundred and eighty-two months, if the amount financed is five thousand dollars ($5,000) or greater, but less than ten thousand dollars ($10,000), or

(5) As the contract provides, if the amount financed is ten thousand dollars ($10,000) or greater.

The provisions of this section shall not apply to a consumer credit installment sale contract executed in connection with any financing which is insured under regulations of the Federal Housing Administration or the Veterans Administration. (1971, c. 796, s. 1; 1973, c. 1446, s. 3.)

§ 25A-34. Balloon payments.

With respect to a consumer credit sale, other than one pursuant to a revolving charge account, no scheduled payment may be more than ten percent (10%) (except the final payment may be twenty-five percent (25%)) larger than the average of earlier scheduled payments. This provision does not apply when the payment schedule is adjusted to the seasonal or irregular income of the buyer. (1971, c. 796, s. 1.)

§ 25A-35. Statement of account.

(a) One time during each 12-month period following execution of a consumer credit installment sale contract and when the buyer repays the debt early, the buyer shall be entitled upon request and without charge to a statement of account from the seller. The statement of account shall contain the following information identified as such in the statement:

(1) The itemized amounts paid by or on behalf of the buyer to the date of the statement of account, except that upon early termination of the contract by prepayment or otherwise, the statement shall include itemized charges for expenses of repossession, storage and legal expenses;

(2) The itemized amounts, if any, which have become due but remain unpaid, including any charges for defaults, expenses of repossession and deferral charges;

(3) The number of installment payments and the dollar amount of each installment not due but still to be paid and the remaining period the contract is to run.

(b) The buyer may request and shall be entitled to additional statements of account but for such additional statements the seller may impose a charge of one dollar ($1.00).

(c) If the buyer requests information for income tax purposes as to the amount of the finance charges, the seller shall provide such information within 30 days without charge but only once in each calendar year. (1971, c. 796, s. 1.)

§ 25A-36. Certificates of insurance and rebates.

(a) Within 45 days following the purchase of insurance by the buyer from or through the seller, the seller shall deliver, send or cause to be sent to the buyer a policy or policies of such insurance or a certificate or certificates thereof. If such insurance is cancelled, or the premium adjusted, any rebate received by the seller shall be promptly applied to the purchase of other similar insurance, credited to the buyer's account, or rebated to the buyer. Unless otherwise required by law or the provisions of the policy, rebates of cancelled insurance shall be computed under the rule of 78's, without the deduction of a prepayment charge.

(b) In those cases where the insurance premium is added in the contract, and the buyer did not actually pay the premium, the return premium plus unearned finance charge on the amount of returned premium (at the same rate as used in the contract) shall be credited to the unpaid balance of the contract. If the required insurance premium is adjusted upward by the insurance company or is added in accordance with the contract, the buyer, after 10 days' notice,

(1) May pay the additional premium, or

(2) Have the additional premium plus finance charge (at the same rate as used in the contract) added to the unpaid balance and spread equally over the remaining installments unpaid, provided, the seller may require a buyer who wishes to finance such additional premium to be financed by the seller in accordance with North Carolina insurance regulations. (1971, c. 796, s. 1; 1977, c. 650.)

§ 25A-37. Referral sales.

The advertisement for sale or the actual sale of any goods or services (whether or not a consumer credit sale) at a price or with a rebate or payment or other consideration to the purchaser that is contingent upon the procurement of prospective customers provided by the purchaser, or the procurement of sales to persons suggested by the purchaser, is declared to be unlawful. Any obligation of a buyer arising under such a sale shall be void and a nullity and a buyer shall be entitled to recover from the seller any consideration paid to the seller upon tender to the seller of any tangible consumer goods made the basis of the sale. (1971, c. 796, s. 1.)

§ 25A-38. "Home-solicitation sale" defined.

"Home-solicitation sale" means a consumer credit sale of goods or services in which the seller or a person acting for him engages in a personal solicitation of the sale at a residence of the buyer and the buyer's agreement or offer to purchase is there given to the seller or a person acting for him. It does not include

(1)   A sale made to a buyer who has previously engaged in a similar business transaction with the seller;

(2)   A sale made pursuant to a preexisting revolving charge account;

(3)   A sale made pursuant to negotiations between the parties on the premises of a business establishment at a fixed location where such goods or services are offered or exhibited for sale;

(4)   A sale which is regulated by the provisions of Section 226.9 of Regulation Z promulgated pursuant to Section 105 of the Consumer Credit Protection Act; or

(5)   Sales of personal wearing apparel, motor vehicles defined in G.S. 20-286(10), farm equipment and goods and services to be utilized within 10 days in connection with funeral services. (1971, c. 796, s. 1; 1973, c. 672.)

§ 25A-39. Buyer's right to cancel.

(a)   Except as provided in subsection (e) of this section, in addition to any right otherwise to revoke an offer, the buyer has the right to cancel a home-solicitation sale until midnight of the third business day after the day on which the buyer signs an agreement or offer to purchase which complies with G.S. 25A-40, or which complies with the requirements of the Federal Trade Commission Trade Regulation Rule Concerning a Cooling-Off Period for Door-to-Door Sales.

(b)   Cancellation occurs when the buyer gives written notice of cancellation to the seller at the address stated in the agreement or offer to purchase.

(c) Notice of cancellation, if given by mail, is given when it is deposited in the United States mail properly addressed and postage prepaid.

(d) Unless the seller complies with G.S. 25A-40(b), notice of cancellation given by the buyer need not take a particular form and is sufficient if it indicates by any form of written expression the intention of the buyer not to be bound by the home-solicitation sale.

(e) The buyer may not cancel a home-solicitation sale if the buyer requests the seller in a separate writing to provide goods or services without delay because of an urgency or an emergency, and

(1) The seller in good faith makes a substantial beginning of performance of the contract before the buyer gives notification of cancellation,

(2) In the case of goods, the goods cannot be returned to the seller in substantially as good condition as when received by the buyer, and

(3) Unless the buyer returns the goods, if any, to the seller at his expense.

(f) A buyer, who has not received delivery of the goods and services from the seller in a home-solicitation sale within 30 days following the execution of the contract (and such delay is the fault of the seller), shall have the right at any time thereafter before acceptance of the goods and services to rescind the contract and to receive a refund of all payments made and to a return of all goods traded in to the seller on account of or in contemplation of such contract, or if the goods traded in cannot or are not returned to the buyer within 10 days after cancellation, the buyer may elect to recover an amount equal to the trade-in allowance stated in the contract. By written agreement, the buyer may agree to a later time for the delivery of goods and services. (1971, c. 796, s. 1; 1975, c. 805, s. 1.)

§ 25A-40. Form of agreement or offer; statement of buyer's rights.

(a) In a home-solicitation sale the seller must present to the buyer and obtain his signature to a fully completed written agreement or offer to purchase which is in the same language as that principally used in the oral sales presentation and which designates as the date of the transaction the date on which the buyer actually signs and which contains the name and address of the seller, and which contains in immediate proximity to the space reserved for the signature of the buyer in bold face type of a minimum size of 10 points, a statement in substantially the following form:

"You, the buyer, may cancel this transaction at any time prior to midnight of the third business day after the date of this transaction. See the attached Notice of Cancellation form for an explanation of this right."

(b)   The seller must, in addition to furnishing the buyer with a copy of the contract or offer to purchase, furnish to the buyer at the time he signs the home-solicitation sale contract or otherwise agrees to buy consumer goods or services from the seller, a completed form in duplicate, captioned "Notice of Cancellation," which shall be attached to the contract and easily detachable, and which shall contain in 10 point bold face type the following information and statements in the same language as that used in the contract:

"Notice of Cancellation

(enter date of transaction)

_____

(date)

You may cancel this transaction, without any penalty or obligation, within three business days from the above date.

If you cancel, any property traded in, and payments made by you under the contract or sale, and any negotiable instrument executed by you will be returned within 10 business days following receipt by the seller of your cancellation notice, and any security interest arising out of the transaction will be canceled.

If you cancel, you must make available to the seller at your residence, in substantially as good condition as when received, any goods delivered to you under this contract or sale; or you may, if you wish, comply with the instructions of the seller regarding the return shipment of the goods at the seller's expense and risk.

If you do make the goods available to the seller and the seller does not pick them up within 20 days of the date of your notice of cancellation, you may retain or dispose of the goods without any further obligation. If you fail to make the goods available to the seller, or if you agree to return the goods to the seller and fail to do so, then you remain liable for performance of all obligations under the contract.

To cancel this transaction, mail or deliver a signed and dated copy of this cancellation notice or any other written notice, or send a telegram to _____

(name of seller)

at_____,

(address of seller's place of business)

not later than midnight of _____

(date)

I hereby cancel this transaction.

_____

(date)

_____

(Buyer's Signature)"

(1971, c. 796, s. 1; 1975, c. 805, s. 2.)

§ 25A-41. Restoration of down payment; retention of goods.

(a) Except as provided in this section, within 10 business days after a home-solicitation sale has been canceled or an offer to purchase revoked in accordance with G.S. 25A-40, the seller must tender to the buyer any payments made by the buyer and any note or other evidence of indebtedness.

(b) If the down payment includes goods traded in, the goods must be tendered at the buyer's residence in substantially as good condition as when received by the seller. If the seller fails to tender the goods as provided by this section, the buyer may elect to recover an amount equal to the trade-in allowance stated in the agreement.

(c) Repealed by Session Laws 1975, c. 805, s. 3.

(d) Until the seller has complied with the obligations imposed by this section, the buyer may retain possession of goods delivered to him by the seller and has a lien on the goods in his possession or control for any recovery to which he is entitled. (1971, c. 796, s. 1; 1975, c. 805, s. 3.)

§ 25A-42. Duties as to care and return of goods; no compensation for services prior to cancellation.

(a) Except as provided by the provisions on retention of goods by the buyer (G.S. 25A-41(d)), within a reasonable time after a home-solicitation sale has been canceled, the buyer must make available to the seller at the buyer's residence in substantially as good condition as received, any goods delivered under the contract or sale, or in the alternative, the buyer may comply with the instructions of the seller regarding the return shipment of the goods at the seller's expense and risk. The seller shall within 10 business days of receipt of the buyer's notice of cancellation notify the buyer whether the seller intends to repossess or to abandon any shipped or delivered goods. If the buyer makes the goods available to the seller and the seller does not pick them up within 20 days of the date of the notice of cancellation, the buyer may retain or dispose of the goods without any further obligation. If the buyer fails to make the goods available to the seller, or agrees to return the goods to the seller and fails to do so, then the buyer shall remain liable for performance of all obligations under the contract.

(b) The buyer has the duty of a bailee to take reasonable care of the goods in his possession before cancellation or revocation and for a reasonable time thereafter, during which time the goods are otherwise at the seller's risk.

(c) If the seller has performed any services pursuant to a home-solicitation sale prior to its cancellation, the seller is entitled to no compensation therefor.

(d) The seller shall not negotiate, transfer, sell, or assign any note, contract, or other evidence of indebtedness arising out of a home-solicitation sale to a finance company or other third party prior to midnight of the fifth business day following the day the contract was signed or the goods or services were purchased. (1971, c. 796, s. 1; 1975, c. 805, s. 4.)

§ 25A-43. Unconscionability.

(a) With respect to a consumer credit sale, if the court finds the agreement or any clause of the agreement to have been unconscionable at the time it was made, the court may refuse to enforce the agreement, or it may enforce the remainder of the agreement without the unconscionable clause, or it may so limit the application of any unconscionable clause as to avoid any unconscionable result.

(b) If it is claimed or appears to the court that the agreement or any clause thereof may be unconscionable, all parties shall be afforded a reasonable opportunity to present evidence as to its setting, purpose and effect to aid the court in making its determination.

(c) As used in this section, "unconscionable" shall mean totally unreasonable under all of the circumstances. (1971, c. 796, s. 1.)

§ 25A-44. Remedies and penalties.

In addition to remedies hereinbefore provided, the following remedies shall apply to consumer credit sales:

(1) In the event that a consumer credit sale contract requires the payment of a finance charge not more than two times in excess of that permitted by this

Chapter, the seller or an assignee of the seller shall not be permitted to recover any finance charge under that contract and, in addition, the seller shall be liable to the buyer in an amount that is two times the amount of any finance charge that has been received by the seller, plus reasonable attorney's fees incurred by the buyer as determined by the court. However, if the requirement of an excess charge results from an accidental or good faith error, the seller shall be liable only for the amount by which the finance charge exceeds the rates permitted by this Chapter.

(2)   In the event that a consumer credit sale contract requires the payment of a finance charge more than two times that permitted by this Chapter, the contract shall be void. The buyer may, at his option, retain without any liability any goods delivered under such a contract and the seller or an assignee of the rights shall not be entitled to recover anything under such contract.

(3)   In the event the seller or an assignee of the seller (i) shall fail to make any rebate required by G.S. 25A-32 or G.S. 25A-36, (ii) shall charge and receive fees or charges in excess of those specifically authorized by this Chapter, or (iii) shall charge and receive sums not authorized by this Chapter, the buyer shall be entitled to demand and receive the rebate due and excessive or unauthorized charges. Ten days after receiving written request therefor, the seller shall be liable to the buyer for an amount equal to three times the sum of any rebate due and all improper charges which have not been rebated or refunded within the 10-day period.

(4)   The knowing and willful violation of any provision of this Chapter shall constitute an unfair trade practice under G.S. 75-1.1.

(5)   Any buyer injured by any violation of G.S. 25A-2(e) may bring an action for recovery of damages, including reasonable attorney's fees. (1971, c. 796, s. 1; 1983, c. 686, s. 4.)

§ 25A-45. Conflict with Consumer Credit Protection Act.

In all cases of irreconcilable conflict between the provisions of this Chapter and the provisions of the Consumer Credit Protection Act, the provisions of the Consumer Credit Protection Act shall control. (1971, c. 796, s. 3.)

Chapter 25B.

Credit.

Article 1.

Credit Rights of Women.

§ 25B-1. Equal availability of credit for women.

(a)   No married woman shall be denied credit in her own name if her uncommingled earnings, separate property or other assets are such that a man possessing the same amount of uncommingled earnings, separate property or other assets would receive credit.

(b)   No unmarried woman shall be denied credit in her own name if her property, earnings or other assets are such that a man possessing the same amount of property, earnings or other assets would receive credit.

(c)   For the purposes of this section, "credit" means the obtaining of money, property, labor or services on a deferred-payment basis. (1973, c. 1394, s. 1.)

§ 25B-2. Responsibility of credit-reporting agency to maintain separate credit histories.

A credit-reporting agency shall, upon written request of a married person, identify within any report delivered by the agency, both the separate credit history of each spouse and the credit history of their joint accounts, if such information is on file with the credit-reporting agency. (1973, c. 1394, s. 2.)

§ 25B-3. Right of action to enforce Article.

(a)   A married or unmarried woman denied credit in violation of this Chapter shall have a right of action on account of such violation in which she shall be entitled to actual damages, and reasonable attorney's fees in the discretion of the court to be taxed as part of the cost.

(b)   Violations of this Chapter may be enjoined by action of the Attorney General brought in behalf of the State pursuant to authority granted in G.S. 114-2. (1973, c. 1394, s. 3.)

§ 25B-4. Granting of credit not otherwise affected.

Nothing contained herein shall be construed to deprive any credit grantor of his right to deny credit or limit its terms based upon its evaluation of the applicant's capability or willingness to repay, or to require any credit grantor to give preferential treatment to any applicant because of sex or marital status. (1973, c. 1394, s. 4.)

Article 2.

Sale of Prints.

§ 25C-10. Definitions.

As used in this Article, the term:

(1)   "Artist" means any person who created or who conceived of and approved:

a.   The master image of a work of art for a print, including but not limited to a photograph or a negative; or

b.   The master image of a work of art which served as the model for a print.

(2)   "Art dealer" means a person:

a.   Who is in the business of dealing in prints to which this Article applies; or

b.   Who holds himself out as having knowledge or skills particular to prints to which this Article applies; or

c.   Who employs an agent or other intermediary who holds himself out as having knowledge or skills particular to prints to which this Article applies; or

d. Who is a professional auctioneer who sells prints to which this Article applies, at auctions.

(3) "Fine print" means a printed image on paper or any other suitable substance which is based on an artist's master image and has been taken off a plate by printing, stamping, casting, or any other process commonly used in the graphic arts, and includes but is not limited to engraving, etching, woodcut, lithograph, or serigraph, or a print developed or created from a negative when such negative is itself an original work of art.

(4) "Person" means an individual, partnership, corporation, association, joint venture, or any other legal or commercial entity.

(5) "Plate" means a plate, stone, block, or other material used to create a fine print or from which a fine print is taken.

(6) "Print" means a fine print or reproduction as defined in this Article.

(7) "Photograph" means the image produced upon a photosensitive surface by the chemical action of light.

(8) "Negative" means any negative image, photographic plate, slide, or other material created by the artist and used for the purpose of creating the print.

(9) "Reproduction" means a copy of a fine print or other work of art made by a commercial mechanical process which does not require the use of an original plate or an original negative.

(10) "Signed print" means a finished fine print autographed by the artist and not by mechanical means of reproduction, whether or not it was signed or unsigned in the plate.

(11) "Work of art" means an original art work that is:

a. A visual rendition, including a painting, drawing, sculpture, mosaic, or photograph;

b. A work of calligraphy;

c. A work of graphic art, including but not limited to a fine print;

d. A craft work in materials, including clay, textile, fiber, wood, metal, plastic, or glass; or

e. A work in mixed media, including a collage or a work consisting of any combination of works included in this subdivision. (1989, c. 464; 1997-456, s. 27.)

§ 25C-11. General prohibitions.

(a) An art dealer may not publish in or distribute in, into or from, this State any catalog, prospectus, circular, advertisement or other publication which solicits a direct sale, by inviting transmittal of payment for a specific print not exempt under G.S. 25C-16, unless it clearly sets forth, in close physical proximity to the place in such publication describing the print, all information required by G.S. 25C-14. This requirement does not apply to general written material or advertising that does not solicit such a direct sale.

(b) An art dealer may not sell or invite offers to buy any print not exempt under G.S. 25C-16, either at retail or wholesale, unless the art dealer clearly and conspicuously discloses in writing to prospective purchasers, all information required by G.S. 25C-14. At public or private auction, an art dealer may not invite offers to buy any non-exempt print unless the art dealer clearly and conspicuously discloses in writing such required information to prospective bidders before any offer is made and until an offer is accepted. (1989, c. 464, s. 1.)

§ 25C-12. Sale by artist; consignments.

(a) The disclosure requirements of this Article do not apply to a sale of a print by the artist who produced the print, directly to a purchaser, without the intervention of a wholesale or retail merchant, unless the artist is an art dealer within the definition of G.S. 25C-10(2)a. or unless the artist consigns a print of his own creation.

(b) An artist or art dealer who consigns a print to an art dealer for the purpose of effecting a sale of such print shall have no liability to a purchaser under this Article if such consignor, as to the consignee, has complied with the disclosure requirements of this Article. (1989, c. 464, s. 1.)

§ 25C-13. Warranties.

(a)   Whenever an art dealer discloses information as required by G.S. 25C-11, such information shall be a part of the basis of the bargain and shall create express warranties as to the information so provided.

(b)   When information is not disclosed as required by G.S. 25C-11, such nondisclosure shall constitute an express warranty that such information is not required to be disclosed.

(c)   Evidence of a warranty made in accordance with this Article shall be prima facie evidence of reliance upon the warranty. (1989, c. 464, s. 1.)

§ 25C-14. Disclosure requirements.

(a)   An art dealer who sells or offers to sell a print not exempt under G.S. 25C-16, shall disclose the following information in a writing to the prospective purchaser:

(1)   The name of the artist;

(2)   The year the plate or negative was created;

(3)   The year when the print was printed or created;

(4)   The process used to create the master image;

(5)   The process used to create the print;

(6)   Whether the print is part of a limited edition.

(b)   If the print or its plate or negative is a mechanical, photomechanical or photographic copy or reproduction of a master image previously created or produced in another medium, this information shall be disclosed as part of the disclosure required by subsection (a) of this section.

(c) If the print is represented to be part of a limited edition, the disclosure required by subsections (a) and (b) of this section shall further state:

(1) The authorized maximum number of numbered or signed prints, or both, in the edition;

(2) The authorized maximum number of unnumbered or unsigned prints, or both, in the edition;

(3) Any authorized maximum number of artist's, publisher's, printer's, or other proofs, exclusive of trial proofs, outside the regular edition;

(4) The total number of prints, either numbered or unnumbered, in the edition;

(5) Whether the plate or negative has been destroyed, effaced, altered, defaced, or cancelled after the current edition;

(6) If there were any prior plates or negatives of the same master image, the total number of plates or negatives and a designation of the plate or negative from which the print was taken;

(7) If there were any prior or later editions from the same plate or negative, the series number of the edition of which the print is a part, and the aggregate size of all other editions;

(8) Whether the print was published as a book illustration or in a magazine article;

(9) Whether the edition is a posthumous edition or a restrike, and, if it is, whether the plate has been reworked;

(10) The name of any workshop where the edition was printed; and

(11) Whether the print has been printed on acid-free paper.

(d) Whenever an art dealer disclaims knowledge as to a particular item about which information is required, such disclaimer shall be clearly and conspicuously stated in unqualified terms as to each of those items of information required by this section and shall be contained in writing in the physical context of other language setting forth the required information to be disclosed under this section. (1989, c. 464, s. 1.)

§ 25C-15. Rights and liabilities not inclusive.

(a) An art dealer who sells a print in violation of this Article shall be liable to the purchaser of the print; the purchaser shall be entitled to recover of the art dealer the consideration paid by the purchaser for the print, with interest at the legal rate thereon, upon the tender of the print in substantially the same condition in which it was received by the purchaser.

(b) If an art dealer liable to a purchaser under the provisions of subsection (a) of this section wrongfully refuses to repay the purchaser's consideration as specified therein, the purchaser who prevails in a civil action to recover such consideration may also recover all expenses incurred in connection with the action, including a reasonable attorney's fee.

(c) A willful violation of this Article shall constitute a prima facie violation of G.S. 75-1.1.

(d) The rights and liabilities created by this Article shall be construed to be in addition to and not in substitution, exclusion, or displacement of other rights and liabilities provided by law. (1989, c. 464, s. 1.)

§ 25C-16. Exemptions.

(a) This Article shall not apply to any print when offered for sale or sold at wholesale or retail for one hundred dollars ($100.00) or less, exclusive of the value of any frame.

(b) This Article shall not apply to any print described clearly and conspicuously in writing by the seller as a "reproduction and not a fine print", unless the print is said or represented to be one in a limited edition, an edition of numbered or signed prints, or any combination thereof.

(c) This Article shall not apply to the sale of any print sold before January 1, 1990. (1989, c. 464, s. 1.)

Chapter 26.

Suretyship.

§ 26-1. Surety and principal distinguished in judgment and execution.

In the trial of actions upon contracts either of the defendants may show in evidence that he is surety, and if it be satisfactorily shown, the jury in their verdict, or the magistrate in his judgment, shall distinguish the principal and surety, which shall be endorsed on the execution by the clerk of superior court. (1826, c. 31, s. 1; R.C., c. 31, s. 124; Code, s. 2100; Rev., s. 2840; C.S., s. 3961; 1973, c. 108, s. 14.)

§ 26-2. Principal liable on execution before surety.

When an execution, indorsed as aforesaid, shall come to the hands of any officer for collection, he shall levy on all the property of the principal, or so much thereof as shall be necessary to satisfy the execution, and, for want of sufficient property of the principal, also on the property of the surety, and make sale of all the property of the principal levied on before that of the surety. (1826, c. 31, s. 2; R.C., c. 31, s. 125; Code, s. 2101; Rev., s. 2841; C.S., s. 3962.)

§ 26-3. Summary remedy of surety against principal.

Any person who may have paid money for and on account of those for whom he became surety, upon producing to the clerk of superior court, a receipt, and showing that an execution has issued, and he has satisfied the same, and making it appear by sufficient testimony that he has expended any sum of money as the surety of such person, may move the clerk for judgment against his principal for the amount which he has actually paid; a citation having previously issued against the principal to show cause why execution should not be awarded; and should the principal not show sufficient cause, the clerk shall award execution against the principal. (1797, c. 487, s. 1, P.R.; R.C., c. 110, s. 1; Code, s. 2093; Rev., s. 2842; C.S., s. 3963; 1973, c. 108, s. 15.)

§ 26-3.1. Surety's recovery on obligation paid; no assignment necessary.

(a)   A surety who has paid his principal's note, bill, bond or other written obligation, may either sue his principal for reimbursement or sue his principal on the instrument and may maintain any action or avail himself of any remedy which the creditor himself might have had against the principal debtor. No assignment of the obligation to the surety or to a third-party trustee for the surety's benefit shall be required.

(b)   The word "surety" as used herein includes a guarantor, accommodation maker, accommodation indorser, or other person who undertakes liability for the written obligation of another. (1959, c. 1120.)

§ 26-4. Subrogation of surety paying debt of deceased principal.

Whenever a surety, or his representative, shall pay the debt of his deceased principal, the claim thus accruing shall have such priority in the administration of the assets of the principal as had the debt before its payment. (1829, c. 23; R.C., c. 110, s. 4; Code, s. 2096; Rev., s. 2843; C.S., s. 3964.)

§ 26-5. Contribution among sureties.

Where there are two or more sureties for the performance of a contract, and one or more of them may have been compelled to perform and satisfy the same, or any part thereof, such surety may have and maintain an action against every other surety for a just and ratable proportion of the same which may have been paid as aforesaid, whether of principal, interest or cost. (1807, c. 722, P.R.; R.C., c. 110, s. 2; Code, s. 2094; Rev., s. 2844; C.S., s. 3965; 1957, c. 981.)

§ 26-6. Dissenting surety not liable to surety on stay of execution.

Whenever any judgment shall be obtained against a principal and his surety, and the principal debtor shall desire to stay the execution thereon, but the surety is unwilling that such stay shall be had, the surety may cause his dissent thereto to be entered by the judge or clerk, which shall absolve him from all liability to the surety who may stay the same. And the sheriff or other officer, who may have the collection of the debt, shall make the money out of the property of the principal debtor, and that of the surety for the stay of execution, if he can, before he shall sell the property of the surety before judgment. (1829, c. 6, ss. 1, 2; R.C., c. 110, s. 3; Code, s. 2095; Rev., s. 2845; C.S., s. 3966; 1973, c. 108, s. 16.)

§ 26-7. Surety, indorser, or guarantor may notify creditor to take action.

(a)   After any note, bill, bond, or other obligation becomes due and payable, any surety, indorser, or guarantor thereof may give written notice to the holder or owner of the obligation requiring him to use all reasonable diligence to recover against the principal and to proceed to realize upon any securities which he holds for the obligation.

(b)   The surety, indorser or guarantor who gives notice to the holder or owner of the obligation as provided by subsection (a) shall forthwith give written notice to all co-sureties, co-indorsers and co-guarantors of the fact that such notice is being given to the holder or owner of the obligation, and such co-sureties, co-indorsers and co-guarantors shall have ten days after receipt of the notice in which themselves to give written notice to the holder or owner of the obligation and to their co-sureties, co-indorsers, and co-guarantors, that they join in or adopt the notice given pursuant to subsection (a). Failure of such surety, indorser or guarantor to give the required notice to co-sureties, co-indorsers or co-guarantors whose names and residences are known to him or can be obtained by due diligence bars such surety indorser or guarantor from any of the benefits of G.S. 26-9.

(c)   The holder or owner of the obligation shall on demand disclose to any surety, indorser, or guarantor of the obligation the names and addresses of all other sureties, indorsers and guarantors which appear on the obligation or of which he has knowledge.

(d) Nothing herein contained shall apply to official bonds, or bonds given by any person acting in a fiduciary capacity. (1868-9, c. 232, s. 1; Code, s. 2097; Rev., s. 2846; C.S., s. 3967; 1951, c. 763, s. 1.)

§ 26-8. Notice; how given; prima facie evidence thereof.

(a) Any notice authorized or required to be given by G.S. 26-7 shall-

(1) Be served by the sheriff by delivering a copy thereof to the person entitled to the notice, or

(2) Be sent by the person giving notice, by registered mail, with return receipt requested, to the last known address of the person being notified.

(b) Upon serving the notice, the sheriff shall return the original thereof, with his return thereon, to the person who caused the notice to be given.

(c) The sheriff's return, when the notice is served by the sheriff, or the return receipt, when the notice is sent by registered mail, shall be prima facie evidence of the giving of the notice. (1868-9, c. 232, s. 3; Code, s. 2099; Rev., s. 2848; C.S., s. 3968; 1951, c. 763, s. 2.)

§ 26-9. Effect of failure of creditor to take action.

(a) If the holder or owner of the obligation refuses or fails, within 30 days from the service or receipt of such notice, to take appropriate action pursuant thereto, the following persons shall be discharged on any such note, bond, bill or other obligation to the extent that they are prejudiced thereby:

(1) The surety, indorser or guarantor giving such notice, and

(2) All co-sureties, co-indorsers or co-guarantors joining therein or adopting such notice as provided by G.S. 26-7, and

(3) All the co-sureties, co-indorsers, or co-guarantors whose names or addresses such holder or owner of the obligation failed to disclose on demand as required by subsection (c) of G.S. 26-7.

(b) The fact that an instrument contains a provision waiving any defense of any surety, indorser or guarantor by reason of the extension of the time for payment does not prevent the operation of this section. Any such notice to the holder or owner of the obligation as is authorized by G.S. 26-7 may be given at or subsequent to the time such obligation is due or at or subsequent to the termination of a period of extension.

(c) The failure of any co-surety, co-indorser or co-guarantor to join in or adopt a notice to the holder or owner of the obligation as authorized by subsection (b) of G.S. 26-7 does not prevent such co-surety, co-indorser or co-guarantor from giving a separate notice as authorized by subsection (a) of G.S. 26-7. (1868-9, c. 232, s. 2; Code, s. 2098; Rev., s. 2847; C.S., s. 3969; 1951, c. 763, s. 3.)

§ 26-10. Repealed by Session Laws 1943, c. 543.

§ 26-11. Cancellation of judgment as to surety.

Whenever a judgment shall be rendered in any court in accordance with the provisions of G.S. 26-1 and the surety, endorser or other person shown in said judgment to be secondarily liable thereon and having the rights as by this chapter prescribed against the person or persons primarily liable, and the surety, endorser or other person so shown in the judgment to be secondarily liable, shall pay the said judgment or shall be compelled to pay an execution issued thereon and such fact shall appear to the satisfaction of the clerk of the superior court of the county in which the said judgment is rendered and docketed, such judgment shall be canceled as to said surety, endorser or other person secondarily liable and shall ceased to be a lien upon his real estate and other property, but such cancellation shall not have the force and effect nor operate as a cancellation and discharge of the judgment as to any other person against whom the said judgment shall be rendered and the person so paying the said judgment shall have all the rights given to a surety who has been compelled to pay a judgment against the principal debtor and co-sureties which are given in this chapter, notwithstanding the cancellation of the said judgment as herein provided for. (1925, c. 38.)

§ 26-12. Joinder of debtor by surety.

(a) As used in this section, "surety" includes guarantors, accommodation makers, accommodation indorsers, or others who undertake liability on the obligation and for the accommodation of another.

(b) When any surety is sued by the holder of the obligation, the court, on motion of the surety may join the principal as an additional party defendant, provided the principal is found to be or can be made subject to the jurisdiction of the court. Upon such joinder the surety shall have all rights, defenses, counterclaims, and setoffs which would have been available to him if the principal and surety had been originally sued together. (1959, c. 1121.)

Chapter 27.

Warehouse Receipts.

Article 1.

General Provisions.

§§ 27-1 through 27-4: Repealed by Session Laws 1965, c. 700, s. 2.

Article 2.

Issue of Warehouse Receipts.

§§ 27-5 through 27-11: Repealed by Session Laws 1965, c. 700, s. 2.

Article 3.

Obligations and Rights of Warehousemen on Receipts.

§§ 27-12 through 27-40: Repealed by Session Laws 1965, c. 700, s. 2.

Article 4.

Negotiation and Transfer of Receipts.

§§ 27-41 through 27-53: Repealed by Session Laws 1965, c. 700, s. 2.

Chapter 27.

Warehouse Receipts.

Article 5.

Criminal Offenses.

§§ 27-54 through 27-59: Repealed by Session Laws 2006-112, s. 58(a), effective October 1, 2006.

Chapter 28.

Administration.

§§ 28-1 through 28-201. Repealed by Session Laws 1973, c. 1329, s. 1.

Chapter 28A.

Administration of Decedents' Estates.

Article 1.

Definitions and Other General Provisions.

§ 28A-1-1. Definitions.

As used in this Chapter, unless the context otherwise requires, the term:

(1) "Collector" means any person authorized to take possession, custody, or control of the personal property of the decedent for the purpose of executing the duties outlined in G.S. 28A-11-3.

(1a) "Devisee" means any person entitled to take real or personal property under the provisions of a valid, probated will.

(1b) "Estate proceeding" means a matter initiated by petition related to the administration, distribution, or settlement of an estate, other than a special proceeding. There may be more than one estate proceeding within the administration of a decedent's estate.

(2) "Foreign personal representative" means a personal representative appointed in another jurisdiction, including a personal representative appointed in another country.

(3) "Heir" means any person entitled to take real or personal property upon intestacy under the provisions of Chapter 29 of the General Statutes.

(4) "Mortgage" includes a deed of trust.

(4a) "Party," in the context of a contested or uncontested estate proceeding pursuant to G.S. 28A-2-6, means a party joined as a petitioner or respondent.

(4b) "Person" means an individual; corporation; business trust; estate; trust; partnership; limited liability company; association; joint venture; government; governmental subdivision, agency, or instrumentality; public corporation; or any other legal or commercial entity.

(5) "Personal representative" includes both an executor and an administrator, but does not include a collector.

(6) Repealed by Session Laws 2011-344, s. 4, effective January 1, 2012, and applicable to estates of decedents dying on or after that date. (1973, c. 1329, s. 3; 1981, c. 955, c. 4; 2011-344, s. 4.)

§ 28A-1-2. Repealed by Session Laws 1979, c. 88, s. 2.

Article 2.

Jurisdiction for Probate of Wills and Administration of Estates of Decedents.

§ 28A-2-1. Clerk of superior court.

The clerk of superior court of each county, ex officio judge of probate, shall have jurisdiction of the administration, settlement, and distribution of estates of decedents including, but not limited to, estate proceedings as provided in G.S. 28A-2-4. (R.C., c. 46, s. 1; C.C.P., s. 433; 1868-9, c. 113, s. 115; Code, s. 1374; Rev., s. 16; C.S., s. 1; 1931, c. 165; 1943, c. 543; 1951, c. 765; 1973, c. 1329, s. 3; 2011-344, s. 4.)

§ 28A-2-2. Assistant clerk of superior court.

An assistant clerk of superior court shall have jurisdiction as provided by G.S. 7A-102. (1973, c. 1329, s. 3.)

§ 28A-2-3. Jurisdiction where clerk interested.

Whenever the clerk of superior court is a subscribing witness to a will offered for probate in the clerk's county or has an interest, direct or indirect, in an estate or trust within the clerk's jurisdiction, jurisdiction with respect thereto shall be vested in the senior resident superior court judge of the clerk's district, and shall extend to all things which the clerk of superior court might have done in the administration of such estate. (R.C., c. 46, s. 1; C.C.P., s. 433; 1868-9, c. 113, s. 115; Code, s. 1374; Rev., s. 16; C.S., s. 1; 1931, c. 165; 1943, c. 543; 1951, c. 765; 1973, c. 1329, s. 3; 1975, c. 300, s. 1; 2011-344, s. 4.)

§ 28A-2-4. Subject matter jurisdiction of the clerk of superior court in estate proceedings.

(a) The clerks of superior court of this State, as ex officio judges of probate, shall have original jurisdiction of estate proceedings. Except as provided in subdivision (4) of this subsection, the jurisdiction of the clerk of superior court is exclusive. Estate proceedings include, but are not limited to, the following:

(1)   Probate of wills.

(2)   Granting and revoking of letters testamentary and letters of administration, or other proper letters of authority for the administration of estates.

(3)   Determination of the elective share for a surviving spouse as provided in G.S. 30-3.

(4)   Proceedings to ascertain heirs or devisees, to approve settlement agreements pursuant to G.S. 28A-2-10, to determine questions of construction of wills, to determine priority among creditors, to determine whether a person is in possession of property belonging to an estate, to order the recovery of property of the estate in possession of third parties, and to determine the existence or nonexistence of any immunity, power, privilege, duty, or right. Any party or the clerk of superior court may file a notice of transfer of a proceeding pursuant to this subdivision to the Superior Court Division of the General Court of Justice as provided in G.S. 28A-2-6(h). In the absence of a transfer to superior court, Article 26 of Chapter 1 of the General Statutes shall apply to a trust proceeding pending before the clerk of superior court to the extent consistent with this Article.

(b)   Nothing in this section shall affect the right of a person to file an action in the Superior Court Division of the General Court of Justice for declaratory relief under Article 26 of Chapter 1 of the General Statutes. In the event that either the petitioner or the respondent in an estate proceeding requests declaratory relief under Article 26 of Chapter 1 of the General Statutes, either party may move for a transfer of the proceeding to the Superior Court Division of the General Court of Justice as provided in Article 21 of Chapter 7A of the General Statutes. In the absence of a removal to superior court, Article 26 of Chapter 1 of the General Statutes shall apply to an estate proceeding to the extent consistent with this Article.

(c)   Without otherwise limiting the jurisdiction of the Superior Court Division of the General Court of Justice, the clerk of superior court shall not have jurisdiction under subsection (a) or (c) of this section of the following:

(1) Actions by or against creditors or debtors of an estate, except as provided in Article 19 of this Chapter.

(2) Actions involving claims for monetary damages, including claims for breach of fiduciary duty, fraud, and negligence.

(3) Caveats, except as provided under G.S. 31-36.

(4) Proceeding to determine proper county of venue as provided in G.S. 28A-3-2.

(5) Recovery of property transferred or conveyed by a decedent with intent to hinder, delay, or defraud creditors, pursuant to G.S. 28A-15-10(b). (2011-344, s. 4; 2012-194, s. 12.)

§ 28A-2-5. Subject matter jurisdiction of the clerk of superior court in special proceedings.

The clerk of superior court also shall have jurisdiction over special proceedings, including, but not limited to, the following:

(1) Special proceedings to obtain possession, custody, or control of assets as provided in G.S. 28A-13-3.

(2) Special proceedings relating to the sale, lease, or mortgage of real estate as provided in G.S. 28A-15-1 and in G.S. 28A-17-1.

(3) Special proceedings against unknown heirs before distribution of estate as provided in G.S. 28A-22-3.

Nothing in this section shall be deemed to limit the jurisdiction of the clerk of superior court in special proceedings. (2011-344, s. 4.)

§ 28A-2-6. Commencement of estate proceedings, pleadings, consolidation, and joinder.

(a) Contested Estate Proceedings. - Contested estate proceedings brought against adverse parties shall be commenced by petition in the existing estate administration file. All parties not joined as petitioners shall be joined as respondents. The clerk of superior court shall issue the estate proceeding summons to the respondents. The clerk of superior court may order that additional persons be joined as respondents and shall issue the estate proceeding summons to the additional persons. The estate proceeding summons shall notify a respondent to appear and answer the petition within 20 days after its service upon the respondents. The estate proceeding summons shall comply with the requirements set forth in G.S. 1-394 for a special proceeding summons except that the summons shall be titled "ESTATE PROCEEDING SUMMONS" and shall be served upon a respondent in accordance with G.S. 1A-1, Rule 4. After the time for responding to the petition or complaint has expired, any party or the clerk of superior court may give notice to all parties of a hearing.

(b) Uncontested Estate Proceedings. - Estate proceedings before the clerk of superior court that are uncontested may be decided without hearing according to practice and procedure provided by law and shall be commenced by the filing of a petition, setting forth the facts entitling the petitioners to relief and the nature of the relief demanded. In these proceedings, the clerk of superior court may hear and decide the petition summarily.

(c) Pleadings. - Any petition, response, or request for hearing in a contested estate proceeding before the clerk of superior court shall contain a short and plain statement of the claim that is sufficiently particular to give the court and the parties notice of the transactions, occurrences, or series of transactions intended to be proved showing that the pleaders are entitled to relief, and a demand for judgment for the relief to which the pleader is entitled. Each averment should be simple, concise, and direct. No technical forms of motions or responses are required. A party may set forth two or more statements of a claim or defense alternatively or hypothetically. The signature of an attorney or party constitutes a certificate by that attorney or party that (i) the attorney or party has read the pleading, motion, or other paper; (ii) to the best of the attorney's or party's knowledge, information, and belief formed after reasonable inquiry, it is well grounded in fact and is warranted by existing law or a good faith argument for the extension, modification, or reversal of existing law; and (iii) it is not interposed for any improper purpose, such as to harass or to cause unnecessary delay or needless increase in the cost of litigation. All motions, responses, and requests for hearing shall be so construed as to do substantial justice.

(d) Extensions of Time. - The clerk of superior court, for cause shown at any time in the clerk's discretion, with or without motion or notice, may enter an order enlarging the period of time within which an act is required or permitted in an estate proceeding, by any applicable rule of G.S. 1A-1, the Rules of Civil Procedure, or by order of the court, if the request is made before the expiration of the period originally prescribed, but not to exceed 10 days, provided that the court can enlarge the time for a period of more than 10 days for good cause shown, but only to the extent that the court in its discretion determines that justice requires. Upon motion made after the expiration of the specified period, the clerk of superior court may permit the act where the failure to act was the result of excusable neglect. Notwithstanding any other provision of this subsection, the parties to a proceeding may enter into binding stipulations, without approval of the clerk of superior court, enlarging the time within which an act is required or permitted by this Article, by any applicable Rules of Civil Procedure or by order of the court, not to exceed 30 days.

(e) Rules of Civil Procedure. - Unless the clerk of superior court otherwise directs, Rules 4, 5, 6(a), 6(d), 6(e), 18, 19, 20, 21, 24, 45, 56, and 65 of G.S. 1A-1, the Rules of Civil Procedure, shall apply to estate proceedings. Upon motion of a party or the clerk of superior court, the clerk may further direct that any or all of the remaining Rules of Civil Procedure shall apply, including, without limitation, discovery rules; however, nothing in Rule 17 requires the appointment of a guardian ad litem for a party represented except as provided in G.S. 28A-2-7. In applying these Rules to an estate proceeding pending before the clerk of superior court, the term "judge" shall mean "clerk of superior court."

(f) Consolidation. - When an estate proceeding pending before the clerk of superior court and a civil action pending before the Superior Court Division of the General Court of Justice involve a common question of law or fact, upon the court's motion or motion of a party to either the estate proceeding or the civil action, a superior court judge may order a consolidation of the estate proceeding and civil action, and the judge may make orders concerning proceedings therein as may tend to avoid unnecessary cost or delay. Upon the entry of an order consolidating an estate proceeding and civil action, the jurisdiction for all matters pending in both the estate proceeding and the civil action shall be vested in the superior court.

(g) Joinder. - In any civil action pending before the Superior Court Division of the General Court of Justice, the party asserting a claim for relief as an original claim, counterclaim, crossclaim, or third-party claim may join, either as independent or alternative claims, as many claims, legal or equitable, as the party may have against the opposing party, notwithstanding the fact that such claims may otherwise be within the exclusive jurisdiction of the clerk of superior court.

(h) Notice of Transfer. - A notice to transfer an estate proceeding brought pursuant to G.S. 28A-2-4(a)(4) must be served within 30 days after the moving party is served with a copy of the pleading requesting relief pursuant to G.S. 28A-2-4(a)(4), or in the case of the clerk of superior court, prior to or at the first hearing duly noticed in such estate proceeding and prior to the presentation of evidence by the parties, including a hearing at which an order of continuance is entered. Failure to timely serve a notice of transfer of a trust proceeding is a waiver of any objection to the clerk of superior court's exercise of jurisdiction over the trust proceeding then pending before the clerk. When a notice of transfer is duly served and filed, the clerk shall transfer the proceeding to the appropriate court. The proceeding after the transfer is subject to the provisions of the General Statutes and to the rules that apply to actions initially filed in the court to which the proceeding was transferred.

(i) Orders Upon Consolidation/Joinder/Transfer. - Upon the consolidation of an estate proceeding in a civil action, joinder of claims under subsection (f) or (g) of this section, or transfer to the Superior Court Division of the General Court of Justice pursuant to subsection (h) of this section, the clerk of superior court or judge may make appropriate orders to protect the interest of the parties and avoid unnecessary cost or delay. Notwithstanding the consolidation or joinder of claims under subsection (f) or (g) of this section, where the estate proceeding is transferred to the Superior Court Division of the General Court of Justice under subsection (h) of this section, the clerk of superior court's exclusive jurisdiction as set forth in G.S. 28A-2-4(a)(1) through (3) shall not be stayed unless so ordered by the court. (2011-344, s. 4; 2013-410, s. 6.)

§ 28A-2-7. Representation of parties.

(a) Notwithstanding any other applicable rule of the Rules of Civil Procedure or provision of Chapter 1 of the General Statutes, in any contested or uncontested estate proceeding or special proceeding, whether brought before the clerk of superior court or in the Superior Court Division of the General Court of Justice, the parties shall be represented as provided in Article 3 of Chapter 36C of the General Statutes.

(b) In the case of any party represented by another as provided in subsection (a) of this section, service of process shall be made by serving such representative. (2011-344, s. 4.)

§ 28A-2-8. Waiver of notice.

A party, or a representative of a party as provided in G.S. 28A-2-7, may waive notice by a writing signed by the party, the representative, or the attorney of the party or the representative and filed in the proceeding. (2011-344, s. 4.)

§ 28A-2-9. Appeals of estate proceedings and special proceedings.

(a) With the exception of appeals of special proceedings heard by the clerk of superior court, appeals in estate matters shall be as provided in G.S. 1-301.3.

(b) Appeals in special proceedings shall be as provided in G.S. 1-301.2.

(c) Any party may appeal from a decision of the clerk of superior court in an estate proceeding or special proceeding to a superior court judge as provided for in G.S. 1-301.3; provided that the appeals from orders of the clerk of superior court in special proceedings shall be as provided in G.S. 1-301.2. (2011-344, s. 4.)

§ 28A-2-10. Approval of settlement agreements by the clerk.

The clerk shall have the authority, in the clerk's discretion, to consider and approve settlement agreements where the following apply:

(1) The controversy arises with respect to a matter over which the clerk has jurisdiction.

(2) The controversy arose in good faith.

Nothing herein shall be construed as giving a clerk the authority to approve a settlement agreement modifying the terms of a last will and testament or resolving a caveat of a last will and testament. (2011-344, s. 4.)

Article 2A.

Probate of Will.

§ 28A-2A-1. Executor may apply for probate.

Any executor named in a will may, at any time after the death of the testator, apply to the clerk of the superior court, having jurisdiction, to have the will admitted to probate. (C.C.P., s. 439; Code, s. 2151; Rev., s. 3122; 1919, c. 15; C.S., s. 4139; 1921, c. 99; 1923, c. 14; 1953, c. 920, s. 2; 1975, c. 300, s. 13; 2011-344, s. 3; 2012-68, s. 1.)

§ 28A-2A-2. Executor failing, beneficiary may apply.

If no executor applies to have the will proved within 60 days after the death of the testator, any devisee named in the will, or any other person interested in the estate, may make such application, upon 10 days' notice thereof to the executor. For good cause shown, the clerk of superior court may shorten the initial 60-day period during which the executor may apply to have the will proved. (C.C.P., s. 440; Code, s. 2152; Rev., s. 3123; C.S., s. 4140; 2011-284, s. 27; 2011-344, ss. 3, 4.)

§ 28A-2A-3. Clerk to notify devisees of probate of wills.

The clerks of the superior court of the State are hereby required and directed to notify by mail, all devisees whose addresses are known, designated in wills filed for probate in their respective counties. All expense incident to such notification shall be deemed a proper charge in the administration of the respective estates. (1933, c. 133; 2011-284, s. 28; 2011-344, s. 3.)

§ 28A-2A-4. Clerk shall compel production of will.

Every clerk of the superior court having jurisdiction, on application by affidavit setting forth the facts, shall, by summons, compel any person in the State, having in possession the last will of any decedent, to exhibit the same in his court for probate; and whoever being duly summoned refuses, in contempt of the court, to produce such will, or (the same having been parted with by him) refuses to inform the court on oath where such will is, or in what manner he has disposed of it, shall, by order of the clerk of the superior court, be committed to the jail of the county, there to remain without bail till such will be produced or accounted for, and due submission made for the contempt. (C.C.P., s. 442; Code, s. 2154; Rev., s. 3124; C.S., s. 4141; 2011-344, ss. 3, 4.)

§ 28A-2A-5. What shown on application for probate.

On application to the clerk of the superior court, he must ascertain by affidavit of the applicant -

(1)   That such applicant is the executor or devisee named in the will, or is some other person interested in the estate, and how so interested.

(2)   The value and nature of the testator's property, as near as can be ascertained.

(3)   The names and residences of all parties entitled to the testator's property, if known, or that the same on diligent inquiry cannot be discovered; which of the parties in interest are minors, and whether with or without guardians, and the names and residences of such guardians, if known.

Such affidavit shall be recorded with the will and the certificate of probate thereof, if the same is admitted to probate. (C.C.P., s. 441; Code, s. 2153; Rev., s. 3125; C.S., s. 4142; 2011-284, s. 29; 2011-344, s. 3.)

§ 28A-2A-6. Proof and examination in writing.

Every clerk of the superior court shall take in writing the proofs and examinations of the witnesses touching the execution of a will, and he shall embody the substance of such proofs and examinations, in case the will is admitted to probate, in his certificate of the probate thereof, which certificate must be recorded with the will. The proofs and examinations as taken must be filed in the office. (C.C.P., s. 437; Code, s. 2149; Rev., s. 3126; C.S., s. 4143; 2011-344, s. 3.)

§ 28A-2A-7. Probate in solemn form.

(a) A person entitled to apply for probate of a will pursuant to G.S. 28A-2A-1 or G.S. 28A-2A-2 may file a petition for probate of the will in solemn form, and the matter shall proceed as an estate proceeding governed by Article 2 of Chapter 28A of the General Statutes. The clerk of superior court shall issue a summons to all interested parties in the estate. The clerk shall schedule a hearing at which the petitioner shall produce the evidence necessary to probate the will.

(b) If an interested party contests the validity of the will, that person must file a caveat before the hearing or raise an issue of devisavit vel non at the hearing. Upon the filing of a caveat or raising of an issue of devisavit vel non, the clerk shall transfer the cause to the superior court, and the matter shall be heard as a caveat proceeding.

(c) If no interested party contests the validity of the will, the probate shall be binding, and no interested party who was properly served may file a caveat of the probated will. Initiation of a probate in common form shall not preclude a person from applying for probate in solemn form. (2011-344, s. 4.)

§ 28A-2A-8. Manner of probate of attested written will.

(a) An attested written will, executed as provided by G.S. 31-3.3, may be probated in the following manner:

(1) Upon the testimony of at least two of the attesting witnesses; or

(2)   If the testimony of only one attesting witness is available, then

a.   Upon the testimony of such witness, and

b.   Upon proof of the handwriting of at least one of the attesting witnesses who is dead or whose testimony is otherwise unavailable, and

c.   Upon proof of the handwriting of the testator, unless he signed by his mark, and

d.   Upon proof of such other circumstances as will satisfy the clerk of the superior court as to the genuineness and due execution of the will; or

(3)   If the testimony of none of the attesting witnesses is available, then

a.   Upon proof of the handwriting of at least two of the attesting witnesses whose testimony is unavailable, and

b.   Upon compliance with paragraphs c. and d. of subsection (a)(2) of this section; or

(4)   Upon a showing that the will has been made self-proved in accordance with the provisions of G.S. 31-11.6.

(b)   Due execution of a will may be established, where the evidence required by subsection (a) of this section is unavoidably lacking or inadequate, by testimony of other competent witnesses as to the requisite facts.

(c)   The testimony of a witness is unavailable within the meaning of this section when the witness is dead, out of the State, not to be found within the State, incompetent, physically unable to testify or refuses to testify. (1953, c. 1098, s. 12; 1977, c. 795, s. 2; 1979, c. 107, s. 4; 2011-344, ss. 3, 4.)

§ 28A-2A-9. Manner of probate of holographic will.

A holographic will may be probated only in the following manner:

(1)   Upon the testimony of at least three competent witnesses that they believe that the will is written entirely in the handwriting of the person whose will

it purports to be, and that the name of the testator as written in or on, or subscribed to, the will is in the handwriting of the person whose will it purports to be; and

(2) Upon the testimony of one witness who may, but need not be, one of the witnesses referred to in subdivision (1) of this section to a statement of facts showing that the will was found after the testator's death as required by G.S. 31-3.4. (1953, c. 1098, s. 12; 2011-344, s. 3.)

§ 28A-2A-10. Manner of probate of nuncupative will.

(a) No nuncupative will may be probated later than six months from the time it was made unless it was reduced to writing within 10 days after it was made.

(b) Before a nuncupative will may be probated

(1) Written notice must be given to the surviving spouse, if any, and to the next of kin, by the clerk of the court in which it is to be probated, notifying them that the will has been offered for probate and that they may, if they desire, oppose the probate thereof, or

(2) When the surviving spouse or next of kin are not known or when for any other reason such notice cannot be given, a notice to the same effect must be published not less than once a week for four consecutive weeks in some newspaper published in the county where the will is offered for probate, or if no newspaper is published in the county, then in some newspaper having general circulation therein.

(c) A nuncupative will may be probated only in the following manner:

(1) Upon the testimony of at least two competent witnesses who establish the terms of such will and who state that they were simultaneously present at the making thereof, that the testator declared he was then making his will, and that they were then and there specially requested by him to bear witness thereto; and

(2) Upon the testimony of one competent witness, who may but need not be one of the witnesses referred to in subdivision (1) of this subsection, that the will was made in the testator's last illness or while he was in imminent peril of death,

and that he did not survive such sickness or imminent peril, but it is not necessary that all such facts be proved by the testimony of the same witness. (1953, c. 1098, s. 12; 2011-344, s. 3.)

§ 28A-2A-11. Probate of wills of members of the Armed Forces of the United States.

In addition to the methods already provided in existing statutes therefor, a will executed by a person while in the Armed Forces of the United States or the United States Merchant Marine, shall be admitted to probate (whether there were subscribing witnesses thereto or not, if they, or either of them, is out of the State at the time said will is offered for probate) upon the oath of at least three credible witnesses that the signature to said will is in the handwriting of the person whose will it purports to be. Such will so proven shall be effective to devise real property as well as to bequeath personal estate of all kinds. This section shall not apply to cases pending in courts and at issue on the date of its ratification. (1919, c. 216; C.S., s. 4151; Ex. Sess. 1921, c. 39; 1943, c. 218; 1945, c. 81; 1953, c. 1098, s. 13; 2011-183, s. 27; 2011-284, s. 30; 2011-344, s. 3.)

§ 28A-2A-12. Probate conclusive until vacated; substitution of consolidated bank as executor or trustee under will.

Such record and probate is conclusive in evidence of the validity of the will, until it is vacated on appeal or declared void by a competent tribunal. Provided, that whenever in a will so probated or recorded a bank or trust company shall be named executor and/or trustee and shall have at the time of such probate and recording become absorbed by or consolidated with another bank or trust company or shall have sold and transferred all its assets and liabilities to another bank or trust company doing business in North Carolina, such latter bank or trust company shall be deemed substituted for and shall have all the rights and powers of the former bank or trust company. (C.C.P., s. 438; Code, s. 2150; Rev., s. 3128; C.S., s. 4145; 1929, c. 150; 1941, c. 79; 2011-344, s. 3.)

§ 28A-2A-13. Wills filed in clerk's office.

All original wills shall remain in the clerk's office, among the records of the court where the same shall be proved, and to such wills any person may have access, as to the other records. If said will contains a devise of real estate, outside said county where said will is probated, then a copy of the said will, together with the probate of the same, certified under the hand and seal of the clerk of the superior court of said county may be recorded in the book of wills and filed in the office of the clerk of the superior court of any county in the State in which said land is situated with the same effect as to passing the title to said real estate as if said will had originally been probated and filed in said county and the clerk of the superior court of said last-mentioned county had had jurisdiction to probate the same. (1777, c. 115, s. 59; R.C., c. 119, s. 19; Code, s. 2173; Rev., s. 3129; 1921, c. 108, s. 1; C.S., s. 4146; 2011-344, s. 3.)

§ 28A-2A-14. Validation of wills heretofore certified and recorded.

All wills which have prior to March 9, 1921, been certified and recorded in the office of the clerk of the superior court of any county, substantially following the provisions of G.S. 28A-2A-13, are hereby validated and approved as to the conveyance and transfer of any title to real estate as contained therein, to the same extent as if said wills had originally been probated and filed in said county, and the clerk of the superior court of said county had had jurisdiction to probate the same, provided the probates and witnesses to the said wills are sufficient and according to law. (1921, c. 108, s. 2; C.S., s. 4146(a); 2011-344, ss. 3, 4.)

§ 28A-2A-15. Certified copy of will proved in another state or country.

When a will, made by a citizen of this State, is proved and allowed in some other state or country, and the original will cannot be removed from its place of legal deposit in such other state or country, for probate in this State, the clerk of the superior court of the county where the testator had his last usual residence or has any property, upon a duly certified copy or exemplification of such will being exhibited to him for probate, shall take every order and proceeding for proving, allowing and recording such copy as by law might be taken upon the production of the original. (1802, c. 623; R.C., c. 44, s. 9; C.C.P., s. 445; Code, s. 2157; Rev., s. 3130; C.S., s. 4147; 2011-344, s. 3.)

§ 28A-2A-16. Examination of witnesses by affidavit.

(a) The examination of witnesses to a will may be taken and subscribed in the form of an affidavit before a notary public or other person who is authorized to administer oaths in the jurisdiction where the examination is held.

(b) A photographic copy of the original will certified to be a true and exact copy thereof by the clerk of superior court of the county in which the will is to be probated may be used in the examination of the witnesses in the procedures set out in subsection (a) of this section; provided, the said clerk has in his possession the original will at the time of examination of the witnesses.

(c) Affidavits taken in accordance with subsection (a) of this section shall be transmitted by the person taking the affidavit to the clerk of superior court of the county in which the will is to be probated.

(d) Testimony submitted in accordance with subsection (a) of this section is competent in regard to all requirements of G.S. 31-3.3 and to establish that a will was executed in compliance with the requirements of G.S. 31-3.3.

(e) Nothing in this section is to limit or otherwise affect the authority of a clerk of superior court in the exercise of his authority as judge of probate under G.S. 28A-2-1 to:

(1) Issue subpoenas under G.S. 7A-103; or

(2) Order the taking of depositions of witnesses. (1917, c. 183; C.S., s. 4149; 1933, c. 114; 1957, c. 587, ss. 1, 1A; 1979, c. 226, s. 1; 1987, c. 78, s. 2; 2011-344, ss. 3, 4.)

§ 28A-2A-17. Certified copy of will of nonresident recorded.

(a) Subject to the provisions of subsection (b) of this section, if the will of a citizen or subject of another state or country is probated in accordance with the laws of that jurisdiction and a duly certified copy of the will and the probate proceedings are produced before a clerk of superior court of any county wherein the testator had property, the copy of the will shall be probated as if it were the original. If the jurisdiction is within the United States, the copy of the will and the probate proceedings shall be certified by the clerk of the court wherein the will was probated. If the jurisdiction is outside the United States, the copy of the will and probate proceedings shall be certified by any ambassador, minister, consul or commercial agent of the United States under his official seal.

(b) For a copy of a will probated under the provisions of subsection (a) of this section to be valid to pass title to or otherwise dispose of real estate in this State, the execution of said will according to the laws of this State either at the time of its execution or at the time of the death of the testator, or as otherwise recognized as valid under the provisions of G.S. 31-46, must appear affirmatively, to the satisfaction of the clerk of the superior court of the county in which such will is offered for probate, from the testimony of a witness or witnesses to such will, or from findings of fact or recitals in the order of probate, or otherwise in such certified copy of the will and probate proceedings.

(c) If the execution of the will in accordance with the laws of this State either at the time of its execution or at the time of the death of the testator, or as otherwise recognized as valid under the provisions of G.S. 31-46, does not appear as required by subsection (b) of this section, the clerk before whom the copy is exhibited shall have power to take proof as prescribed in G.S. 28A-2A-16, and the will may be adjudged duly proved, and if so proved, the will shall be recorded as herein provided.

(d) Any copy of a will of a nonresident heretofore allowed, filed and recorded in this State in compliance with the foregoing shall be valid to pass title to or otherwise dispose of real estate in this State. (C.C.P., s. 444; 1883, c. 144; Code, s. 2156; 1885, c. 393; Rev., s. 3133; C.S., s. 4152; 1941, c. 381; 1965, c. 995; 1987, c. 78, s. 3; 2011-344, ss. 3, 4; 2013-91, s. 1(h).)

§ 28A-2A-18. Probates validated where proof taken by commissioner or another clerk.

In all cases of the probate of any will made prior to March 8, 1899, in common form before any clerk of the superior courts of this State, where the testimony of the subscribing witnesses has been taken in the State or out of it by any commissioner appointed by said clerk or taken by any other clerk of the superior court in any other county of this State, and the will admitted to probate upon such testimony, the proceedings are validated. (1899, c. 680; Rev., s. 3134; C.S., s. 4153; 2011-344, s. 3.)

§ 28A-2A-19. Probates in another state before 1860 validated.

In all cases where any will devises land in this State, and the original will was duly admitted to probate in some other state prior to the year 1860, and a certified copy of such will and the probate thereof has been admitted to probate and record in any county in this State, and it in any way appears from such recorded copy that there were two subscribing witnesses to such will, and its execution was proved by the examination of such witnesses when the original was admitted to probate, such will shall be held and considered, and is hereby declared to be, good and valid for the purpose of passing title to the lands devised thereby, situated in this State, as fully and completely as if the original will had been duly executed and admitted to probate and recorded in this State in accordance with the laws of this State. (1913, c. 93, s. 1; C.S., s. 4155; 2011-344, s. 3.)

§ 28A-2A-20. Validation of wills recorded without probate by subscribing witnesses.

In all cases where wills and testaments were executed prior to the first day of January, 1875, and which appear as recorded in the record of last wills and testaments to have had two or more witnesses thereto, and such last wills and testaments were admitted to probate and recorded in the record of wills in the proper county in this State prior to the first day of January, 1888, without having been duly proven as provided by law, and such wills were presented to the clerk of the superior court in any county in this State where the makers of said wills owned property, and where the makers of such wills lived and died, and were by such clerks recorded in the record of wills for that county, said wills and testaments or exemplified copies or certified true copies thereof, so recorded, if otherwise sufficient, shall have the effect to pass the title to real or personal property, or both, therein devised, to the same extent and as completely as if the execution thereof had been duly proven by the two subscribing witnesses thereto in the manner provided by law of this State. Nothing herein shall be construed to prevent such wills from being impeached for fraud. (1921, c. 66; C.S., s. 4157(a); 1997-81, s. 3; 2011-284, s. 31; 2011-344, s. 3.)

§ 28A-2A-21. Validation of wills admitted on oath of one subscribing witness.

In all cases where last wills and testaments which appear as recorded in the record of last wills and testaments to have had two witnesses thereto and such last wills and testaments were admitted to probate and recorded in the record of wills in the proper county in this State prior to the first day of January, 1890, upon the oath and examination of one of the witnesses, such proof being taken in writing and recorded, and the certificate of probate of the clerk of the court states that such a will is proven by one of the subscribing witnesses thereto and the handwriting of the other subscribing witness being a nonresident is proven under oath, and such a will and certificate has been recorded in the record of wills of the proper county, such probate is hereby validated as fully as if the proof of the handwriting of the nonresident witness had been taken in regular form in writing and recorded. (1929, c. 41, ss. 1, 2; 2011-344, s. 3.)

§ 28A-2A-22. Validation of probates of wills when witnesses examined before notary public; acts of deputy clerks validated.

Whenever any last will and testament has been probated, based upon the examination of the subscribing witness or the subscribing witnesses, taken before a notary public in the county in which the will is probated, or taken before a notary public of any other county, it is hereby in all respects validated and shall be sufficient to pass the title to all real and personal property purported to be transferred thereby.

All acts heretofore performed by deputy clerks of the superior court in taking acknowledgments, examining witnesses and probate of any wills, deeds and other instruments required or permitted by law to be recorded, are hereby validated. Nothing herein contained shall affect pending litigation. (1945, c. 822; 1973, c. 445; 1977, c. 734, s. 1; 1979, c. 226, s. 2; 2011-344, s. 3.)

§ 28A-2A-23. Validation of wills when recorded without order of probate or registration upon oath and examination of subscribing witness or witnesses.

Whenever any last will and testament has been duly presented to the clerk of the superior court, and the said will together with the oath and examination of the subscribing witness or witnesses thereto taken before a notary public in the county in which the will is probated, or taken before a notary public of any other county, or before the clerk of the superior court of said county, or any other county, is duly recorded in the office of the clerk of the superior court of the said county, without a formal order of probate or registration, such will, if executed in accordance with the laws of this State, is hereby validated with respect to the probate and registration thereof and shall be sufficient to pass title to all real and personal property purported to be transferred thereby to the same extent that the said will would have done so if there had been a formal order of probate and registration. This section shall apply only to wills presented to the clerk of the superior court and recorded prior to the first day of January, 1943. (1951, c. 725; 2011-344, s. 3.)

Article 3.

Venue for Probate of Wills and Administration of Estates of Decedents.

§ 28A-3-1. Proper county.

The venue for the probate of a will and for all proceedings relating to the administration of the estate of a decedent shall be:

(1) In the county in this State where the decedent was domiciled at the time of the decedent's death; or

(2) If the decedent had no domicile in this State at the time of death, then in any county wherein the decedent left any property or assets or into which any property or assets belonging to this estate may have come. If there be more than one such county, that county in which proceedings are first commenced shall have priority of venue; or

(3) If the decedent was a nonresident motorist who died in the State, then in any county in the State. (R.C., c. 46, s. 1; C.C.P., s. 433; 1868-9, c. 113, s. 115; Code, s. 1374; Rev., s. 16; C.S., s. 1; 1931, c. 165; 1943, c. 543; 1951, c. 765; 1973, c. 1329, s. 3; 2011-344, s. 4.)

§ 28A-3-2. Proceedings to determine venue.

(a) If proceedings are commenced in more than one county or if upon commencement of a proceeding a question arises as to the proper county of venue, or if for any other reason a delay arises in determining venue, the matter shall be referred by the clerk of superior court for a hearing and determination by the senior resident superior court judge or any judge assigned to hold the superior courts of the district which includes the county where the proceedings were first commenced. Upon the filing of a motion or petition to determine venue, the judge shall determine which is the proper county for administration of the estate and stay proceedings in all other counties. The judge shall make such orders as are necessary to transfer the entire proceedings to the proper county. The clerk of superior court of each county in which proceedings are stayed shall retain a true copy of the entire file and transmit the original to the clerk of superior court of such county as the judge directs.

(a1) Any interested person may file a petition to determine proper venue within the time prescribed by G.S. 28A-3-5. The matter shall be referred by the clerk of superior court by or before whom the petition is filed for a hearing and determination by the senior resident superior court judge or any judge assigned to hold the superior courts of the district that includes the county where the proceedings were first commenced.

(b) A proceeding shall be deemed commenced by the offering of a will for probate or by applying for letters of administration as provided by G.S. 28A-6-1 through 28A-6-5 or by applying for letters of collection as provided by G.S. 28A-11-1 through 28A-11-4 and the proceeding first legally commenced shall extend to all of the property or assets of the decedent in this State. (1973, c. 1329, s. 3; 1975, c. 19, s. 7; 2011-344, s. 4.)

§ 28A-3-3. Procedure after determination of improper appointment.

Where a person has been improperly appointed, and a different person in another county is determined under G.S. 28A-3-2(a) to be the properly appointed personal representative, such improperly appointed personal representative shall surrender to the properly appointed personal representative all assets of the estate under control of the improperly appointed personal representative. In addition such improperly appointed personal representative shall file an accounting with the clerk of superior court in the proper county according to the form prescribed for collectors by G.S. 28A-11-4. (1973, c. 1329, s. 3; 2011-344, s. 4.)

§ 28A-3-4. Liability of personal representative appointed in improper county.

When a personal representative has been appointed in an improper county, and a different person in another county is determined under G.S. 28A-3-2(a) to be the properly appointed personal representative, such improperly appointed personal representative shall not thereby incur personal liability for administrative acts performed prior to the transfer except as provided in G.S. 28A-13-10. (1973, c. 1329, s. 3.)

§ 28A-3-5. Waiver of venue.

If questions as to priority of venue are not raised within three months after the issuance of letters testamentary or letters of administration to the personal representative, the validity of the proceeding shall not be affected by any error in venue. (1973, c. 1329, s. 3.)

Article 4.

Qualification and Disqualification for Letters Testamentary and Letters of Administration.

§ 28A-4-1. Order of persons qualified to serve.

(a)   Letters Testamentary. - Letters testamentary shall be granted to the executor or executors named or designated in the will, or if no such person qualifies, to any substitute or successor executor named or designated in the will. If no person so named or designated qualifies, letters testamentary shall be granted to some other person nominated by a person upon whom the will expressly confers the authority to make such nomination. If none of the foregoing persons qualifies, the clerk shall grant letters of administration in accordance with subsection (b) of this section.

(b) Letters of Administration. - Letters of administration shall be granted to persons who are qualified to serve, in the following order, unless the clerk of superior court in the discretion of the clerk of superior court determines that the best interests of the estate otherwise require:

(1) The surviving spouse of the decedent;

(2) Any devisee of the testator;

(3) Any heir of the decedent;

(3a) Any next of kin, with a person who is of a closer kinship as computed pursuant to G.S. 104A-1 having priority;

(4) Any creditor to whom the decedent became obligated prior to the decedent's death;

(5) Any person of good character residing in the county who applies therefor; and

(6) Any other person of good character not disqualified under G.S. 28A-4-2.

When applicants are equally entitled, letters shall be granted to the applicant who, in the judgment of the clerk of superior court, is most likely to administer the estate advantageously, or they may be granted to any two or more of such applicants.

(c) Any interested person may file a petition pursuant to Article 2 of this Chapter alleging that all or any of the persons described in subsection (b) of this section is disqualified in accordance with G.S. 28A-4-2. (R.C., c. 46, ss. 2, 3; C.C.P., s. 456; 1968-9, c. 113, s. 115; Code, s. 1376; Rev., s. 3; C.S., s. 6; 1949, c. 22; 1973, c. 1329, s. 3; 1987, c. 357; 2011-344, s. 4.)

§ 28A-4-2. Persons disqualified to serve as personal representative.

No person is qualified to serve as a personal representative who:

(1) Is under 18 years of age;

(2) Has been adjudged incompetent in a formal proceeding and remains under such disability;

(3) Is a convicted felon, under the laws either of the United States or of any state or territory of the United States, or of the District of Columbia and whose citizenship has not been restored;

(4) Is a nonresident of this State who has not appointed a resident agent to accept service of process in all actions or proceedings with respect to the estate, and caused such appointment to be filed with the court; or who is a resident of this State who has, subsequent to appointment as a personal representative, moved from this State without appointing such process agent;

(5) Is a corporation not authorized to act as a personal representative in this State;

(6) Repealed by Session Laws 1999-133, s. 1.

(7) Has lost that person's rights as provided by Chapter 31A;

(8) Is illiterate;

(9) Is a person whom the clerk of superior court finds otherwise unsuitable; or

(10) Is a person who has renounced either expressly or by implication as provided in G.S. 28A-5-1 and 28A-5-2. (C.C.P., s. 457; Code, ss. 1377, 1378, 2162; Rev., s. 5; C.S., s. 8; 1973, c. 1329, s. 3; 1999-133, s. 1; 2011-344, s. 4.)

Article 5.

Renunciation by Personal Representative.

§ 28A-5-1. Renunciation by executor.

(a) Express Renunciation by Executor. - Any person named or designated as executor in a duly probated will may renounce the office by filing with the clerk of superior court a writing signed by such person, and acknowledged or proved to the satisfaction of the clerk.

(b) Implied Renunciation by Executor. - If any person named or designated as executor fails to qualify or to renounce within 30 days after the will had been admitted to probate, (i) the clerk of superior court may issue a notice to that person to qualify or move for an extension of time to qualify within 15 days, or (ii) any other person named or designated as executor in the will or any interested person may file a petition in accordance with Article 2 of this Chapter for an order finding that person named or designated as executor to be deemed to have renounced. If that person does not file a response to the notice or petition within 15 days from the date of service of the notice or petition, the clerk of superior court shall enter an order adjudging that the person has renounced. If the person files a response within 15 days from the date of service of the notice or petition requesting an extension of time within which to qualify or renounce, upon hearing, the clerk of superior court may grant to that person a reasonable extension of time within which to qualify or renounce for cause shown. If that person qualifies within 15 days of the date of service of the notice or petition, the clerk of superior court shall dismiss that notice or petition, without prejudice, summarily and without hearing.

(c) Procedure upon Renunciation. - Upon renunciation by a person named or designated as executor, letters shall be issued to some other person as provided in G.S. 28A-4-1. (C.C.P., ss. 450, 451; Code, ss. 2163, 2164; Rev., ss. 10, 13; C.S., ss. 13, 16; 1931, c. 183; 1953, c. 78, s. 1; 1973, c. 1329, s. 3; 2011-344, s. 4; 2012-194, s. 13(a).)

§ 28A-5-2. Renunciation of right to administer.

(a) Express Renunciation. - Any person entitled to apply for letters of administration may renounce the office by filing with the clerk of superior court a writing signed by such person, and acknowledged or proved to the satisfaction of the clerk.

(b) Implied Renunciation. -

(1) If any person entitled to apply for letters of administration fails to apply therefor within 30 days from the date of death of the intestate, (i) the clerk of superior court may issue a notice to the person to qualify or move for an extension of time to qualify within 15 days, or (ii) any interested person may file a petition in accordance with Article 2 of this Chapter for an order finding that person to be deemed to have renounced. If the person does not file a response to the notice or petition within 15 days from the date of service of the notice or petition, the clerk of superior court shall enter an order adjudging that the person has renounced. If the person files a response within 15 days from the date of service of the notice or petition requesting an extension of time within which to qualify or renounce, upon hearing, the clerk of superior court may grant to that person a reasonable extension of time within which to qualify or renounce for cause shown. If the person qualifies within 15 days of the date of service of the notice or petition, the clerk of superior court shall dismiss the notice or petition, without prejudice, summarily and without hearing and the clerk of superior court shall issue letters to some other person as provided in G.S. 28A-4-1. No notice shall be required to be given to any interested person, but the clerk may give notice as the clerk in the clerk's discretion may determine.

(2) If no person entitled to administer applies for letters of administration within 90 days after the date of death of an intestate, then the clerk of superior court may, in the clerk's discretion, enter an order declaring all prior rights to apply for letters of administration to be renounced, and issue letters to some suitable person as provided in G.S. 28A-4-1.

(c) Nomination by Person Renouncing. - Any person who expressly renounces the person's prior right to apply for letters of administration may at the same time nominate in writing some other person not disqualified under G.S. 28A-4-2 to be named as personal representative, and such designated person shall be entitled to the same priority of right to apply for letters of administration as the person making the nomination. (R.C., c. 46, ss. 2, 3; C.C.P., ss. 456, 460(a); 1868-9, c. 113, s. 115; c. 203; Code, ss. 1376, 1380; Rev., ss. 3, 12; C.S., ss. 6, 15; 1949, c. 22; 1973, c. 1329, s. 3; 2011-344, s. 4; 2012-194, s. 13(b).)

Article 6.

Appointment of Personal Representative.

§ 28A-6-1. Application for letters; grant of letters.

(a) The application for letters of administration or letters testamentary shall be in the form of an affidavit sworn to before an officer authorized to administer oaths, signed by the applicant or the applicant's attorney, which may be supported by other proof under oath in writing, all of which shall be recorded and filed by the clerk of superior court, and shall allege the following facts:

(1) The name, and to the extent known, the domicile and the date and place of death of the decedent;

(2) The legal residence and mailing address of the applicant;

(3) The names, ages and mailing addresses of the decedent's heirs and devisees, including the names and mailing addresses of the guardians of those having court-appointed guardians, so far as all of these facts are known or can with reasonable diligence be ascertained;

(4) That the applicant is the person entitled to apply for letters, or that the applicant applies after persons having prior right to apply are shown to have renounced under Article 5 of this Chapter, or that the applicant applies subject to the provisions of G.S. 28A-6-2(1), and that the applicant is not disqualified under G.S. 28A-4-2.

(5) The nature and probable value of the decedent's property, both real and personal, and the location of such property, so far as all of these facts are known or can with reasonable diligence be ascertained; and

(6) If the decedent was not domiciled in this State at the time of the decedent's death, a schedule of the decedent's property located in this State, and the name and mailing address of the decedent's domiciliary personal representative, or if there is none, whether a proceeding to appoint one is pending.

(b) If it appears to the clerk of superior court that the application and supporting evidence comply with the requirements of subsection (a) of this section and on the basis thereof the clerk finds that the applicant is entitled to appointment, the clerk shall issue letters of administration or letters testamentary to the applicant unless in the clerk's discretion the clerk determines that the best interests of the estate would be served by delaying the appointment of a personal representative, in which case the clerk may appoint a collector as provided in Article 11.

(c)   The clerk of superior court may rely upon the following as evidence of death:

(1)   A certified or authenticated copy of a death certificate purporting to be issued by an official or agency of the place where the death purportedly occurred.

(2)   A certified or authenticated copy of any record or report of a governmental agency, domestic or foreign, evidencing the date of death.

(3)   A certificate or authenticated copy of medical records, including a record of death, evidencing the date of death.

(4)   Any other evidence that the clerk of superior court deems sufficient to confirm the date of death. (C.C.P., s. 461; Code, s. 1381; Rev., s. 26; C.S., s. 28; 1973, c. 1329, s. 3; 2011-344, s. 4.)

§ 28A-6-2. Letters issued without notice; exceptions.

Letters of administration or letters testamentary may be issued without notice, including upon a finding of implied renunciation under G.S. 28A-5-1(b) or G.S. 28A-5-2(b), except:

(1)   When the applicant is not entitled to priority of appointment under G.S. 28A-4-1, all persons entitled to an equal or higher preference shall be given 15 days prior to written notice of that application, unless they have renounced in accordance with the provisions of Article 5 of this Chapter.

(2)   The clerk of superior court may in any case require that prior written notice be given to such interested persons as the clerk, in the clerk's discretion, may designate prior to the granting of letters. (1973, c. 1329, s. 3; 2011-344, s. 4.)

§ 28A-6-3. Appointment of successor to personal representative.

When the appointment of a sole or last surviving personal representative is terminated by death, resignation pursuant to Article 10 of this Chapter, or revocation pursuant to Article 9 of this Chapter, the clerk of superior court shall appoint another personal representative as provided by G.S. 28A-4-1 to act as successor to the sole or last surviving personal representative. When two or more personal representatives have qualified, and the appointment of one or more of them is terminated by death, resignation or revocation, leaving in office one or more personal representatives, the appointment of successors shall not be required unless:

(1) The clerk of superior court determines, in the clerk's discretion, that it is in the best interest of the estate to appoint a successor or successors to such personal representative or personal representatives, or

(2) In the case of executors, the will so provides. (1868-9, c. 113, s. 92; Code, s. 1521; Rev., s. 35; C.S., s. 32; 1973, c. 1329, s. 3; 2011-344, s. 4.)

§ 28A-6-4. Right to contest appointment; procedure.

Prior to the issuance of letters, any interested person may, by written petition filed with the clerk of superior court, and served upon such interested persons as the clerk of superior court may direct, contest the issuance of letters of administration or letters testamentary to a person otherwise entitled to apply for letters of administration or letters testamentary. After a petition has been duly filed, the clerk of superior court shall conduct a hearing and determine to whom letters shall be issued. Appeal may be taken from the order of the clerk as in an estate proceeding pursuant to G.S. 1-301.3. (C.C.P., s. 462; Code, s. 1382; Rev., s. 27; C.S., s. 29; 1973, c. 1329, s. 3; 1975, c. 300, s. 2; 2011-344, s. 4.)

§ 28A-6-5. Letters not subject to collateral attack.

The validity of letters issued shall not be subject to collateral attack. (1973, c. 1329, s. 3.)

Article 7.

Oath.

§ 28A-7-1. Oath required before letters issue.

Before letters testamentary, letters of administration or letters of collection are issued to any person, the person shall take and subscribe an oath or affirmation before the clerk of superior court, or before any other officer of any state or country authorized by the laws of North Carolina to administer oaths, that the person will faithfully and honestly discharge the duties of the person's office. Such oath or affirmation shall be in the form prescribed in G.S. 11-11, and shall be filed in the office of the clerk of superior court. (C.C.P., ss. 467, 468; 1870-1, c. 93; Code, ss. 1387, 1388, 2169; Rev., s. 29; C.S., s. 39; 1923, c. 56; 1967, c. 41, s. 1; 1973, c. 1329, s. 3; 2011-344, s. 4.)

Article 8.

Bond.

§ 28A-8-1. Bond required before letters issue; when bond not required.

(a) Except as otherwise provided in subsection (b) of this section, every personal representative, before letters are issued, shall give bond, conditioned as provided in G.S. 28A-8-2.

(b) No bond shall be required of:

(1) A resident executor, unless the express terms of the will require a resident executor to give bond;

(2) A nonresident executor (or a resident executor who moves from this State subsequent to that executor's appointment) who has appointed a resident agent to accept service of process as provided in G.S. 28A-4-2(a) [28A-4-2(4)], when the express terms of the will excuse a nonresident executor from giving bond;

(3) A nonresident executor, when there is a resident executor named who has qualified as coexecutor unless the express terms of the will require them to give bond, or the clerk of superior court finds that such bond is necessary for the protection of the estate; or

(4) A personal representative appointed solely for the purpose of bringing an action for the wrongful death of the deceased until such time as the personal representative shall receive property into the estate of the deceased; or

(5) A personal representative that is a trust institution licensed under G.S. 53-159;

(6) A personal representative of an intestate who resides in the State of North Carolina when all of the heirs of the decedent are over 18 years of age and file with the clerk of superior court a written waiver instrument agreeing to relieve the personal representative from the necessity of giving bond; or

(7) A personal representative where the personal representative receives all the property of the decedent;

(8) An administrator with the will annexed who resides in the State of North Carolina when all of the devisees of the decedent are over 18 years of age and file with the clerk of superior court a written waiver instrument agreeing to relieve the administrator with the will annexed of the necessity of giving bond. (C.C.P., ss. 467, 468; 1870-1, c. 93; Code, ss. 1387, 1388, 2169; Rev., s. 29; C.S., s. 39; 1923, c. 56; 1967, c. 41, s. 1; 1973, c. 1329, s. 3; 1975, c. 300, s. 3; 1977, c. 29; 1981, c. 428; c. 599, ss. 5, 6; 2011-339, s. 5; 2011-344, s. 4.)

§ 28A-8-2. Provisions of bond.

A bond given pursuant to this Article shall be:

(1) Payable to the State to the use of all persons interested in the estate; and

(2) Conditioned that the personal representative giving the bond shall faithfully execute the trust reposed in the personal representative and obey all lawful orders of the clerk of superior court or other court touching the administration of the estate committed to the personal representative; and

(3) In an amount not less than:

a. One and one-fourth times the value of all personal property of the decedent when the bond is secured by a suretyship bond executed by a corporate surety company authorized by the Commissioner of Insurance to do business in this State, provided that the clerk of superior court, when the value of the personal property to be administered by the personal representative exceeds one hundred thousand dollars ($100,000), may accept bond in an amount equal to the value of the personal property plus ten percent (10%) thereof; or

b. Double the value of all personal property of the decedent when the bond is secured by one of the methods provided in subdivision (4)b, (4)c or (4)d; such value of said personal property to be ascertained by the clerk of superior court by examination, on oath, of the applicant or of some other person determined by the clerk to be qualified to testify as to its value; and

(4) Secured by one or more of the following:

a. Suretyship bond executed, at the expense of the estate, by a corporate surety company authorized by the Commissioner of Insurance to do business in this State;

b. Suretyship bond executed and justified upon oath before the clerk of superior court by two or more sufficient personal sureties each of whom shall reside in and own real estate in North Carolina and shall have assets with an aggregate value above encumbrances of not less than the amount of the penalty of the required bond;

c. A first mortgage or first deed of trust in form approved by the administrative officer of the courts on real estate located in North Carolina:

1. Executed by the owner, and conditioned on the performance of the obligations of the bond, and

2. Containing a power of sale which, in the case of a mortgage, is exercisable by the clerk of superior court upon a breach of any condition thereof, or, in the case of a deed of trust, is exercisable by the trustee after notice by the clerk of superior court that a breach of condition has occurred.

The clerk of superior court shall not accept such mortgage or deed of trust until it shall have been properly registered in the county or counties in which the real estate is located, and the clerk of superior court is satisfied that the real estate subject to the mortgage or deed of trust is worth the amount to be secured thereby, and that the mortgage or deed of trust is a first charge on said real estate. No such mortgage or deed of trust shall be cancelled or surrendered until the approval of the final account, unless substitution is permitted as provided in G.S. 28A-8-3(d).

d. A deposit by the owner with the clerk of superior court of negotiable securities, of a kind permitted by law to be proper investments for fiduciaries exercising due care, having a fair market value determined by the clerk to be equal to the amount of the penalty of the bond. Such securities shall be properly endorsed, delivered to the clerk of superior court, and accompanied by a security agreement containing a power of sale authorizing the clerk of superior court to sell them in the event the person to whom letters are being issued commits a breach of any duty imposed upon that person by law in respect of that person's office. Such securities shall not be surrendered by the clerk of superior court to the owner until the approval of the final account, unless substitution is permitted as provided in G.S. 28A-8-3(d). For the purposes of determining the value of the assets of the personal sureties in subdivision (4)b, or the value of the real estate in subdivision (4)c, or the value of the negotiable securities in subdivision (4)d, the clerk of superior court may require a certificate of the value of such property by one or more persons not interested in the estate determined by the clerk to be qualified to certify such value. (C.C.P., s. 468; 1870-1, c. 93; Code, s. 1388; Rev., s. 319; C.S., s. 33; 1935, c. 386; 1949, c. 971; 1967, c. 41, s. 1; 1973, c. 1329, s. 3; 2011-344, s. 4.)

§ 28A-8-3. Modification of bond requirements.

(a) Increase of Bond or Security in Case of Inadequacy or Insufficiency. -

(1) The clerk of superior court, on the clerk's own motion, may require the personal representative to give a new bond or to furnish additional security if the clerk of superior court finds that the bond filed pursuant to this Article, or its security, is insufficient, inadequate in amount, or that any of the individual sureties has become or is about to become a nonresident or, in the case of a corporate surety, has withdrawn or is about to withdraw from doing business in this State.

(2) Any interested person may file a verified petition in accordance with Article 2 of this Chapter requesting modification of bond requirements. Upon the filing of a verified petition, the clerk of superior court shall conduct a hearing in accordance with Article 2 of this Chapter. If the clerk of superior court finds that the bond filed or its security is insufficient or inadequate, the clerk shall make an order requiring the personal representative to give a new bond or to furnish additional security within a reasonable time to be fixed in the order.

(b) Increase of Bond upon Sale of Real Estate. - When a personal representative makes application for an order to sell real estate, the provisions of G.S. 1-339.10 shall govern.

(c) Reduction of Bond. - On application of the personal representative the penalty of the bond may be reduced from time to time when the clerk of superior court finds that such reduction is clearly justified, but in no event shall the penalty of the bond be reduced below the amount required by G.S. 28A-8-2(3).

(d) Substitution of Security. - When a bond is secured by a mortgage or deed of trust on real estate as provided in G.S. 28A-8-2(4)c or a deposit of negotiable securities as provided in G.S. 28A-8-2(4)d, the clerk of superior court may, on application of the personal representative, order that such real estate or negotiable securities, or a part thereof, be released upon the substitution therefor of other security in compliance with G.S. 28A-8-2(4)a, (4)c, or (4)d. Such substitution may be allowed in conjunction with any other modification of bond requirements permitted by this section. (1868-9, c. 113, s. 89; Code, s. 1518; Rev., s. 32; C.S., s. 43; 1973, c. 1329, s. 3; 2011-344, s. 4.)

§ 28A-8-4. Failure to give additional bond; letters revoked.

If any personal representative fails to give an additional bond or new bond or to furnish additional security as ordered by the clerk of superior court pursuant to the provisions of this Article, within the time specified in any such order (not less than five days or more than 15 days), the clerk of superior court shall proceed as provided in G.S. 28A-9-2. (1868-9, c. 113, s. 91; Code, s. 1520; Rev., s. 34; C.S., s. 44; 1973, c. 1329, s. 3; 2011-344, s. 4.)

§ 28A-8-5. Rights of surety in danger of loss.

Any surety on the bond of a personal representative who is in danger of loss under the surety's suretyship may file a verified petition with the clerk of superior court setting forth the facts, and asking that such personal representative be removed from office, or that the personal representative be required to give security to indemnify the petitioner against apprehended loss, or that the petitioner be discharged as surety and be released from liability for any future breach of the bond. The clerk of superior court shall conduct a hearing in accordance with Article 2 of this Chapter. If, upon the hearing, the clerk of superior court determines that the surety is entitled to relief, the clerk may grant the same in such manner as to serve the best interest of the estate. In any event, however, the previous surety shall not be released from liability for any breach of duty by the personal representative occurring prior to the filing of bond with a new surety unless the new surety assumes liability for the earlier breaches. (1868-9, c. 113, s. 90; Code, s. 1519; Rev., s. 33; C.S., s. 41; 1973, c. 1329, s. 3; 2011-344, s. 4.)

§ 28A-8-6. Action against obligors on bond of personal representative.

Any person injured by the breach of any bond given by a personal representative or collector may institute a civil action against one or more of the obligors of the bond and recover such damages as the person may have sustained. Any successor personal representative, or any other personal representative of the same decedent, may institute such action on behalf of the persons interested in the estate. Any such action against one or more of the obligors of the bond shall be brought in the name of the State of North Carolina and shall be instituted in the county in which letters were issued to the personal representative or collector, and the clerk of superior court shall give notice of the institution of the action in such manner as the clerk may determine to all other persons shown by the clerk's records to be interested in the estate. The bond of the personal representative is not void after the first or any subsequent recovery thereon until the entire penalty is recovered. If the plaintiff fails to prevail, costs may be taxed against the person or persons for whose benefit the action on a personal representative's bond is prosecuted. (1868-9, c. 113, ss. 87, 88; Code, ss. 1516, 1517; Rev., ss. 30, 31; C.S., ss. 40, 42; 1973, c. 1329, s. 3; 2011-344, s. 4.)

§ 28A-8-1.1. Deposited money; exclusion in computing amount of bond.

Notwithstanding the provisions of G.S. 28A-8-1, in any proceeding for the determination of the amount of bond to be required of the personal representative or testamentary trustee, whether at the time of appointment or subsequently, when it appears that the estate of the decedent or the testamentary trust includes money which has been or will be deposited in a bank or banks in this State, or money which has been or will be invested in an account or accounts in an insured savings and loan association or associations upon condition that such money will not be withdrawn except on authorization of the court, the court may, in its discretion, order such money so deposited or so invested and shall exclude such deposited money from the computation of the amount of such bond or reduce the amount of bond to be required in respect of such money to such an amount as it may deem reasonable.

The petitioner for letters testamentary, of administration, or of trusteeship may deliver to any such bank or association any such money in the petitioner's possession, or may allow such bank to retain any such money already in its possession, or may allow such association to retain any such money already invested with it; and, in either event, the petitioner shall secure and file with the court a written receipt including the agreement of the bank or association that such money shall not be allowed to be withdrawn except on authorization of the court. In so receiving and retaining such money, the bank or association shall be protected to the same extent as though it had received the same from a person to whom letters testamentary, of administration, or of trusteeship had been issued.

The term "account in an insured savings and loan association" as used in this section means an account insured by the Federal Deposit Insurance Corporation, the Federal Savings and Loan Insurance Corporation or by a mutual deposit guaranty association authorized by Article 7A of Chapter 54 of the General Statutes of North Carolina.

The term "money" as used in this section means the principal of the decedent's estate and does not include the income earned by the principal of the decedent's estate which may be withdrawn without any authorization of the court. (1977, c. 870, s. 1; 2011-344, s. 4.)

Article 9.

Revocation of Letters.

§ 28A-9-1. Revocation after hearing.

(a)   Grounds. - Letters testamentary, letters of administration, or letters of collection may be revoked after hearing on any of the following grounds:

(1)   The person to whom they were issued was originally disqualified under the provisions of G.S. 28A-4-2 or has become disqualified since the issuance of letters.

(2)   The issuance of letters was obtained by false representation or mistake.

(3)   The person to whom they were issued has violated a fiduciary duty through default or misconduct in the execution of the person's office, other than acts specified in G.S. 28A-9-2.

(4)   The person to whom they were issued has a private interest, whether direct or indirect, that might tend to hinder or be adverse to a fair and proper administration. The relationship upon which the appointment was predicated shall not, in and of itself, constitute such an interest.

(b)   Procedure. -

(1)   The clerk of superior court may, on the clerk's own motion, conduct a hearing in accordance with Article 2 of this Chapter to determine whether any of the grounds set forth in subsection (a) of this section exist with regard to any personal representative or collector within the jurisdiction of the clerk of superior court.

(2)   Upon the verified petition of any person interested in the estate for an order finding that any of the grounds set forth in subsection (a) of this section exist with regard to any personal representative or collector within the jurisdiction of the clerk of superior court, the clerk shall conduct a hearing in accordance with Article 2 of this Chapter.

(3)   Notice of the time and date of the hearing shall be given in accordance with Article 2 of this Chapter and to such persons as the clerk of superior court shall determine. If at the hearing the clerk of superior court finds any one of the

grounds set forth in subsection (a) of this section to exist, the clerk of superior court shall revoke the letters issued to such personal representative or collector. (C.C.P., s. 470; Code, s. 2171; Rev., s. 38; C.S., s. 31; 1921, c. 98; 1953, c. 795; 1973, c. 1329, s. 3; 2011-344, s. 4.)

§ 28A-9-2. Summary revocation.

(a)   Grounds. - Letters testamentary, letters of administration, or letters of collection, shall be revoked by the clerk of superior court without hearing when:

(1)   After letters of administration or collection have been issued, a will is subsequently admitted to probate.

(2)   After letters testamentary have been issued:

a.   The will is set aside, or

b.   A subsequent testamentary paper revoking the appointment of the executor is admitted to probate.

(3)   Any personal representative or collector required to give a new bond or furnish additional security pursuant to G.S. 28A-8-3 fails to do so within the time ordered.

(4)   A nonresident personal representative refuses or fails to obey any citation, notice, or process served on that nonresident personal representative or the process agent of the nonresident personal representative.

(5)   A trustee in bankruptcy, liquidating agent, or receiver has been appointed for any personal representative or collector, or any personal representative or collector has executed an assignment for the benefit of creditors.

(6)   A personal representative has failed to file an inventory or an annual account with the clerk of superior court, as required by Article 20 and Article 21 of this Chapter, and proceedings to compel such filing pursuant to G.S. 28A-20-2 or 28A-21-4 cannot be had because service cannot be completed because the personal representative cannot be found.

(b) Procedure. - Upon the occurrence of any of the acts set forth in subsection (a) of this section, the clerk of superior court shall enter an order revoking the letters issued to such personal representative or collector and shall cause a copy of the order to be served on the personal representative or collector or the personal representative's or collector's process agent. (C.C.P., s. 469; Code, s. 2170; Rev., s. 37; C.S., s. 30; 1973, c. 1329, s. 3; 1975, c. 19, s. 8; 2011-344, s. 4.)

§ 28A-9-3. Effect of revocation.

Upon entry of the order revoking a personal representative's or collector's letters, the authority of the personal representative or collector shall cease. The personal representative or collector shall surrender all assets of the estate under the control of the personal representative or collector to the personal representative's or collector's successor, or the remaining personal representative or collector or to the clerk of superior court; and shall file an accounting in the form prescribed by Article 21 of this Chapter. A personal representative or collector whose letters are revoked pursuant to G.S. 28A-9-2(a)(1) or 28A-9-2(a)(2) shall not thereby incur personal liability for administrative acts performed prior to revocation except as provided in G.S. 28A-13-10. (1973, c. 1329, s. 3; 2011-344, s. 4.)

§ 28A-9-4. Appeal; stay effected.

Any interested person may appeal from the order of the clerk of superior court granting or denying revocation as a special proceeding pursuant to G.S. 28A-2-9(b). The clerk of superior court may issue a stay of an order revoking the letters upon the appellant posting an appropriate bond set by the clerk until the cause is heard and determined upon appeal. (1973, c. 1329, s. 3; 2011-344, s. 4.)

§ 28A-9-5. Interlocutory orders.

Pending any proceeding or appeal with respect to revocation of letters, the clerk of superior court may enter such interlocutory orders as are necessary to preserve the assets of the estate. (1868-9, c. 113, s. 92; Code, s. 1521; Rev., s. 35; C.S., s. 32; 1973, c. 1329, s. 3.)

§ 28A-9-6. Appointment of successor to personal representative or collector whose letters have been revoked; when not required.

Upon the revocation of letters issued to a sole or last surviving personal representative or collector, the clerk of superior court shall appoint another personal representative or collector as provided by G.S. 28A-4-1 to act as successor to the sole or last surviving personal representative or collector. When two or more personal representatives or collectors have qualified, and the letters of one or more personal representatives or collectors are revoked, leaving in office one or more personal representatives or collectors, the appointment of successors shall not be required unless:

(1)   The clerk of superior court determines, in the discretion of the clerk of superior court, that it is in the best interest of the estate to appoint a successor or successors to the personal representatives or collectors whose letters have been revoked, or

(2)   In the case of executors, the will so provides. (1868-9, c. 113, s. 92; Code, s. 1521; Rev., s. 35; C.S. 32; 1973, c. 1329, s. 3; 2011-344, s. 4.)

§ 28A-9-7. Rights and duties devolve on successor.

After the revocation of letters pursuant to this Article and upon the qualification and appointment of a successor, the substituted personal representative or collector shall succeed to all the powers stated in G.S. 28A-13-7. The substituted personal representative or collector shall be subject to all the duties, responsibilities and liabilities of the original personal representative or collector, other than liabilities arising out of the grounds for revocation. (1973, c. 1329, s. 3; 2011-344, s. 4.)

Article 10.

Resignation.

§ 28A-10-1. Clerk's power to accept resignation.

The clerk of superior court in the county where a person has been appointed personal representative shall have the power to accept that person's resignation. (1973, c. 1329, s. 3; 2011-344, s. 4.)

§ 28A-10-2. Contents of petition; notice.

(a) When a personal representative desires to resign the personal representative's office, the personal representative shall file a verified petition in the office of the clerk of the superior court, setting forth:

(1) The facts relating to the personal representative's appointment and qualifications;

(2) The names and residences of all interested persons known to the personal representative;

(3) A full statement of the reasons why the petitioner should be permitted to resign the petitioner's office; and

(4) A statement that the personal representative has filed with the clerk of superior court the personal representative's accounts and a record of the personal representative's conduct of the office.

(b) Notice of the petition for resignation, together with the date and time of the hearing thereon, shall be served upon all interested persons named in the petition in such manner as the clerk of superior court shall determine. (1973, c. 1329, s. 3; 2011-344, s. 4.)

§ 28A-10-3. Statement of account; record of conduct.

When the personal representative files the personal representative's petition requesting permission to resign the personal representative's office, the personal representative shall also file a verified statement of:

(1) The personal representative's accounts since that personal representative's qualification, or if the personal representative has previously filed an account, a statement of the personal representative's accounts since the date thereof;

(2) The assets of the estate and their location;

(3) The debts and liabilities of the estate;

(4) All facts and circumstances known to the personal representative the disclosure of which is necessary for a full and fair assessment of the personal representative's conduct of the office; and

(5) All additional facts and circumstances known to the personal representative the disclosure of which is necessary for a full and fair understanding of all matters concerning the estate. (1973, c. 1329, s. 3; 2011-344, s. 4.)

§ 28A-10-4. Hearing; order.

The clerk of superior court shall conduct a hearing in accordance with Article 2 of this Chapter on the petition not sooner than 10 days nor later than 20 days after notice to interested persons pursuant to G.S. 28A-10-2(b). If the clerk of superior court finds all the accounts proper, including accounts subsequent to the filing of the petition, and determines that the resignation of the personal representative is in the best interest of the estate and can be allowed, the resignation may be approved subject to the provisions of G.S. 28A-10-5. Except in cases governed by G.S. 28A-10-8, the clerk of superior court shall appoint a successor pursuant to G.S. 28A-4-1. (1973, c. 1329, s. 3; 2011-344, s. 4.)

§ 28A-10-5. When resignation becomes effective.

The resignation shall not become effective until:

(1) A successor has been duly qualified, unless G.S. 28A-10-8 is applicable; and

(2) The clerk of superior court is satisfied that the accounts of the personal representative are true and correct; and

(3) The personal representative has accounted to the personal representative's successor in full for all assets of the estate, or if pursuant to G.S. 28A-10-8 no successor is appointed, to the remaining personal representative or representatives, and the personal representative's final account has been filed with and approved by the clerk of superior court. (1973, c. 1329, s. 3; 2011-344, s. 4.)

§ 28A-10-6. Appeal; stay effected.

Any interested person who has appeared at the hearing and objected to the order of the clerk of superior court granting or denying resignation may appeal an order denying or allowing the resignation as a special proceeding pursuant to G.S. 28A-2-9(b). The clerk of superior court may issue a stay of an order allowing the resignation upon the appellant posting an appropriate bond set by the clerk until the cause is heard and determined upon appeal. (1973, c. 1329, s. 3; 2011-344, s. 4.)

§ 28A-10-7. Rights and duties devolve on successor.

Upon the qualification and appointment of a successor to a personal representative whose resignation has been allowed as provided in G.S. 28A-10-4, the substituted personal representative shall succeed to all the powers as provided in G.S. 28A-13-7 and shall also be subject to all the duties, responsibilities, and liabilities as provided in Article 13. (1973, c. 1329, s. 3; 2011-344, s. 4.)

§ 28A-10-8. When appointment of successor to personal representative who has resigned is not required.

When two or more personal representatives have qualified, and one or more personal representatives resign pursuant to this Article, leaving in office one or more personal representatives, the appointment of successors shall not be required unless:

(1) The clerk of superior court determines, in the clerk's discretion, that it is in the best interest of the estate to appoint a successor or successors to the personal representative or representatives who have resigned, or

(2) In the case of executors, the will so provides. (1973, c. 1329, s. 3; 2011-344, s. 4.)

Article 11.

Collectors.

§ 28A-11-1. Appointment and qualifications of collectors.

When for any reason other than a situation provided for in Chapter 28B or Chapter 28C entitled "Estates of Absentees in Military Service" and "Estates of Missing Persons" a delay is encountered in the issuance of letters to a personal representative or when, in any case, the clerk of superior court finds that the best interest of the estate would be served by the appointment of a collector, the clerk of superior court may issue letters of collection to any person or persons not disqualified to act as a personal representative under G.S. 28A-4-2. (R.C., c. 46, s. 9; C.C.P., s. 463; 1868-9, c. 113, s. 115; Code, s. 1383; Rev., s. 22; C.S., s. 24; 1924, c. 43; 1965, c. 815, s. 2; 1967, c. 24, s. 14; 1973, c. 1329, s. 3; 2011-344, s. 4.)

§ 28A-11-2. Oath and bond.

Every collector shall take an oath as prescribed in G.S. 28A-7-1 and give bond as required in Article 8 of this Chapter for personal representatives. (C.C.P., s. 464; Code, s. 1384; Rev., s. 23; C.S., s. 25; 1973, c. 1329, s. 3.)

§ 28A-11-3. Duties and powers of collectors.

(a) Every collector shall:

(1) Take such possession, custody, or control of the personal property of the decedent as in the exercise of reasonable judgment the collector deems necessary to its preservation;

(2) Publish notices to creditors as provided by Article 14 of this Chapter;

(3) Collect claims payable to the estate;

(4) Maintain and defend actions in behalf of the estate;

(5) File inventories, accounts, and other reports in the same manner as is required of personal representatives;

(6) Renew obligations of the decedent in the same manner as the personal representative is allowed to do under the provisions of Article 13 of this Chapter; and

(7) Under the express direction and supervision of the clerk of superior court, possess, exercise and perform all other powers, duties and liabilities given to personal representatives by Article 13 of this Chapter. (R.C., c. 46, s. 6; C.C.P., s. 465; 1868-9, c. 113, s. 115; Code, s. 1385; Rev., s. 24; C.S., s. 26; 1973, c. 1329, s. 3; 2011-344, s. 4.)

§ 28A-11-4. When collectors' powers cease; settlement of accounts.

(a) When letters testamentary or letters of administration are issued, or when in any case the clerk of superior court terminates the appointment of the collector, the powers of the collector cease.

(b) Upon the termination of the collector's appointment, the collector shall surrender to the personal representative or to the person otherwise entitled thereto or to the clerk all assets of the estate under this control and shall file with the clerk a verified statement of:

(1) The collector's accounts since the collector's qualification, or if the collector has previously filed an account, a statement of the collector's accounts since the date thereof;

(2) The assets of the estate and their location;

(3) The debts and liabilities of the estate;

(4) All facts and circumstances known to the collector the disclosure of which is necessary for a full and fair assessment of the collector's conduct of the office; and

(5) All additional facts and circumstances known to the collector the disclosure of which is necessary for a full and fair understanding of all matters concerning the estate.

(c) The clerk of superior court shall examine the account of the collector and if the clerk finds all of the accounts proper, the clerk shall by order approve the account. (R.C., c. 46, s. 7; C.C.P., s. 466; 1868-9, c. 113, s. 115; Code, s. 1386; Rev., s. 25; C.S., s. 27; 1973, c. 1329, s. 3; 2011-344, s. 4.)

§ 28A-11-5. Compensation.

A collector shall be compensated in accordance with Article 23 of this Chapter. (1977, c. 814, s. 4.)

Article 12.

Public Administrator.

§ 28A-12-1. Appointment and term.

There shall be a public administrator in every county, appointed by the clerk of superior court, with the written approval of the senior resident superior court judge of the district in which the appointment is made, for a term of four years. (1868-9, c. 113; Code, s. 1389; Rev., s. 18; C.S, s. 17; 1925, c. 253; 1973, c. 1329, s. 3.)

§ 28A-12-2. Oath of office.

The public administrator shall take and subscribe an oath or affirmation in the form provided in G.S. 11-11 for administrators and in the manner provided in G.S. 28A-7-1; and the oath or affirmation so taken and subscribed shall be filed in the office of the clerk of superior court. (1868-9, c. 113, ss. 2, 5; Code, s. 1393; Rev., s. 19; C.S., s. 18; 1973, c. 1329, s. 3.)

§ 28A-12-3. Qualification and bond.

(a) The public administrator shall qualify and give bond with regard to each estate administered by the public administrator as provided in Article 8 of this Chapter, at the expense of such estate.

(b) As an alternative to and in lieu of the bonding requirement provided in subsection (a), the administrator may, in the discretion of the clerk of superior court, enter into a single permanent bond, secured by any of the methods provided in G.S. 28A-8-2(4), payable to the State of North Carolina, conditioned upon the faithful performance of the duties of the administrator's office and obedience to all lawful orders of the clerk of superior court or other court touching the administration of any estate committed to the administrator. The amount of the permanent bond shall be determined by the clerk, based on the total value of all the estates administered by the public administrator, and may be increased or decreased from time to time as the clerk determines is necessary. The expense of the bond shall be borne by the estates administered by the administrator, as determined by the clerk. (1868-9, c. 113, ss. 2, 3, 4; Code, ss. 1390, 1391, 1392; Rev., s. 320; 1915, c. 216; C.S., s. 19; 1941, c. 243; 1973, c. 1329, s. 3; 1979, cc. 111, 726; 2011-344, s. 4.)

§ 28A-12-4. When public administrator shall apply for letters.

The public administrator shall apply for and may, with the approval of the clerk of superior court, obtain letters on the estates of decedents when:

(1) It is brought to the public administrator's attention that a period of six months has elapsed from the death of any decedent who has died owning

property, and no letters testamentary, or letters of administration or collection, have been applied for or issued to any person; or

(2)   Any person without known heirs shall die intestate owning property; or

(3)   Any person entitled to apply for letters of administration shall, in writing, request the clerk to issue letters to the public administrator as provided in G.S. 28A-5-2(c). (1868-9, c. 113, s. 6; Code, s. 1394; Rev., s. 20; C.S., s. 20; 1973, c. 1329, s. 3; 2011-344, s. 4.)

§ 28A-12-5. Powers and duties.

(a)   The public administrator shall have, in respect to the several estates in the public administrator's hands, all the rights and powers and shall be subject to all the duties and liabilities of other personal representatives.

(b)   After the expiration of the term of office of a public administrator or the public administrator's resignation as public administrator, the public administrator shall continue, subject to the provisions of Articles 9 and 10 of this Chapter, to administer the several estates previously committed to the public administrator until the public administrator has fully administered the same, and the public administrator's bonds shall continue in effect as to all such estates. (1868-9, c. 113, s. 7; 1876-7, c. 239; Code, s. 1395; Rev., s. 21; C.S., s. 21; 1973, c. 1329, s. 3; 2011-344, s. 4.)

§ 28A-12-6. Removal from office.

If letters of administration issued to the public administrator with respect to any estate are subsequently revoked on the grounds that they were obtained by false representation as provided in G.S. 28A-9-1(a)(2), or on the grounds as specified in G.S. 28A-9-1(a)(1), 28A-9-1(a)(3), 28A-9-2(a)(3), 28A-9-2(a)(5), or 28A-9-2(a)(6) or if the public administrator becomes a nonresident of the State, the clerk of superior court shall order the removal of the public administrator from office upon notice and hearing in accordance with Article 2 of this Chapter. (1973, c. 1329, s. 3; 2011-344, s. 4.)

§ 28A-12-7. Procedure after removal from office.

The clerk of superior court shall require of any public administrator who is removed from office pursuant to G.S. 28A-12-6 a complete accounting of all of the public administrator's activities as public administrator and for the property remaining under the public administrator's control by reason of the public administrator's appointment under this Article as administrator of any estate that has not been fully administered at the time of the public administrator's removal. If it appears to the clerk of superior court that grounds exist for revocation of letters of administration issued with respect to any such estate, the clerk shall proceed in accordance with the provisions of Article 9 of this Chapter. If letters of administration are revoked pursuant to such proceedings, the clerk of superior court shall issue letters of administration to the successor public administrator or to some other person not disqualified under G.S. 28A-4-2. (1973, c. 1329, s. 3; 2011-344, s. 4.)

§ 28A-12-8. Compensation.

A public administrator shall be compensated in accordance with Article 23 of this Chapter. (1977, c. 814, s. 5.)

Article 13.

Representative's Powers, Duties and Liabilities.

§ 28A-13-1. Time of accrual of duties and powers.

The duties and powers of a personal representative commence upon the personal representative's appointment. The powers of a personal representative relate back to give acts by the person appointed which are beneficial to the estate occurring prior to appointment the same effect as those occurring thereafter. However, a person named executor in a will may, prior to appointment, carry out written instructions of the decedent relating to the decedent's body, funeral and burial arrangements; provided that a health care agent authorized in a valid health care power of attorney to make body, funeral, and burial arrangements shall have precedence in making these arrangements, both before and after qualification of the decedent's personal representative, to the extent provided in G.S. 32A-19(b). A personal representative may ratify and accept acts on behalf of the estate done by others where the acts would have been proper for a personal representative. (1973, c. 1329, s. 3; 2007-502, s. 17; 2011-344, s. 4.)

§ 28A-13-2. General duties; relation to persons interested in estate.

A personal representative is a fiduciary who, in addition to the specific duties stated in this Chapter, is under a general duty to settle the estate of the personal representative's decedent as expeditiously and with as little sacrifice of value as is reasonable under all of the circumstances. A personal representative shall use the authority and powers conferred upon the personal representative by this Chapter, by the terms of the will under which the personal representative is acting, by any order of court in proceedings to which the personal representative is party, and by the rules generally applicable to fiduciaries, for the best interests of all persons interested in the estate, and with due regard for their respective rights. (1973, c. 1329, s. 3; 2011-344, s. 4.)

§ 28A-13-3. Powers of a personal representative or fiduciary.

(a) Except as qualified by express limitations imposed in a will of the decedent or a court order, and subject to the provisions of G.S. 28A-13-6 respecting the powers of joint personal representatives, a personal representative has the power to perform in a reasonable and prudent manner every act which a reasonable and prudent person would perform incident to the collection, preservation, liquidation or distribution of a decedent's estate so as to accomplish the desired result of settling and distributing the decedent's estate in a safe, orderly, accurate and expeditious manner as provided by law, including the powers specified in the following subdivisions:

(1) To take possession, custody or control of the personal property of the decedent. If in the opinion of the personal representative the personal representative's possession, custody or control of such property is not necessary for purposes of administration, such property may be left with or surrendered to the heir or devisee presumptively entitled thereto. The personal representative has the power to take possession, custody or control of the real

property of the decedent if the personal representative determines such possession, custody or control is in the best interest of the administration of the estate, including the power to eject occupants of real property. Prior to exercising such power over real property the procedure as set out in subsection G.S. 28A-13-3(c) shall be followed, except with respect to real property that is devised to the personal representative in the decedent's will or title to which is acquired by the personal representative during the estate administration, in which case the personal representative shall be immediately entitled to custody, possession, and control, and may institute an estate proceeding under subsection (d) of this section to enforce those rights. If the personal representative determines that such possession, custody or control is not in the best interest of the administration of the estate such property may be left with or surrendered to the heir or devisee presumptively entitled thereto.

(2)   To retain assets owned by the decedent pending distribution or liquidation even though such assets may include items which are otherwise improper for investment of trust funds.

(3)   To receive assets from other fiduciaries or other sources.

(4)   To complete performance of contracts entered into by the decedent that continue as obligations of the decedent's estate, or to refuse to complete such contracts, as the personal representative may determine to be in the best interests of the estate, but such refusal shall not limit any cause of action which might have been maintained against decedent if the decedent had refused to complete such contract. In respect to enforceable contracts by the decedent to convey an interest in land, the provisions of G.S. 28A-17-9 are controlling.

(5)   To deposit, as a fiduciary, funds of the estate in a bank, including a bank operated by the personal representative pursuant to G.S. 53-163.1.

(6)   To make, as a fiduciary, any form of investment allowed by law to the State Treasurer under G.S. 147-69.1, with funds of the estate, when such are not needed to meet debts and expenses immediately payable and are not immediately distributable, including money received from the sale of other assets; or to enter into other short-term loan arrangements that may be appropriate for use by trustees or beneficiaries generally. Provided, that in addition to the types of investments hereby authorized, deposits in interest-bearing accounts of any credit union authorized to do business in this State, when such deposits are insured in the same manner as required by G.S. 147-69.1 for deposits in a savings and loan association, are hereby authorized.

(7) To abandon or relinquish all rights in any property when, in the opinion of the personal representative acting reasonably and in good faith, it is valueless, or is so encumbered or is otherwise in such condition that it is of no benefit to the estate.

(8) To vote shares of stock or other securities in person or by general or limited proxy, and to execute waivers, consents or objections with respect to such stock or securities.

(9) To pay calls, assessments, and any other sums chargeable or accruing against or on account of securities.

(10) To hold shares of stock or other securities in the name of a nominee, without mention of the estate in the instrument representing stock or other securities or in registration records of the issuer thereof; provided, that

a. The estate records and all reports or accounts rendered by the personal representative clearly show the ownership of the stock or other securities by the personal representative and the facts regarding its holdings, and

b. The nominee shall not have possession of the stock or other securities or access thereto except under the immediate supervision of the personal representative or when such securities are deposited by the personal representative in a clearing corporation as defined in G.S. 25-8-102.

Such personal representative shall be personally liable for any acts or omissions of such nominee in connection with such stock or other securities so held, as if such personal representative had done such acts or been guilty of such omissions.

(11) To insure, at the expense of the estate, the assets of the estate in the personal representative's possession, custody or control against damage or loss.

(12) To borrow money for such periods of time and upon such terms and conditions as to rates, maturities, renewals, and security as the personal representative shall deem advisable, including the power of a corporate personal representative to borrow from its own banking department, for the purpose of paying debts, taxes, and other claims against the estate, and to mortgage, pledge or otherwise encumber such portion of the estate as may be

required to secure such loan or loans. In respect to the borrowing of money on the security of the real property of the decedent, G.S. 28A-17-11 is controlling.

(13)   To renew obligations of the decedent for the payment of money.

(14)   To advance the personal representative's own money for the protection of the estate, and for all expenses, losses and liabilities sustained in the administration of the estate or because of the holding or ownership of any estate assets. For such advances, with any interest, the personal representative shall have a lien on the assets of the estate as against a devisee or heir.

(15)   To compromise, adjust, arbitrate, sue on or defend, abandon, or otherwise deal with and settle claims in favor of or against the estate.

(16)   To pay taxes, assessments, the personal representative's own compensation, and other expenses incident to the collection, care, administration and protection of the assets of the estate in the personal representative's possession, custody or control.

(17)   To sell or exercise stock subscription or conversion rights; consent, directly or through a committee or other agent, to the reorganization, consolidation, merger, dissolution, or liquidation of a corporation or other business enterprise.

(18)   To allocate items of income or expense to either estate income or principal, as permitted or provided by law.

(19)   To employ persons, including attorneys, auditors, investment advisors, appraisers or agents to advise or assist the personal representative in the performance of the personal representative's administrative duties.

(20)   To continue any business or venture in which the decedent was engaged at the date of the decedent's death, where such continuation is reasonably necessary or desirable to preserve the value, including goodwill, of the decedent's interest in such business. With respect to the use of the decedent's interest in a continuing partnership, the provisions of G.S. 59-71 and 59-72 qualify this power; and with respect to farming operations engaged in by the decedent at the time of the decedent's death, the provisions of G.S. 28A-13-4 qualify this power.

(21) To incorporate or participate in the incorporation of any business or venture in which the decedent was engaged at the time of the decedent's death.

(22) To provide for the exoneration of the personal representative from personal liability in any contract entered into on behalf of the estate.

(23) To maintain actions for the wrongful death of the decedent according to the provisions of Article 18 of this Chapter and to compromise or settle any such claims, whether in litigation or not. Unless all persons who would be entitled to receive any damages recovered under G.S. 28A-18-2(b)(4) are competent adults and have consented in writing, any such settlement shall be subject to the approval of a judge of the court or tribunal exercising jurisdiction over the action or a judge of the district or superior court in cases where no action has previously been filed. If the claim is brought under Article 31 of Chapter 143 of the General Statutes, the settlement is subject to the approval of the Industrial Commission in accordance with that Article. It shall be the duty of the personal representative in distributing the proceeds of such settlement in any instance to take into consideration and to make a fair allocation to those claimants for funeral, burial, hospital and medical expenses which would have been payable from damages which might have been recovered had a wrongful death action gone to judgment in favor of the plaintiff.

(24) To maintain any appropriate action or proceeding to recover possession of any property of the decedent, or to determine the title thereto; to recover damages for any injury done prior to the death of the decedent to any of the decedent's property; and to recover damages for any injury done subsequent to the death of the decedent to such property.

(25) To purchase at any public or private sale of any real or personal property belonging to the decedent's estate or securing an obligation of the estate as a fiduciary for the benefit of the estate when, in the personal representative's opinion, it is necessary to prevent a loss to the estate.

(26) To sell or lease personal property of the estate in the manner prescribed by the provisions of Article 16 of this Chapter.

(27) To sell or lease real property of the estate in the manner prescribed by the provisions of Article 17 of this Chapter.

(28) To enter into agreements with taxing authorities to secure the benefit of the federal marital deduction pursuant to G.S. 28A-22-6.

(29) To pay or satisfy the debts and claims against the decedent's estate in the order and manner prescribed by Article 19 of this Chapter.

(30) To distribute any sum recovered for the wrongful death of the decedent according to the provisions of G.S. 28A-18-2; and to distribute all other assets available for distribution according to the provisions of this Chapter or as otherwise lawfully authorized.

(31) To exercise such additional lawful powers as are conferred upon the personal representative by the will.

(32) To execute and deliver all instruments which will accomplish or facilitate the exercise of the powers vested in the personal representative.

(33) Repealed by Session Laws 2009-48, s. 10, effective October 1, 2009, and applicable to renunciations and powers of attorney executed on or after that date.

(a1) Except as qualified by express limitations imposed in a will of the decedent, and subject to the provisions of G.S. 28A-13-6 respecting the powers of joint personal representatives, a personal representative shall have absolute discretion to make the election as to which items of the decedent's personal and household effects shall be excluded from the carry over basis provision of the federal income tax law and such election shall be conclusive and binding on all concerned.

(a2) Subject to the provisions of G.S. 28A-13-6 respecting the powers of joint personal representatives, a personal representative has the power to renounce in accordance with the provisions of Chapter 31B of the General Statutes.

(b) Repealed by Session Laws 2012-18, s. 3.7, effective June 11, 2012.

(c) Except with respect to real property that is devised to the personal representative in the decedent's will, or title to which is acquired by the personal representative during the estate administration, in which case the personal representative shall be immediately entitled to custody, possession, and control and may institute an estate proceeding under subsection (d) of this section to enforce those rights, prior to the personal representative exercising possession, custody or control over real property of the estate, the personal representative shall petition the clerk of court to obtain an order authorizing such possession, custody or control. The petition shall include:

(1) A description of the real property which is the subject of the petition;

(2) The names, ages, and addresses, if known, of the devisees and heirs of the decedent;

(3) A statement by the personal representative that the personal representative has determined that such possession, custody or control is in the best interest of the administration of the estate.

The devisees and heirs will be made parties to the proceeding by service of summons in the manner prescribed by law. If the clerk of court determines that it is in the best interest of the administration of the estate to authorize the personal representative to take possession, custody or control, the clerk of court shall grant an order authorizing that power. If a special proceeding has been instituted by the personal representative pursuant to G.S. 28A-15-1(c), the personal representative may petition for possession, custody, or control of any real property as a part of that proceeding and is not required to institute a separate special proceeding.

(d) The personal representative has the power to institute a proceeding pursuant to Article 2 of this Chapter to enforce the rights set forth in this section. The clerk of superior court may enter orders necessary to enforce the rights set forth in this section. If the person occupying the real property is a tenant or lessee of the property, the personal representative may seek ejectment of the tenant or lessee only pursuant to the provisions of Article 3 of Chapter 42 of the General Statutes. (1868-9, c. 113, ss. 73, 77; Code, ss. 1501, 1505; Rev., ss. 85, 159; C.S., ss. 170, 171; 1925, c. 86; 1933, cc. 161, 196, 498; 1973, c. 1329, s. 3; 1975, c. 19, s. 9; c. 371, s. 4; 1977, c. 556; 1979, c. 467, s. 21; c. 717, s. 3; 1985, c. 689, s. 8; 1991, c. 460, s. 3; 1995, c. 401, s. 1; 1997-181, s. 22; 2001-413, s. 2; 2002-159, s. 8; 2007-106, s. 1; 2009-48, s. 10; 2011-344, s. 4; 2012-18, s. 3.7.)

§ 28A-13-4. Continuance of farming operations of deceased persons.

When any person dies while engaged in farming operations, the decedent's personal representative is authorized to continue such farming operations until the end of the current calendar year, and until all crops grown during that year are harvested. The net income from such farming operations shall be personal assets of the estate. Any indebtedness incurred in connection with such farming operations after the date of death shall be preferred over the claims of any heir, devisee, distributee, general or unsecured creditor of said estate. Nothing herein contained shall limit the powers of a personal representative under the terms of a will. (1935, c. 163; 1973, c. 1329, s. 3; 2011-284, s. 15; 2011-344, s. 4.)

§ 28A-13-5. Personal representatives hold in joint tenancy.

Any estate or interest in property which becomes vested in two or more personal representatives shall be held by them in joint tenancy with the incident of survivorship. (1868-9, c. 113, s. 74; Code, s. 1502; Rev., s. 166; C.S., s. 172; 1973, c. 1329, s. 3.)

§ 28A-13-6. Exercise of powers of joint personal representatives by one or more than one.

(a) Repealed by Session Laws 2005-192, s. 5, effective January 1, 2006.

(b) If a will expressly makes provision for the execution of any of the powers of personal representatives by all of them or by any one or more of them, the provisions of the will govern.

(c) Repealed by Session Laws 2005-192, s. 5, effective January 1, 2006.

(c1) If there is no governing provision in the will, personal representatives may, by written agreement signed by all of them and filed with and approved by the clerk of superior court of the county in which the personal representatives qualified, provide that any designated one or more of the personal representatives may exercise one or more of the following powers:

(1) Establish and maintain bank accounts for the estate and issue checks for the estate.

(2) Maintain inventories, accountings, and income and expense records of the estate.

(3)   Enter any safety deposit box rented by the estate.

(4)   Employ persons as advisors or assistants in the performance of administrative duties, including agents, attorneys, accountants, brokers, appraisers, and custodians.

(5)   List estate property for taxes and prepare and file tax returns for the estate.

(6)   Collect and give receipts for claims and debts of the estate.

(7)   Pay debts, claims, costs of administration, and taxes of the estate.

(8)   Compromise, adjust, or otherwise settle any claim by or against the estate and release, in whole or in part, a claim belonging to the estate.

(9)   Have custody of the estate property.

(10)   Perform any function relating to investment of estate assets.

(d)   Subject to subsection (b) of this section, if two or more personal representatives own shares of corporate stock or other securities, their acts with respect to voting shall have the following effect:

(1)   If only one votes, in person or by proxy, that personal representative's act binds all;

(2)   If more than one vote, in person or by proxy, the act of the majority so voting binds all;

(3)   If more that [than] one vote, in person or by proxy, but the vote is evenly split on any particular matter, each faction is entitled to vote the stock or other securities in question proportionately.

(e)   Subject to subsections (b), (c1), and (d) of this section, all other acts and duties must be performed by both of the personal representatives if there are two, and by a majority of them if there are more than two. No personal representative who has not joined in exercising a power shall be liable for the consequences of such exercise, nor shall a dissenting personal representative be liable for the consequences of an act in which the personal representative joins at the direction of the majority of the personal representatives, if that personal representative expressed his or her dissent in writing to any other personal representative at or before the time of such joinder.

(f) No personal representative shall be relieved of liability on his or her bond or otherwise by entering into any agreement under this section. (1959, c. 1160; 1973, c. 1329, s. 3; 1977, c. 446, s. 1; 1991, c. 460, s. 1; 2005-192, s. 5; 2011-326, s. 5; 2011-344, s. 4.)

§ 28A-13-7. Powers and duties of successor personal representative.

A successor personal representative is one appointed to succeed a personal representative whose appointment has terminated by death, resignation or revocation. Unless a contrary intent clearly appears from the will, a successor personal representative has all the powers and duties, discretionary or otherwise, of the original personal representative. (1973, c. 1329, s. 3.)

§ 28A-13-8. Powers and duties of administrator with will annexed.

When an administrator with the will annexed has been appointed, whether or not the administrator is succeeding a previously appointed personal representative, that administrator has the same powers and duties, discretionary or otherwise, as if the administrator had been named executor in the will, unless a contrary intent clearly appears from the will. (C.C.P., s. 468; 1870-1, c. 93; Code, s. 1388; Rev., s. 319; C.S., s. 33; 1935, c. 386; 1949, c. 971; 1967, c. 41, s. 1; 1973, c. 1329, s. 3; 2011-344, s. 4.)

§ 28A-13-9. Powers of surviving personal representative.

When one or more of those nominated as coexecutors in a will is not appointed, or when the appointment of one or more joint personal representatives is terminated, every power granted to such joint personal representatives may be exercised by the surviving representative or representatives; provided that nothing to the contrary appears in the will of a testate decedent. (C.C.P., s. 451;

Code, s. 2164; Rev., s. 13; C.S., s. 16; 1931, c. 183; 1953, c. 78, s. 1; 1973, c. 1329, s. 3.)

§ 28A-13-10. Liability of personal representative.

(a) Property of Estate. - A personal representative shall be liable for and chargeable in the personal representative's accounts with all of the estate of the decedent which comes into the personal representative's possession at any time, including all the income therefrom; but the personal representative shall not be liable for any debts due to the decedent or other assets of the estate which remain uncollected without the personal representative's fault. Except for commissions allowable by law, the personal representative shall not be entitled to any profits caused by an increase in values, nor be chargeable with loss by a decrease in value or destruction without the personal representative's fault, of any part of the estate.

(b) Property Not a Part of Estate. - A personal representative shall be chargeable in the personal representative's accounts with property not a part of the estate which comes into the personal representative's possession at any time and shall be liable to the persons entitled thereto if:

(1) The property was received under a duty imposed on the personal representative by law in the capacity of personal representative; or

(2) The personal representative has commingled such property with the assets of the estate.

(c) Breach of Duty. - A personal representative shall be liable and chargeable in the personal representative's accounts for any loss to the estate arising from the personal representative's embezzlement or commingling of the estate with other property; for loss to the estate through self-dealing; for any loss to the estate from wrongful acts or omissions of the personal representative's joint personal representatives which the personal representative could have prevented by the exercise of ordinary care; and for any loss to the estate arising from the personal representative's failure to act in good faith and with such care, foresight and diligence as an ordinarily reasonable and prudent person would act with the ordinarily reasonable and prudent person's own property under like circumstances. If the exercise of power concerning the estate is improper, the personal representative is liable for breach of fiduciary duty to interested persons for resulting damage or loss to the same extent as a trustee of an express trust. (1973, c. 1329, s. 3; 1975, c. 300, s. 4; 2011-344, s. 4.)

Article 14.

Notice to Creditors.

§ 28A-14-1. Notice for claims.

(a) Every personal representative and collector after the granting of letters shall notify all persons, firms and corporations having claims against the decedent to present the same to such personal representative or collector, on or before a day to be named in such notice, which day must be at least three months from the day of the first publication or posting of such notice. The notice shall set out a mailing address for the personal representative or collector. The notice shall be published once a week for four consecutive weeks in a newspaper qualified to publish legal advertisements, if any such newspaper is published in the county. If there is no newspaper published in the county, but there is a newspaper having general circulation in the county, then at the option of the personal representative, or collector, the notice shall be published once a week for four consecutive weeks in the newspaper having general circulation in the county and posted at the courthouse or the notice shall be posted at the courthouse and four other public places in the county. Personal representatives are not required to publish or mail notice to creditors if the only asset of the estate consists of a claim for damages arising from death by wrongful act. When any collector or personal representative of an estate has published or mailed the notice provided for by this section, no further publication or mailing shall be required by any other collector or personal representative.

(b) Prior to filing the proof of notice required by G.S. 28A-14-2, every personal representative and collector shall personally deliver or send by first class mail to the last known address a copy of the notice required by subsection (a) of this section to all persons, firms, and corporations having unsatisfied claims against the decedent who are actually known or can be reasonably ascertained by the personal representative or collector within 75 days after the granting of letters and, if at the time of the decedent's death the decedent was receiving medical assistance as defined by G.S. 108A-70.5(b)(1), to the Department of Health and Human Services, Division of Medical Assistance. Provided, however, no notice shall be required to be delivered or mailed with respect to any claim that is recognized as a valid claim by the personal representative or collector.

(c) The personal representative or collector may personally deliver or mail by first class mail a copy of the notice required by subsection (a) of this section to all creditors of the estate whose names and addresses can be ascertained with reasonable diligence. If the personal representative or collector in good faith believes that the notice required by subsection (b) of this section to a particular creditor is or may be required and gives notice based on that belief, the personal representative or collector is not liable to any person for giving the notice, whether or not the notice is actually required by subsection (b) of this section. If the personal representative or collector in good faith fails to give notice required by subsection (b) of this section, the personal representative or collector is not liable to any person for such failure. (1868-9, c. 113, s. 29; 1881, c. 278, s. 2; Code, ss. 1421, 1422; Rev., s. 39; C.S., s. 45; 1945, c. 635; 1949, c. 47; c. 63, s. 1; 1955, c. 625; 1961, c. 26, s. 1; c. 741, s. 1; 1973, c. 1329, s. 3; 1977, c. 446, s. 1; 1985, c. 319; 1987 (Reg. Sess., 1988), c. 1077, s. 1; 1989, c. 378, s. 1; c. 770, s. 8; 1991, c. 282, s. 1; 2013-378, s. 3.)

§ 28A-14-2. Proof of notice.

A copy of the notice directed by G.S. 28A-14-1(a) to be posted or published, together with an affidavit or affidavits of one of the persons authorized by G.S. 1-600(a) to make affidavits to the effect that such notice was posted or published in accordance with G.S. 28A-14-1(a), and an affidavit of the personal representative or collector, or the attorney for the personal representative or collector, to the effect that a copy of the notice was personally delivered or mailed to each creditor entitled to notice in accordance with G.S. 28A-14-1(b) shall be filed in the office of the clerk of superior court by the personal representative or collector at the time the inventory required by G.S. 28A-20-1 is filed. The copy of the notice, together with the affidavit or affidavits, shall be deemed a record of the court and a copy thereof, duly certified by the clerk of superior court, shall be received as prima facie evidence of the fact of publication or mailing in all the courts of this State. (1868-9, c. 113, s. 31; Code, s. 1423; Rev., s. 40; C.S., s. 46; 1951, c. 1005, s. 3; 1961, c. 26, s. 2; 1973, c. 1329, s. 3; 1987 (Reg. Sess., 1988), c. 1077, s. 2; 1989, c. 378, s. 2.)

§ 28A-14-3. Personal notice to creditor.

The personal representative or collector may cause the notice to be personally served on any creditor. (1868-9, c. 113, s. 32; Code, s. 1424; 1885, c. 96; Rev., s. 41; C.S., s. 47; 1961, c. 741, s. 2; 1973, c. 1329, s. 3; 1977, c. 446, s. 1; c. 798; 1979, c. 509, s. 2.)

§ 28A-14-1.1. Validation of certain notices.

(a) Any notice to creditors published or posted under G.S. 28A-14-1 which did not, in the advertisement, name the day after which claims could not be presented is validated.

(b) This section applies to all notices published and posted between October 1, 1975, and January 1, 1991, except that it does not affect any pending litigation or any litigation instituted within 90 days of January 1, 1991. (1981, c. 96, ss. 1, 2; 1987, c. 277, s. 8; 1989, c. 390, s. 8; 1991, c. 489, s. 8.)

Article 15.

Assets; Discovery of Assets.

§ 28A-15-1. Assets of the estate generally.

(a) All of the real and personal property, both legal and equitable, of a decedent shall be assets available for the discharge of debts and other claims against the decedent's estate in the absence of a statute expressly excluding any such property. Provided that before real property is selected the personal representative must determine that such selection is in the best interest of the administration of the estate.

(b) In determining what property of the estate shall be sold, leased, pledged, mortgaged or exchanged for the payment of the debts of the decedent and other claims against the decedent's estate, the personal representative shall select the assets which in the personal representative's judgment are calculated to promote the best interests of the estate. In the selection of assets for this purpose, there shall be no necessary distinction between real and personal property, absent any contrary provision in the will.

(c) If it shall be determined by the personal representative that it is in the best interest of the administration of the estate to sell, lease, or mortgage any real estate or interest therein to obtain money for the payment of debts and other claims against the decedent's estate, the personal representative shall institute a special proceeding before the clerk of superior court for such purpose pursuant to Article 17 of this Chapter, except that no such proceeding shall be required for a sale made pursuant to authority given by will. A general provision granting authority to the personal representative to sell the testator's real property, or incorporation by reference of the provisions of G.S. 32-27(2) shall be sufficient to eliminate the necessity for a proceeding under Article 17. If a special proceeding has been instituted by the personal representative pursuant to G.S. 28A-13-3(c), the personal representative may petition for sale, lease, or mortgage of any real property as a part of that proceeding and is not required to institute a separate special proceeding.

(d) The crops of every deceased person, remaining ungathered at the person's death, shall, in all cases, belong to the personal representative or collector, as part of the personal assets of the decedent's estate; and shall not pass to the devisee by virtue of any devise of the land, unless such intent be manifest and specified in the will. (1868-9, c. 113, ss. 14, 15; Code, ss. 1406, 1407; Rev., ss. 45, 47; C.S., ss. 52, 54; 1973, c. 1329, s. 3; 1975, c. 300, s. 5; 1985, c. 426; 2001-413, s. 2.1; 2002-159, s. 9; 2011-344, s. 4.)

§ 28A-15-2. Title and possession of property.

(a) Personal Property. - Subsequent to the death of the decedent and prior to the appointment and qualification of the personal representative or collector, the title and the right of possession of personal property of the decedent is vested in the decedent's heirs; but upon the appointment and qualification of the personal representative or collector, the heirs shall be divested of such title and right of possession which shall be vested in the personal representative or collector relating back to the time of the decedent's death for purposes of administering the estate of the decedent. But, if in the opinion of the personal representative, the personal representative's possession, custody and control of any item of personal property is not necessary for purposes of administration, such possession, custody and control may be left with or surrendered to the heir or devisee presumptively entitled thereto.

(b) Real Property. - The title to real property of a decedent is vested in the decedent's heirs as of the time of the decedent's death; but the title to real property of a decedent devised under a valid probated will becomes vested in the devisees and shall relate back to the decedent's death, subject to the provisions of G.S. 31-39. (1973, c. 1329, s. 3; 2011-344, s. 4.)

§ 28A-15-3. Nonexoneration of encumbered property.

When real or personal property subject to any lien or security interest, except judgment liens, is specifically devised, the devisee takes the property subject to the encumbrance and without a right to have other assets of the decedent applied to discharge the secured obligation, unless an express provision of the will confers such right of exoneration. A general testamentary direction to pay the debts of the decedent is not sufficient to confer such right. (1973, c. 1329, s. 3.)

§ 28A-15-4. Encumbered assets.

When any assets of the estate are encumbered by mortgage, pledge, lien or other security interest, the personal representative may pay the encumbrance or any part thereof, renew or extend any obligation secured by the encumbrance, or convey or transfer the encumbered assets to the creditor in satisfaction of the creditor's lien, in whole or in part, whether or not the holder of the encumbrance has filed a claim, if it appears to be for the best interest of the estate; provided that payment of an encumbrance shall not increase the share of the distributee entitled to the encumbered assets unless the distributee is entitled to exoneration by express provisions of the will. (1973, c. 1329, s. 3; 2011-344, s. 4.)

§ 28A-15-5. Order in which assets appropriated; abatement.

(a) General Rules. - In the absence of testamentary indication as to the order of abatement, or some other controlling statute, shares of devisees and of heirs abate, without any preference or priority as between real and personal property, in the following order:

(1) Property not disposed of by the will;

(2) Residuary devises;

(3) General devises;

(4) Specific devises.

For purposes of abatement, a demonstrative devise of money or property payable out of or charged on a particular fund or other property is treated as a specific devise; but if the particular fund or property out of which the demonstrative devise is to be paid is nonexistent or insufficient at the death of the testator, the deficiency is to be payable out of the general estate of the decedent and is to be regarded as a general devise and must abate pro rata with other general devises. Abatement within each classification is in proportion to the amounts of property each of the beneficiaries would have received, had full distribution of the property been made in accordance with the terms of the will.

(b) Abatement; Sales; Contribution. - When property which has been specifically devised is sold, leased, or mortgaged, or a security therein is created, by the personal representative, abatement shall be achieved by ratable adjustments in, or contributions from other interest in the remaining assets. The clerk of superior court shall, at the time of the hearing on the petition for final distribution, determine the amounts of the respective contributions and whether the same shall be made before distribution or shall constitute a lien on specific property which is distributed. (1973, c. 1329, s. 3.)

§ 28A-15-6. Federal income tax refunds - joint returns.

Upon the determination by the United States Treasury Department of an overpayment of income tax by a married couple filing a joint federal income tax return, one of whom has died since the filing of such return or where a joint federal income tax return is filed on behalf of a husband and wife, one of whom has died prior to the filing of the return, any refund of the tax by reason of such overpayment, if not in excess of five hundred dollars ($500.00), shall be the sole and separate property of the surviving spouse. In the event that both spouses are dead at the time such overpayment is determined, such refund, if not in excess of five hundred dollars ($500.00), shall be the sole and separate property of the estate of the spouse who died last and may be paid directly by the Treasury Department to the executor or administrator of such estate, or to the person entitled to the possession of the assets of a small estate pursuant to the provisions of Article 25 of this Chapter. (1955, c. 720; 1957, c. 986; 1973, c. 1329, s. 3.)

§ 28A-15-7. Federal income tax refunds - separate returns.

Upon the determination by the United States Treasury Department of an overpayment of income tax by any married person filing a separate return, any refund of the tax by reason of such overpayment, if not in excess of two hundred fifty dollars ($250.00), exclusive of interest, shall be the sole and separate property of the surviving spouse, and the United States Treasury Department may pay said sum directly to such surviving spouse, and such payment to the extent thereof shall operate as a complete acquittal and discharge of the United States Treasury Department. (1961, c. 643; 1973, c. 1329, s. 3.)

§ 28A-15-8. State income tax returns.

Upon the determination by the Secretary of Revenue of North Carolina of an overpayment of income tax by any married person, any refund of the tax by reason of such overpayment, if not in excess of two hundred dollars ($200.00) exclusive of interest, shall be the sole and separate property of the surviving spouse, and said Secretary of Revenue may pay said sum directly to such surviving spouse, and such payment to the extent thereof shall operate as a complete acquittal and discharge of the Secretary of Revenue. (1961, c. 735; 1973, c. 1329, s. 3.)

§ 28A-15-9. Excess funds.

If the amount of any refund exceeds the sums specified in G.S. 28A-15-6, 28A-15-7 or 28A-15-8, the sums specified therein and one half of any additional sums shall be the sole and separate property of the surviving spouse. The remaining one half of such additional sums shall be the property of the estate of the decedent spouse. (1973, c. 1329, s. 3.)

§ 28A-15-9.1: Repealed by Session Laws 2011-326, s. 6, effective June 27, 2011.

§ 28A-15-10. Assets of decedent's estate for limited purposes.

(a)   When needed to satisfy claims against a decedent's estate, assets may be acquired by a personal representative or collector from the following sources:

(1)   Tentative trusts created by the decedent in savings accounts for other persons.

(2)   Gifts causa mortis made by the decedent.

(3)   Joint deposit accounts with right of survivorship created by decedent pursuant to the provisions of G.S. 41-2.1 or otherwise; and joint tenancies with right of survivorship created by decedent in corporate stocks or other investment securities.

(4)   An interest in a security passing to a beneficiary pursuant to the provisions of Article 4 of Chapter 41 of the General Statutes.

Such assets shall be acquired solely for the purpose of satisfying such claims, however, and shall not be available for distribution to heirs or devisees.

(b)   Where there are not sufficient personal and real assets of the decedent to satisfy all the debts and other claims against the decedent's estate, the personal representative shall have the right to sue for and recover any and all personal property or real property, or interest therein, which the decedent may in any manner have transferred or conveyed with intent to hinder, delay, or defraud the decedent's creditors, and any personal property or real property, or interest therein, so recovered shall constitute assets of the estate in the hands of the personal representative for the payment of debts and other claims against the estate of the decedent. But if the alienee has sold the personal property or real property, or interest therein, so fraudulently acquired by the alienee from the decedent to a bona fide purchaser for value without notice of the fraud, then such personal property or real property, or interest therein, may not be recovered from such bona fide purchaser but the fraudulent alienee shall be liable to the personal representative for the value of the personal property or real property, or interest therein, so acquired and disposed of to a bona fide purchaser. If the whole recovery from the fraudulent alienee shall not be necessary for the payment of the debts and other claims against the estate of the decedent, the surplus shall be returned to such fraudulent alienee or the fraudulent alienee's assigns.

(c)   Where there has been a recovery in an action for wrongful death, the same shall not be applied to the payment of debts and other claims against the estate of decedent or devises, except as to the payment of reasonable burial and funeral expenses and reasonable hospital and medical expenses incident to the injury resulting in death and as limited and provided in G.S. 28-18-2 [G.S. 28A-18-2]. (1973, c. 1329, s. 3; 2005-411, s. 2; 2011-344, s. 4.)

§ 28A-15-11. Debt due from personal representative not discharged by appointment.

The appointment of any person as personal representative does not discharge any debt or demand due from such person to the decedent. (1868-9, c. 113, s. 40; Code, s. 1431; Rev., s. 51; C.S., s. 58; 1973, c. 1329, s. 3.)

§ 28A-15-12. Actions to recover property of decedent.

(a)   Repealed by Session Laws 2011-344, s. 4, effective January 1, 2012, and applicable to estates of decedents dying on or after that date.

(a1) A personal representative or collector shall have the right to bring an action to sue for and recover any property of any kind belonging to the estate of the personal representative's decedent, by action filed in the Superior Court Division of the General Court of Justice and shall be entitled to such other provisional remedies as provided for under Subchapter 13 of Chapter 1 of the General Statutes.

(b) Repealed by Session Laws 2011-344, s. 4, effective January 1, 2012, and applicable to estates of decedents dying on or after that date.

(b1) A personal representative, collector, or any interested person shall have the right to bring an estate proceeding seeking the examination of any persons reasonably believed to be in possession of property of any kind belonging to the estate of the decedent including a demand for the recovery of such property. An estate proceeding brought under the provisions of this subsection shall be instituted by the filing of a verified petition and shall be conducted in accordance with the provisions of Article 2 of this Chapter. The court may enter orders requiring the examination of persons consistent with this subsection and, if the court determines that a person is in possession of property of the estate of the decedent, shall have the authority to order recovery of that property. Orders issued by the clerk of superior court shall be enforceable by proceedings as for contempt of court.

(c) The party against whom the final judgment is rendered shall be adjudged to pay the costs of the proceedings hereunder.

(d) The remedies provided in this section shall not be exclusive, but shall be in addition to any remedies which are now or may hereafter be provided. (1937, c. 209, s. 1; 1973, c. 1329, s. 3; 2011-344, s. 4.)

§ 28A-15-13. Opening and inventory of decedent's safe-deposit box.

(a) Definitions. - The following definitions apply to this section:

(1) Institution. - Any entity or person having supervision or possession of a safe-deposit box to which a decedent had access.

(1a) Deputy. - A person appointed in writing by a lessee or cotenant of a safe-deposit box as having right of access to the safe-deposit box without further authority or permission of the lessee or cotenant, in a manner and form designated by the institution.

(2) Letter of authority. - Letters of administration, letters testamentary, an affidavit of collection of personal property, an order of summary administration, or a letter directed to the institution designating a person entitled to receive the contents of a safe-deposit box to which the decedent had access. The letter of authority must be signed by the clerk of superior court or by the clerk's representative.

(3) Qualified person. - A person possessing a letter of authority or a person named as a deputy, lessee or cotenant of the safe-deposit box to which the decedent had access.

(b) Presence of Clerk Required. - Any safe-deposit box to which a decedent had access shall be sealed by the institution having supervision or possession of the box. Except as provided in subsection (c) of this section, the presence of the clerk of superior court of the county where the safe-deposit box is located or the presence of the clerk's representative is required before the box may be opened. The clerk or the clerk's representative shall open the safe-deposit box in the presence of the person possessing a key to the box and a representative of the institution having supervision or possession of the box. The clerk shall make an inventory of the contents of the box and furnish a copy to the institution and to the person possessing a key to the box.

(c) Presence of Clerk Not Required. - The presence of the clerk of superior court or the clerk's representative is not required when the person requesting the opening of the decedent's safe-deposit box is a qualified person. In that event, the qualified person shall make an inventory of the contents of the box and furnish a copy to the institution and to the person possessing a key to the box if that person is someone other than the qualified person.

(d) Testamentary Instrument in Box. - If the safe-deposit box contains any writing that appears to be a will, codicil, or any other instrument of a testamentary nature, then the clerk of superior court or the qualified person shall file the instrument in the office of the clerk of superior court.

(e) Release of Contents. - Except as provided in subsection (d) for testamentary instruments, the institution shall not release any contents of the safe-deposit box to anyone other than a qualified person.

(f) No Tax Waiver Required. - No tax waiver is required for the release of the contents of the decedent's safe-deposit box. (1998-212, s. 16.14(a); 2003-255, s. 1.)

Article 16.

Sales or Leases of Personal Property.

§ 28A-16-1. Sales or leases without court order.

(a) A personal representative has the power to sell, at either a public or private sale, or to lease, personal property of the decedent without a court order.

(b) A personal representative who sells or leases personal property of the decedent without a court order is not required to file a special report or have the transaction confirmed by the clerk of superior court, or to follow any of the procedure set forth in Article 29A of Chapter 1 of the General Statutes, entitled "Judicial Sales," but shall include in the personal representative's next account, either annual or final, a record of the receipts and disbursements incident to the transaction. (1868-9, c. 113, s. 16; Code, s. 1408; Rev., s. 62; C.S., s. 66; 1973, c. 1329, s. 3; 1975, c. 300, s. 6; 2011-344, s. 4.)

§ 28A-16-2. Sales or leases by court order.

(a) All sales or leases of personal property of the decedent by a collector shall be made only upon order obtained, by motion, from the clerk of superior court.

(b) A personal representative may, if the personal representative so desires, request the clerk of superior court to issue to the personal representative an order to sell or lease personal property of the decedent.

(c) Sales or leases of personal property of the decedent held pursuant to court order shall be conducted as provided in Article 29A of Chapter 1 of the General Statutes, entitled "Judicial Sales."

(d)   A personal representative may, for the personal representative's own benefit, purchase or lease personal property belonging to the decedent at a public sale conducted under an order of the clerk of superior court, if the transaction is reported to the clerk of superior court and confirmed by the clerk of superior court. (1868-9, c. 113, s. 17; Code, s. 1409; Rev., s. 61; C.S., s. 67; 1949, c. 719, s. 2; 1973, c. 1329, s. 3; 2011-344, s. 4.)

§ 28A-16-3. Sales of household furnishings.

If the decedent is survived by a spouse, no sale or lease shall be made of the household furnishings in the usual dwelling house occupied by the surviving spouse at the time of the death of the deceased spouse, if such dwelling house was owned by the deceased spouse at the time of his or her death, until the expiration of the time limits set forth in G.S. 29-30(c) for the filing by the surviving spouse of an election in regard to the property of the decedent. (1973, c. 1329, s. 3.)

Article 17.

Sales, Leases or Mortgages of Real Property.

§ 28A-17-1. Sales of real property.

Pursuant to authority contained in G.S. 28A-15-1 the personal representative may, at any time, apply to the clerk of superior court of the county where the decedent's real property or some part thereof is situated, by petition, to sell such real property for the payment of debts and other claims against the decedent's estate. (1868-9, c. 113, s. 42; Code, s. 1436; Rev., s. 68, C.S., s. 74; 1923, c. 55; 1935, c. 43; 1937, c. 70; 1943, c. 637; 1949, c. 719, s. 2; 1955, c. 302, s. 1; 1959, c. 879, s. 7; 1963, c. 291, s. 1; 1973, c. 1329, s. 3.)

§ 28A-17-2. Contents of petition for sale.

The petition to sell real property shall include:

(1)   A description of the real property and interest therein sought to be sold;

(2)   The names, ages and addresses, if known, of the devisees and heirs of the decedent;

(3)   A statement that the personal representative has determined that it is in the best interest of the administration of the estate to sell the real property sought to be sold. (1868-9, c. 113, s. 43; Code, s. 1437; Rev., s. 77; C.S., s. 79; 1973, c. 1329, s. 3.)

§ 28A-17-3. Petition for partition.

When it is alleged that the real property of the decedent sought to be sold consists in whole or in part of an undivided interest in real property, the personal representative of the decedent may include, in the petition to sell the real property for the payment of debts and other claims against the decedent's estate, a request for partition of the lands sought to be sold. (1868-9, c. 113, s. 42; Code, s. 1436; Rev., s. 68; C.S., s. 74; 1923, c. 55; 1935, s. 43; 1937, c. 70; 1943, c. 637; 1949, c. 719, s. 2; 1955, c. 302, s. 1; 1959, c. 879, s. 7; 1963, c. 291, s. 1; 1973, c. 1329, s. 3.)

§ 28A-17-4. Heirs and devisees necessary parties.

No order to sell real property shall be granted until the heirs and devisees of the decedent have been made parties to the special proceeding by service of summons in the manner required by law, in accordance with G.S. 1A-1, Rule 4. Upon such service, the court shall appoint a guardian ad litem for heirs and devisees who are unknown or whose addresses are unknown, and summons shall issue to the guardian ad litem as such. The guardian ad litem shall file answer for such heirs and devisees and defend for them, and the guardian ad litem shall be paid such sum as the court may fix, to be paid as costs of the proceeding. (1868-9, c. 113, s. 44; Code, s. 1438; Rev., s. 74; C.S., s. 80; Ex. Sess. 1924, c. 3, s. 1; 1973, c. 1329, s. 3; 1975, c. 300, s. 7; 2011-344, s. 4.)

§ 28A-17-5. Property subject to sale; conveyance by deceased in fraud of creditors.

The real property subject to sale under this Article shall include real property recovered from a fraudulent alienee pursuant to G.S. 28A-15-10(b). (1868-9, c. 113, s. 51; Code, s. 1446; Rev., s. 72; C.S., s. 77; 1973, c. 1329, s. 3.)

§ 28A-17-6. Adverse claimant to be heard; procedure.

When the real property sought to be sold, or any interest therein, is claimed by another person, such claimant may be made a party to the proceeding, and in any event may become a party upon the claimant's own motion. When an issue of law or fact is joined between the parties, the procedure shall be as prescribed for other special proceedings. (1868-9, c. 113, ss. 46, 47; Code, ss. 1440, 1441; Rev., ss. 76, 78; C.S., ss. 81, 82; 1973, c. 1329, s. 3; 2011-344, s. 4.)

§ 28A-17-7. Order granted if petition not denied; public or private sale; procedure for sale.

If, by default or admission, the allegations in the petition are not controverted, the clerk of superior court may summarily order a sale. The procedure for the sale shall be as is provided in Article 29A of Chapter 1 of the General Statutes, entitled "Judicial Sales." If it is made to appear to the clerk by petition and by satisfactory proof that it will be for the best interest of the estate to sell by private sale, the clerk may authorize a private sale in accordance with the provisions of G.S. 1-339.33 through 1-339.40. (1868-9, c. 113, s. 48; Code, s. 1443; Rev., s. 79; C.S., s. 83; 1949, c. 719, s. 2; 1973, c. 1329, s. 3.)

§ 28A-17-8. Under power in will, sales public or private.

Sales of real property made pursuant to authority given by will may be either public or private, unless the will otherwise directs, and may be on such terms as in the opinion of the personal representative are most advantageous to those interested in the decedent's estate. (1868-9, c. 113, s. 75; Code, s. 1503; Rev., s. 84; C.S., s. 89; 1973, c. 1329, s. 3.)

§ 28A-17-9. Death of vendor under contract; representative to convey.

When any decedent has contracted to sell any real property and has given bond or other enforceable written contract to the purchaser to convey the same, the decedent's personal representative may execute and deliver a deed to such real property and such deed shall convey the title as fully as if it had been executed and delivered by the decedent. No deed shall be made unless the purchaser complies with the terms of the bond or other written contract. If the contract for conveyance requires the giving of a warranty deed, the deed given by the personal representative shall contain such warranties as required by the contract and the warranties shall be binding on the estate and not on the personal representative personally. (1868-9, c. 113, s. 65; 1874-5, c. 251; Code, s. 1492; Rev., s. 83; C.S., s. 91; 1973, c. 1329, s. 3; 2011-344, s. 4.)

§ 28A-17-10. Title in personal representative for estate; he or successor to convey.

When real property is conveyed to a personal representative for the benefit of the estate the personal representative represents, the personal representative or any successor personal representative may sell and convey it upon such terms as the personal representative may deem just and for the advantage of the estate. The procedure shall be as is provided in Article 29A of Chapter 1 of the General Statutes, entitled "Judicial Sales." If it is made to appear to the clerk of superior court by petition and by satisfactory proof that it will be for the best interest of the estate to sell by private sale, the clerk may authorize a private sale in accordance with the provisions of G.S. 1-339.33 through 1-339.40. (1905, c. 342; Rev., s. 71; C.S., s. 92; 1949, c. 719, s. 2; 1973, c. 1329, s. 3; 2011-344, s. 4.)

§ 28A-17-11. Personal representative may lease or mortgage.

In lieu of asking for an order of sale of real property, the personal representative may request the clerk of superior court to issue to the personal representative an order to lease or to mortgage real property of the decedent. The clerk of superior court is authorized to issue an order to lease or mortgage on such terms as the clerk deems to be in the best interest of the estate. (1913, c. 49, s. 1; C.S., s.75; 1927, c. 222, s. 1; 1973, c. 1329, s. 3; 2011-344, s. 4.)

§ 28A-17-12. Sale, lease or mortgage of real property by heirs or devisees.

(a) If the first publication or posting of the general notice to creditors as provided for in G.S. 28A-14-1 occurs within two years after the death of the decedent:

(1) All sales, leases or mortgages of real property by heirs or devisees of any resident or nonresident decedent made after the death of the decedent and before the first publication or posting of the general notice to creditors are void as to creditors and personal representatives; and

(2) All sales, leases or mortgages of real property by heirs or devisees of any resident or nonresident decedent made after such first publication or posting and before approval of the final account shall be void as to creditors and personal representatives unless the personal representative joins in the sale, lease or mortgage.

(b) If the first publication or posting of the general notice to creditors as provided for in G.S. 28A-14-1 does not occur within two years after the death of the decedent, all sales, leases or mortgages of real property by heirs or devisees of any resident or nonresident decedent shall be valid as to creditors and personal representatives of the decedent. (1973, c. 1329, s. 3; 1979, 2nd Sess., c. 1246, s. 1.)

§ 28A-17-13. Prior validating acts.

Chapter 70 of the Public Laws of 1923, Chapter 48 of the Public Laws of 1925, Chapter 146 of the Public Laws of 1931, and Chapters 31 and 381 of the Public Laws of 1935, all validating certain prior sales of real property by executors or administrators and heretofore codified as G.S. 28-100 through 28-104, shall remain in full force and effect, though no longer carried forward as part of the General Statutes. (1973, c. 1329, s. 3.)

Article 18.

Actions and Proceedings.

§ 28A-18-1. Survival of actions to and against personal representative.

(a) Upon the death of any person, all demands whatsoever, and rights to prosecute or defend any action or special proceeding, existing in favor of or against such person, except as provided in subsection (b) hereof, shall survive to and against the personal representative or collector of the person's estate.

(b) The following rights of action in favor of a decedent do not survive:

(1) Causes of action for libel and for slander, except slander of title;

(2) Causes of action for false imprisonment;

(3) Causes of action where the relief sought could not be enjoyed, or granting it would be nugatory after death. (1868-9, c. 113, ss. 63, 64; Code, ss. 1490, 1491; Rev., ss. 156, 157; 1915, c. 38; C.S., ss. 159, 162; 1965, c. 631; 1973, c. 1329, s. 3; 2011-344, s. 4.)

§ 28A-18-2. Death by wrongful act of another; recovery not assets.

(a) When the death of a person is caused by a wrongful act, neglect or default of another, such as would, if the injured person had lived, have entitled the injured person to an action for damages therefor, the person or corporation that would have been so liable, and the personal representatives or collectors of the person or corporation that would have been so liable, shall be liable to an action for damages, to be brought by the personal representative or collector of the decedent; and this notwithstanding the death, and although the wrongful act, neglect or default, causing the death, amounts in law to a felony. The personal representative or collector of the decedent who pursues an action under this section may pay from the assets of the estate the reasonable and necessary expenses, not including attorneys' fees, incurred in pursuing the action. At the termination of the action, any amount recovered shall be applied first to the reimbursement of the estate for the expenses incurred in pursuing the action, then to the payment of attorneys' fees, and shall then be distributed as provided in this section. The amount recovered in such action is not liable to be applied as assets, in the payment of debts or devises, except as to burial expenses of the deceased, and reasonable hospital and medical expenses not exceeding four thousand five hundred dollars ($4,500) incident to the injury resulting in death, except that the amount applied for hospital and medical expenses shall not exceed fifty percent (50%) of the amount of damages recovered after deducting attorneys' fees, but shall be disposed of as provided in the Intestate Succession Act. The limitations on recovery for hospital and medical expenses under this subsection do not apply to subrogation rights exercised pursuant to G.S. 135-48.37. All claims filed for burial expenses of the decedent and reasonable hospital and medical expenses shall be subject to the approval of the clerk of the superior court and any party adversely affected by any decision of said clerk as to said claim may appeal to the superior court in term time.

(b)   Damages recoverable for death by wrongful act include:

(1)   Expenses for care, treatment and hospitalization incident to the injury resulting in death;

(2)   Compensation for pain and suffering of the decedent;

(3)   The reasonable funeral expenses of the decedent;

(4)   The present monetary value of the decedent to the persons entitled to receive the damages recovered, including but not limited to compensation for the loss of the reasonably expected;

a.   Net income of the decedent,

b.   Services, protection, care and assistance of the decedent, whether voluntary or obligatory, to the persons entitled to the damages recovered,

c.   Society, companionship, comfort, guidance, kindly offices and advice of the decedent to the persons entitled to the damages recovered;

(5)   Such punitive damages as the decedent could have recovered pursuant to Chapter 1D of the General Statutes had the decedent survived, and punitive damages for wrongfully causing the death of the decedent through malice or willful or wanton conduct, as defined in G.S. 1D-5;

(6)   Nominal damages when the jury so finds.

(c) All evidence which reasonably tends to establish any of the elements of damages included in subsection (b), or otherwise reasonably tends to establish the present monetary value of the decedent to the persons entitled to receive the damages recovered, is admissible in an action for damages for death by wrongful act.

(d) In all actions brought under this section the dying declarations of the deceased shall be admissible as provided for in G.S. 8-51.1. (R.C., c. 1, s. 10; c. 46, ss. 8, 9; 1868-9, c. 113, ss. 70-72, 115; Code, ss. 1498-1500; Rev., ss. 59, 60; 1919, c. 29; C.S., ss. 160, 161; 1933, c. 113; 1951, c. 246, s. 1; 1959, c. 879, s. 9; c. 1136; 1969, c. 215; 1973, c. 464, s. 2; c. 1329, s. 3; 1981, c. 468; 1985, c. 625; 1993, c. 299, s. 1; 1995, c. 514, s. 2; 1997-456, s. 7; 2006-264, s. 66(b); 2011-284, s. 16; 2011-344, s. 4; 2013-91, s. 1(a).)

§ 28A-18-3. To sue or defend in representative capacity.

All actions and proceedings brought by or against personal representatives or collectors upon any cause of action or right to which the estate of the decedent is the real party in interest, must be brought by or against them in their representative capacity. (1868-9, c. 113, s. 79; Code, s. 1507; Rev., s. 160; C.S., s. 164; 1973, c. 1329, s. 3.)

§ 28A-18-4. Service on or appearance of one binds all.

In actions against personal representatives or collectors, they are all to be considered as one person, representing the decedent; and if the summons is served on one or more, but not all, the plaintiff may proceed against those served, and if the plaintiff recovers, judgment may be entered against all. (1868-9, c. 113, s. 81; Code, s. 1508; Rev., s. 161; C.S., s. 165; 1973, c. 1329, s. 3; 2011-344, s. 4.)

§ 28A-18-5. When creditors may sue on claim; execution in such action.

An action may be brought by a creditor against the personal representative or collector on a demand at any time after it is due, but no execution shall issue against the personal representative or collector on a judgment therein against the personal representative or collector without leave of the court, upon notice of 20 days and upon proof that the defendant has refused to pay such judgment or its ratable part, and such judgment shall be a lien on the property of the estate of the decedent only from the time of such leave granted. (1868-9, c. 113, s. 82; Code, s. 1509; Rev., s. 162; C.S., s. 166; 1973, c. 1329, s. 3; 2011-344, s. 4.)

§ 28A-18-6. Service by publication on executor without bond.

Whenever process may issue against an executor who has not given bond, and the same cannot be served upon the executor by reason of the executor's absence or concealment, service of such process may be made by publication in the manner prescribed in other civil actions. (1868-9, c. 113, s. 94; Code, s. 1523; Rev., s. 163; C.S., s 167; 1973, c. 1329, s. 3; 2011-344, s. 4.)

§ 28A-18-7. Execution by successor in office.

Any personal representative or collector may have execution issued on any judgment recovered by any person who preceded the personal representative or collector in the administration of the estate, or by the decedent, in the same cases and the same manner as the original plaintiff might have done. (1868-9, c. 113, s. 84; Code, s. 1513; Rev., s. 164; C.S., s. 168; 1973, c. 1329, s. 3; 2011-344, s. 4.)

§ 28A-18-8. Action to continue, though letters revoked.

In case the letters of a personal representative or collector are revoked, pending an action to which the personal representative or collector is a party, the adverse party may, notwithstanding, continue the action against the personal representative or collector in order to charge the personal representative or collector personally. If such party does not elect so to do, within six months after notice of such revocation, the action may be continued against the successor of the personal representative or collector in the administration of the estate, in the same manner as in case of death. (1868-9, c. 113, s. 85; Code, s. 1514; Rev., s. 165; C.S., s. 169; 1973, c. 1329, s. 3; 2011-344, s. 4.)

Article 19.

Claims Against the Estate.

§ 28A-19-1. Manner of presentation of claims.

(a) A claim against a decedent's estate must be in writing and state the amount or item claimed, or other relief sought, the basis for the claim, and the name and address of the claimant; and must be presented by one of the following methods:

(1) By delivery in person or by mail to the personal representative, collector or the clerk of superior court. Such claim will be deemed to have been presented from the time of such delivery.

(2) By mailing, registered or certified mail, return receipt requested, to the personal representative or collector at the address set out in the general notice to creditors. Such claim will be deemed to have been presented from the time when the return receipt is signed by the personal representative, collector, or agent of the personal representative or collector, or is refused by the personal representative, collector, or agent of the personal representative or collector.

(3) By delivery to the clerk of court of the county in which the estate is pending, which notice shall be filed in the appropriate estate file and copy mailed first class by the clerk of superior court at the expense of the claimant to the personal representative, collector, or agent of the personal representative or collector. The claim will be deemed to have been presented from the time of delivery to the clerk of court.

(b) In an action commenced after the death of the decedent against the decedent's personal representative or collector as such, the commencement of the action in the court in which such personal representative or collector qualified will constitute the presentation of a claim and no further presentation is necessary. In an action filed in any other court such claim will be deemed to have been presented at the time of the completion of service of process on such personal representative or collector.

(c) In an action pending against the decedent at the time of the decedent's death, which action survives at law, the court may order the substitution of the personal representative or collector for the decedent on motion therefor and that motion will constitute the presentation of a claim, provided that substitution occurs within the time specified for the presentation of claims under G.S. 28A-19-3, and no further presentation is necessary. Such claim will be deemed to have been presented from the time of the substitution, or motion therefor. (1973, c. 1329, s. 3; 1977, c. 446, s. 1; 1985, c. 645, s. 1; 2011-344, s. 4.)

§ 28A-19-2. Further information or affidavit of claim may be required.

(a) If the personal representative or collector so elects, the personal representative or collector may demand any or all of the following prior to taking action on the claim:

(1) If the claim is not yet due, that the date when it will become due be stated;

(2) If the claim is contingent or unliquidated, that the nature of the uncertainty be stated;

(3) If the claim is secured, that the security be described.

(b) Upon any claim being presented against the estate in the manner prescribed in G.S. 28A-19-1, the personal representative or collector may require the affidavit of the claimant or other satisfactory evidence that such claim is justly due, that no payments have been made thereon, and that there are no offsets against the same, to the knowledge of the claimant; or if any payments have been made, or any offsets exist that their nature and amount be shown by the evidence or stated in the affidavit. (1868-9, c. 113, s. 33; Code, s. 1425; Rev., s. 91; C.S., s. 98; 1973, c. 1329, s. 3; 1977, c. 446, s. 1; 2011-344, s. 4.)

§ 28A-19-3. Limitations on presentation of claims.

(a) All claims against a decedent's estate which arose before the death of the decedent, except contingent claims based on any warranty made in connection with the conveyance of real estate and claims of the United States and tax claims of the State of North Carolina and subdivisions thereof, whether due or to become due, absolute or contingent, liquidated or unliquidated, secured or unsecured, founded on contract, tort, or other legal basis, which are not presented to the personal representative or collector pursuant to G.S. 28A-19-1 by the date specified in the general notice to creditors as provided for in G.S. 28A-14-1(a) or in those cases requiring the delivery or mailing of notice as provided for in G.S. 28A-14-1(b), within 90 days after the date of the delivery or mailing of the notice if the expiration of said 90-day period is later than the date specified in the general notice to creditors, are forever barred against the estate, the personal representative, the collector, the heirs, and the devisees of the decedent. Provided further, if the expiration of said 90-day period is later than the date specified in the general notice to creditors, the notice delivered or mailed to each creditor, if any, shall be accompanied by a statement which specifies the deadline for filing the claim of the affected creditor.

(b) All claims against a decedent's estate which arise at or after the death of the decedent, except claims of the United States and tax claims of the State of North Carolina and subdivisions thereof whether due or to become due, absolute or contingent, liquidated or unliquidated, secured or unsecured, founded on contract, tort, or other legal basis are forever barred against the estate, the personal representative, the collector, the heirs, and the devisees of the decedent unless presented to the personal representative or collector as follows:

(1) With respect to any claim based on a contract with the personal representative or collector, within six months after the date on which performance by the personal representative or collector is due;

(2) With respect to any claim other than a claim based on a contract with the personal representative or collector, within six months after the date on which the claim arises.

(c) Except as otherwise provided by subsection (f) of this section, no claim shall be barred by the statute of limitations which was not barred thereby at the time of the decedent's death, if the claim is presented within the period provided by subsection (a) hereof.

(d) All claims of creditors upon whom there has been personal service of notice as provided in G.S. 28A-14-3 are forever barred unless presented to the personal representative or collector within the time and manner set out in this Article.

(e) Except as otherwise provided by subsection (f) of this section, unless a claim has been presented pursuant to G.S. 28A-19-1 giving notice of an action or special proceeding pending against a decedent at the time of the decedent's death and surviving under G.S. 28A-18-1 within the time provided by subsection (a) of this section, no recovery may be had upon any judgment obtained in any such action or proceeding against the estate, the personal representative, the collector, the heirs, and the devisees of the decedent.

(f) All claims barrable under the provisions of subsections (a) and (b) hereof shall, in any event, be barred if the first publication or posting of the general notice to creditors as provided for in G.S. 28A-14-1 does not occur within three years after the death of the decedent.

(g) Nothing in this section affects or prevents any action or proceeding to enforce any mortgage, deed of trust, pledge, lien (including judgment lien), or other security interest upon any property of the decedent's estate, but no deficiency judgment will be allowed if the provisions of this section are not complied with.

(h) The word "claim" as used in this section does not apply to claims of heirs or devisees to their respective shares or interests in the decedent's estate in their capacity as such heirs or devisees.

(i) Nothing in this section shall bar:

(1) Any claim alleging the liability of the decedent or personal representative; or

(2) Any proceeding or action to establish the liability of the decedent or personal representative; or

(3) The recovery on any judgment against the decedent or personal representative

to the extent that the decedent or personal representative is protected by insurance coverage with respect to such claim, proceeding or judgment or where there is underinsured or uninsured motorist coverage that might extend to such claim, proceeding, or judgment.

(j) Except as otherwise specifically provided in this section, the limitations on presentation of claims set forth in this section apply to claims by the State of North Carolina, its subdivisions, and its agencies. (1973, c. 1329, s. 3; 1977, c. 446, s. 1; 1979, c. 509, s. 1; 1989, c. 378, s. 3; c. 485, s. 65; 2011-344, s. 4.)

§ 28A-19-4. Payment of claims and charges.

As soon as the personal representative or collector is possessed of sufficient means over and above the other costs of administration, the personal representative or collector shall pay the year's allowances in the amounts and in the manner prescribed in G.S. 30-15 to 30-33. Prior to the date specified in the general notice to creditors as provided for in G.S. 28A-14-1, the personal representative or collector may pay such other claims and charges as the personal representative or collector deems in the best interest of the estate if the total assets are sufficient to pay all claims and charges against the estate. (1973, c. 1329, s. 3; 1977, c. 446, s. 1; 2011-344, s. 4.)

§ 28A-19-5. Contingent or unliquidated claims.

(a) If a contingent or unliquidated claim becomes absolute before the distribution of the estate of the decedent, it shall be paid in the same manner as absolute claims of the same class. In other cases the clerk of superior court may provide for the payment of contingent or unliquidated claims in any one of the following ways:

(1) The creditor and the personal representative or collector may determine, by agreement, arbitration, or compromise, the value of the contingent or unliquidated claim, according to its probable present worth, and with the approval of the clerk of superior court, it may be allowed and paid in the same manner as an absolute claim.

(2) The clerk of superior court may order the personal representative or collector to retain sufficient funds to pay the claim if and when the same becomes absolute, and order distribution of the balance of the estate.

(3) The clerk of superior court may order distribution of the estate as though the contingent or unliquidated claim did not exist, but the heirs and devisees of the estate of the decedent are liable to the creditor to the extent of the estate received by them, if the contingent or unliquidated claim thereafter becomes absolute; and the court may require such heirs and devisees to give bond for the performance of their liability to the contingent or unliquidated creditor.

(4) Such other method as the clerk of superior court may order.

(b) With respect to a contingent or unliquidated claim rejected by a personal representative pursuant to G.S. 28A-19-16, the claimant may, within the three-month period prescribed by G.S. 28A-19-16, file a petition for an order of the clerk of superior court in accordance with subsection (a) of this section, provided that nothing in this section shall require the clerk of superior court to hear and determine the validity of, priority of, or amount of a contingent or unliquidated claim that has yet become absolute. (1973, c. 1329, s. 3; 2011-344, s. 4.)

§ 28A-19-6. Order of payment of claims.

(a) After payment of costs and expenses of administration, the claims against the estate of a decedent must be paid in the following order:

First class. Claims which by law have a specific lien on property to an amount not exceeding the value of such property.

Second class. Funeral expenses to the extent of three thousand five hundred dollars ($3,500). This limitation shall not include burial place or gravestone. The preferential limitation herein granted shall be construed to be only a limit with respect to preference of payment and shall not be construed to be a limitation on reasonable funeral expenses which may be incurred; nor shall the preferential limitation of payment in the amount of three thousand five hundred dollars ($3,500) be diminished by any Veterans Administration, social security or other federal governmental benefits awarded to the estate of the decedent or to the decedent's beneficiaries.

Third class. Costs associated with gravestones and reasonable costs for the purchase of a suitable burial place as provided in G.S. 28A-19-9 to the extent of one thousand five hundred dollars ($1,500). The preferential limitation herein granted shall be construed to be only a limit with respect to preference of payment and shall not be construed to be a limitation on reasonable gravestone or burial place expenses which may be incurred; nor shall the preferential limitation of payment in the amount of one thousand five hundred dollars ($1,500) be diminished by any Veterans Administration, social security or other federal governmental benefits awarded to the estate of the decedent or to the decedent's beneficiaries.

Fourth class. All dues, taxes, and other claims with preference under the laws of the United States.

Fifth class. All dues, taxes, and other claims with preference under the laws of the State of North Carolina and its subdivisions.

Sixth class. Judgments of any court of competent jurisdiction within the State, docketed and in force, to the extent to which they are a lien on the property of the decedent at the decedent's death. The Department of Health and Human Services is a sixth-class creditor for purposes of determining the order of claims against the estate; provided, however, that judgments in favor of other sixth-class creditors docketed and in force before the Department seeks recovery for medical assistance shall be paid prior to recovery by the Department.

Seventh class. Wages due to any employee employed by the decedent, which claim for wages shall not extend to a period of more than 12 months next preceding the death; or if such employee was employed for the year current at the decease, then from the time of such employment; for medical services within the 12 months preceding the decease; for drugs and all other medical supplies necessary for the treatment of such decedent during the last illness of such decedent, said period of last illness not to exceed 12 months.

Eighth class. A claim for equitable distribution.

Ninth class. All other claims.

(b)   Notwithstanding subsection (a) of this section, if payment of the commissions of the personal representative under G.S. 28A-23-3(g) would cause the estate to be unable to pay all claims against the estate of a decedent, then the commissions shall be limited to the amount allowed under G.S. 28A-23-3(a). (1868-9, c. 113, s. 24; Code, s. 1416; Rev., s. 87; C.S., s. 93; 1941, c. 271; 1955, c. 641, s. 1; 1967, c. 1066; 1973, c. 1329, s. 3; 1981, c. 383, ss. 1, 2;

1987, c. 286; 1995, c. 262, s. 8; 2005-180, s. 1; 2005-388, s. 2; 2009-288, s. 1; 2011-344, s. 4; 2013-378, s. 4.)

§ 28A-19-7. Satisfaction of claims other than by payment.

Notwithstanding any provision of law to the contrary,

(1)   If a decedent was liable in person at the time of the decedent's death for the payment or satisfaction of any claim or the performance, satisfaction, or discharge of any liability or obligation, whether joint or several, primary or secondary, direct or contingent, or enforceable in any other manner or form whatsoever, or

(2)   If only the property of a decedent or some part thereof was liable at the time of the decedent's death for the payment or satisfaction of any claim or the performance, satisfaction, or discharge or any liability or obligation, whether joint or several, primary or secondary, direct or contingent, or enforceable in any other manner or form against the property of the decedent but not against the decedent or the decedent's estate as a personal liability, and

(3)   If any person other than the personal representative of the decedent is willing to assume the liability of the decedent and of the decedent's estate or to receive or accept property of the decedent subject to such liability in cases where the decedent was not personally liable and the creditor, obligee, or other person for whose benefit such liability exists is willing to accept an agreement with that effect and to discharge the personal representative of the decedent and the estate of the decedent from the payment, satisfaction, or discharge of such liability, and

(4)   If such creditor, obligee, or other person for whose benefit such liability exists and the person assuming the liability or the person receiving or accepting property of the decedent subject to such liability shall execute, acknowledge, and deliver in the form and manner required for deeds conveying real property in North Carolina, an agreement between themselves as to such assumption of liability or the receipt or acceptance of property of the decedent subject to such liability which shall contain a release, as hereinafter defined, discharging the personal representative of the decedent and the decedent's estate from the payment, satisfaction, or discharge of the liability, and thereafter the said creditor, obligee, or other person for whose benefit such liability exists shall

have no remedy for the enforcement thereof except against the person assuming it or against the property subject to it as provided in the said agreement; then upon the filing with the clerk of superior court having jurisdiction over the estate and the personal representative of one duplicate original of the said agreement, or of a certified copy thereof if it is a duly recorded instrument, the same shall be accepted in the same manner as a voucher showing payment or discharge of the said liability in the accounts of the personal representative of the decedent.

The word "person" as used in this section shall include one or more natural persons, corporations, partnerships, or entities having the power to own property or to make contracts in regard thereto. The word "release" as used in this section shall include a covenant not to sue in any case in which an unqualified release or discharge of one obligee would discharge another, and if the liability involved is a negotiable instrument or other instrument transferable to a holder in due course, such release shall not be effective unless notice thereof is endorsed on the instrument involved, dated, and signed by the creditor or the holder of the indebtedness or person for whose benefit the property is encumbered. (1965, c. 1149; 1973, c. 1329, s. 3; 2011-344, s. 4.)

§ 28A-19-8. Funeral expenses of decedent.

(a) Any person authorized under G.S. 130A-420 to dispose of a decedent's body may bind a decedent's estate for funeral expenses and related charges, including interest and finance charges, in accordance with this section, including the execution and delivery on behalf of the estate of any agreements, promissory notes, and other instruments relating to the estate. Whether or not a personal representative of the estate has been appointed at the time the expenses are incurred, funeral expenses of a decedent, together with interest or finance charges if financed by the funeral establishment or a third-party creditor, or advanced by a health care agent exercising authority described in G.S. 32A-19(b), shall be considered as an obligation of the estate of the decedent and the decedent's estate shall be primarily liable for those expenses to the funeral establishment that provided the funeral service, to any third-party creditor that finances the payment of those expenses, or to any other person described in this section who has paid such expenses.

(b) The provisions of this section shall not affect the application of G.S. 28A-19-6 or G.S. 130A-420. (1969, c. 610, s. 1; 1973, c. 1329, s. 3; 1999-166, s. 1; 2011-344, s. 4.)

§ 28A-19-9. Gravestone and burial place authorized.

(a) If the decedent has duly appointed a health care agent pursuant to Article 3 of Chapter 32A of the General Statutes to provide for these expenses, the health care agent may make arrangements to provide a suitable gravestone to mark the grave of the testator or intestate, and the personal representative shall reimburse the health care agent subject to the monetary limitations and procedures contained in this section. If the decedent did not have a health care agent, or if the health care agent does not act, it is lawful for a personal representative or the decedent's duly appointed health care agent to provide a suitable gravestone to mark the graves of the testator or intestate and to pay for the cost of erecting the same. The cost thereof shall be treated as a third class claim under G.S. 28A-19-6 and credited as such in final accounts. The costs thereof shall be in the sound discretion of the personal representative or health care agent, having due regard to the value of the estate and to the interests of creditors and needs of the surviving spouse and the heirs and devisees of the estate. Where the personal representative or health care agent desires to spend more than one thousand five hundred dollars ($1,500) for the purpose of a gravestone, and the will does not grant specific authority to the personal representative for such expenditures in excess of one thousand five hundred dollars ($1,500), the personal representative shall file a petition before the clerk of the court, and such order as will be made by the court shall specify the amount to be expended for such purpose. In specifying the amount, the clerk may consider the value of the estate. To the extent that the personal representative or health care agent advances the costs for providing a suitable gravestone to mark the graves of the testator or intestate and for erecting the same, the advancement shall be considered as an obligation of the decedent's estate, and the decedent's estate shall be primarily liable for the costs for providing a suitable gravestone to mark the graves of the testator or intestate and for erecting the same.

(b) It is lawful for the decedent's duly appointed health care agent to provide a suitable burial place for the testator or intestate. If the decedent did not have a health care agent, or if the health care agent does not act, then the personal representative may provide a suitable burial place for the testator or intestate.

The cost of a suitable burial place shall be in the sound discretion of the personal representative or the decedent's health care agent, having due regard to the value of the estate and to the interests of creditors and needs of the surviving spouse and the heirs and devisees of the estate, and shall be treated as a third class claim under G.S. 28A-19-6. (1905, c. 444; Rev., s. 102; C.S., s. 108; 1925, c. 4; 1941, c. 102; 1951, c. 373; 1973, c. 1329, s. 3; 2009-288, s. 2; 2011-344, s. 4.)

§ 28A-19-10. Perpetual care of cemetery lot.

It shall be lawful for a personal representative to provide for perpetual care for the lot upon which is located the grave of the testator or intestate, and the cost thereof shall be paid and credited as such in final accounts: Provided, that the provisions of this section shall be applicable to an interment made in a cemetery authorized by law to operate as a perpetual-care cemetery or association, and the cost thereof shall be in the sound discretion of the personal representative having due regard to the value of the estate and to the interest of the surviving spouse and the heirs and devisees of the estate. Provided, where the personal representative desires to spend more than two hundred fifty dollars ($250.00) for such purpose, and the will does not grant specific authority to the personal representative for such expenditure in excess of two hundred fifty dollars ($250.00), the personal representative shall file the personal representative's petition before the clerk of the superior court and such order as will be made by the court shall specify the amount to be expended for such purpose. (1945, c. 756; 1973, c. 1329, s. 3; 2011-344, s. 4.)

§ 28A-19-11. Pleading statute of limitations.

When claims are not barred pursuant to G.S. 28A-19-3, it shall be within the discretion of the personal representative or collector acting in good faith to determine whether or not any applicable statute of limitations shall be pleaded to bar a claim which the personal representative or collector believes to be just. The personal representative's or collector's admission of such claim or the personal representative's or collector's decision not to plead the statute in an action brought on the claim shall, in the absence of any showing of collusion or bad faith, be binding on all persons interested in the estate. (1973, c. 1329, s. 3; 2011-344, s. 4.)

§ 28A-19-12. Claims due representative not preferred.

No property or assets of the decedent shall be retained by the personal representative or collector in satisfaction of the personal representative's or collector's own claim, in preference to others of the same class. Prior to payment of the personal representative's or collector's own claim the personal representative or collector shall receive written approval of the clerk of superior court. If the clerk does not approve the claim the personal representative or collector may refer the claim as a disputed claim under the provisions of G.S. 28A-19-15. The provisions of G.S. 28A-19-1 and G.S. 28A-19-3 shall not apply to such claims and the personal representative or collector may present the personal representative's or collector's own claim at any time prior to the filing of the personal representative's or collector's final account. (1868-9, c. 113, s. 28; Code, s. 1420; Rev., s. 89; C.S., s. 96; 1973, c. 1329, s. 3; 1979, c. 525, s. 4; 2011-344, s. 4.)

§ 28A-19-13. No preference within class.

No personal representative or collector shall give to any claim any preference whatever, either by paying it out of its class or by paying thereon more than a pro rata proportion in its class. (1868-9, c. 113, ss. 25, 26; Code, ss. 1417, 1418; Rev., s. 88; C.S., s. 94; 1973, c. 1329, s. 3.)

§ 28A-19-14. Claims not due rebated.

Claims owed by the estate but not yet due may be paid by the personal representative on a rebate of interest thereon for the time unexpired. (1868-9, c. 113, s. 27; Code, s. 1419; Rev., s. 90; C.S., s. 97; 1973, c. 1329, s. 3.)

§ 28A-19-15. Disputed claim may be referred.

If the personal representative doubts the justness of any claim so presented, the personal representative may enter into an agreement, in writing, with the claimant, to refer the matter in controversy, whether the same be of a legal or equitable nature, to one or more disinterested persons, not exceeding three, whose proceedings shall be the same in all respects as if such reference had been ordered in an action. Such agreement to refer, and the award thereupon, shall be filed in the clerk's office where the letters were granted, and shall be a lawful voucher for the personal representative. The same may be impeached in any proceeding against the personal representative for fraud therein: Provided, that the right to refer claims under this section shall extend to claims in favor of the estate as well as those against the estate. (1868-9, c. 113, s. 34; 1872-3, c. 141; Code, s. 1426; Rev., s. 92; C.S., s. 99; 1973, c. 1329, s. 3; 2011-344, s. 4.)

§ 28A-19-16. Disputed claim not referred barred in three months.

If a claim is presented to and rejected by the personal representative or collector, and not referred as provided in G.S. 28A-19-15, the claimant must, within three months, after due notice in writing of such rejection, commence an action for the recovery thereof, or in the case of a contingent or unliquidated claim, file a petition for an order from the clerk of superior court pursuant to G.S. 28A-19-5(b), or be forever barred from maintaining an action thereon. (1868-9, c. 113, s. 35; Code, s. 1427; Rev., s. 93; 1913, c. 3, s.1; C.S., s. 100; 1961, c. 742; 1973, c. 1329, s. 3; 2011-344, s. 4.)

§ 28A-19-17. No lien by suit against representative.

No lien shall be created by the commencement of a suit against a personal representative or collector. (1868-9, c. 113, s. 41; Code, s. 1432; Rev., s. 95; C.S., s. 102; 1973, c. 1329, s. 3.)

§ 28A-19-18. When costs against representative allowed.

No costs shall be recovered in any action against a personal representative or collector unless it appears that payment was unreasonably delayed or neglected, or that the defendant refused to refer the matter in controversy, in which case the court may award such costs against the defendant personally, or against the estate, as may be just. (1868-9, c. 113, s. 38; Code, s. 1429; Rev., s. 97; C.S., s. 103; 1973, c. 1329, s. 3.)

§ 28A-19-19. Claims for equitable distribution.

(a)   The provisions of G.S. 28A-19-5 and G.S. 28A-19-7 shall not apply to claims for equitable distribution.

(b)   The personal representative may enter into an agreement, in writing, with a claimant providing for distribution of marital or divisible property, or both, in a manner deemed by the personal representative and the claimant to be equitable. The agreement shall be filed in the clerk's office where the letters were granted and shall be a lawful voucher for the personal representative. The same may be impeached in any proceeding against the personal representative for fraud therein.

(c)   Unless the claim for equitable distribution has been referred as provided in G.S. 28A-19-15, the claimant may at anytime, subject to the provisions of G.S. 28A-19-16, file an action with the district court for distribution of marital or divisible property in accordance with the provisions of G.S. 50-20. (2003-168, s. 3.)

Article 20.

Inventory.

§ 28A-20-1. Inventory within three months.

Every personal representative and collector, within three months after the qualification of that personal representative or collector, shall return to the clerk, on oath, a just, true and perfect inventory of all the real and personal property of the deceased, which have come to the hands of the personal representative or collector, or to the hands of any person for the personal representative or collector, which inventory shall be signed by the personal representative or collector and be recorded by the clerk. (R.C., c. 46, s. 16; 1868-9, c. 113, s. 8; Code, s. 1396; Rev., s. 42; C.S., s. 48; 1973, c. 1329, s. 3; 1975, c. 300, s. 8; 2011-344, s. 4.)

§ 28A-20-2. Compelling the inventory.

(a) If the inventory specified in G.S. 28A-20-1 is not filed as prescribed, the clerk of superior court must issue an order requiring the personal representative or collector to file it within the time specified in the order, not less than 20 days, or to show cause why the personal representative or collector should not be removed from office. If, after due service of the order, the personal representative or collector does not on or before the return day of the order file such inventory or obtain further time in which to file it, the clerk may remove the personal representative or collector from office or may issue an attachment against the personal representative or collector for a contempt and commit the personal representative or collector until the personal representative or collector files said inventory report.

(b) The personal representative or collector shall be personally liable for the costs of any proceeding incident to the personal representative's or collector's failure to file the inventory required by G.S. 28A-20-1. Such costs shall be taxed against the personal representative or collector by the clerk of superior court and may be collected by deduction from any commissions which may be found due the personal representative or collector upon final settlement of the estate. (1868-9, c. 113, s. 9; Code, s. 1397; Rev., s. 43; C.S., s. 49; 1929, c. 9, s. 1; 1933, c. 100; 1973, c. 1329, s. 3; 2011-344, s. 4.)

§ 28A-20-3. Supplemental inventory.

(a) Whenever any property not included in the original inventory report becomes known to any personal representative or collector or whenever the personal representative or collector learns that the valuation or description of any property or interest therein indicated in the original inventory is erroneous or misleading, the personal representative or collector shall prepare and file with the clerk of superior court a supplementary inventory in the same manner as prescribed for the original inventory. The clerk shall record the supplemental report with the original inventory.

(b) The making of the supplemental inventory shall be enforced in a manner specified in G.S. 28A-20-2. (1868-9, c. 113, s. 10; Code, s. 1398; Rev., s. 44; C.S., s. 50; 1973, c. 1329, s. 3; 2011-344, s. 4.)

§ 28A-20-4. Employment of appraisers.

A personal representative or collector may, but shall not be required to, employ qualified and disinterested appraisers to assist in ascertaining the fair market value as of the date of the decedent's death of any asset the value of which may be subject to reasonable doubt. Different persons may be employed to appraise different kinds of assets. The name and address of any appraiser shall be indicated in the inventory with the asset or assets the appraiser appraised. (1973, c. 1329, s. 3; 2011-344, s. 4.)

Article 21.

Accounting.

§ 28A-21-1. Annual accounts.

Until the final account has been filed pursuant to G.S. 28A-21-2, the personal representative or collector shall, for so long as any of the property of the estate remains in the control, custody or possession of the personal representative or collector, file annually in the office of the clerk of superior court an inventory and account, under oath, of the amount of property received by the personal representative or collector, or invested by the personal representative or collector, and the manner and nature of such investment, and the receipts and disbursements of the personal representative or collector for the past year. Such accounts shall be due by the fifteenth day of the fourth month after the close of the fiscal year selected by the personal representative or collector, and annually thereafter. The election of a fiscal year shall be made by the personal representative or collector upon filing of the first annual account. In no event may a personal representative or collector select a fiscal year-end which is more than twelve months from the date of death of the decedent or, in the case of trust administration, the date of the opening of the trust. Any fiscal year selected may not be changed without the permission of the clerk of superior court.

The personal representative or collector shall produce vouchers for all payments or verified proof for payments in lieu of vouchers. The clerk of superior court may examine, under oath, such accounting party, or any other person, concerning the receipts, disbursements or any other matter relating to the estate. The clerk of superior court must carefully review and audit such account and, if the clerk approves the account, the clerk must endorse the approval of the clerk thereon, which shall be prima facie evidence of correctness, and cause the same to be recorded. (C.C.P., s. 478; 1871-2, c. 46; Code, s. 1399; Rev., s. 99; C.S., s. 105; 1957, c. 783, s. 5; 1973, c. 1329, s. 3; 1977, c. 446, s. 1; 1981, c. 955, s. 1; 1987, c. 783, s. 1; 1991, c. 485, s. 1; 2011-344, s. 4.)

§ 28A-21-2. Final accounts.

(a) Unless the time for filing the final account has been extended by the clerk of superior court, the personal representative or collector must file the final account for settlement within one year after qualifying or within six months after receiving a State estate or inheritance tax release, or in the time period for filing an annual account pursuant to G.S. 28A-21-1, whichever is later. If no estate or inheritance tax return was required to be filed for the estate, the personal representative or collector shall so certify in the final account filed with the clerk of superior court. Such certification shall list the amount and value of all of the decedent's property, and with respect to real estate, its particular location within or outside the State, including any property transferred by the decedent over which the decedent had retained any interest, or any property transferred within three years prior to the date of the decedent's death, and after being filed and accepted by the clerk of superior court shall be prima facie evidence that such property is free of any State inheritance or State estate tax liability. The personal representative or collector shall produce vouchers for all payments or verified proof for all payments in lieu of vouchers. With the approval of the clerk of superior court, such account may be filed voluntarily at any time. In all cases, the accounting shall be reviewed, audited and recorded by the clerk of superior court in the manner prescribed in G.S. 28A-21-1.

(b) Except as provided in subsection (a), after the date specified in the general notice to creditors as provided for in G.S. 28A-14-1, if all of the debts and other claims against the estate of the decedent duly presented and legally owing have been paid in the case of a solvent estate or satisfied pro rata according to applicable statutes in the case of an insolvent estate, the personal representative or collector may file the personal representative's or collector's final account to be reviewed, audited and recorded by the clerk of superior court. Nothing in this subsection shall be construed as limiting the right of the surviving spouse or minor children to file for allowances under G.S. 30-15 through 30-18 and the right of a surviving spouse to file for property rights under G.S. 29-30. (C.C.P., s. 481; Code, s. 1402; Rev., s. 103; C.S., s. 109; 1973, c. 1329, s. 3; 1975, c. 637, s. 5; 1977, c. 446, s. 1; 1979, c. 801, s. 13; 1981, c. 955, s. 2; 1981 (Reg. Sess., 1982), c. 1221, s. 3; 1985, c. 82, s. 3; c. 656, s. 3.1; 1985 (Reg. Sess., 1986), c. 822, s. 3; 1989, c. 770, s. 9; 1999-337, s. 4; 2011-344, s. 4.)

§ 28A-21-3. What accounts must contain.

Accounts filed with the clerk of superior court pursuant to G.S. 28A-21-1, signed and under oath, shall contain:

(1)   The period which the account covers and whether it is an annual accounting or a final accounting;

(2)   The amount and value of the property of the estate according to the inventory and appraisal or according to the next previous accounting, the amount of income and additional property received during the period being accounted for, and all gains from the sale of any property or otherwise;

(3)   All payments, charges, losses, and distributions;

(4)   The property on hand constituting the balance of the account, if any; and

(5)   Such other facts and information determined by the clerk to be necessary to an understanding of the account. (1973, c. 1329, s. 3.)

§ 28A-21-3.1: Repealed by Session Laws 2011-326, s. 6, effective June 27, 2011.

§ 28A-21-4. Clerk may compel account.

If any personal representative or collector fails to account as directed in G.S. 28A-9-3, 28A-21-1 or 28A-21-2 or renders an unsatisfactory account, the clerk of superior court shall, upon motion of the clerk of superior court or upon the request of one or more creditors of the decedent or other interested party, promptly order such personal representative or collector to render a full satisfactory account within 20 days after service of the order. If, after due service of the order, the personal representative or collector does not on or before the return day of the order file such account, or obtain further time in which to file it, the clerk may remove the personal representative or collector from office or may issue an attachment against the personal representative or collector for a contempt and commit the personal representative or collector until the personal representative or collector files said account. (C.C.P., s. 479; Code, s. 1400; Rev., s. 100; C.S., s. 106; 1933, c. 99; 1973, c. 1329, s. 3; 2011-344, s. 4.)

§ 28A-21-5. Vouchers presumptive evidence.

Vouchers, without other proof, are presumptive evidence of disbursement, unless impeached. If lost, the accounting party must, if required, make oath to that fact setting forth the manner of loss, and state the contents and purport of the voucher. (C.C.P., s. 480; Code, s. 1401; Rev., s. 101; C.S., s. 107; 1973, c. 1329, s. 3.)

§ 28A-21-2.1: Reserved for future codification purposes.

§ 28A-21-2.2. Final accounting by limited personal representative.

(a) Filing Requirement. - A limited personal representative appointed pursuant to Article 29 of this Chapter shall file a sworn affidavit or report listing all debts and other claims duly presented to the limited personal representative and providing proof that the debts and other claims were satisfied, compromised, or denied, and that the time for filing suit thereon has expired. The sworn affidavit or report shall be filed within 30 days of the later of the following:

(1) The date by which a claim must be presented as set forth in the general notice to creditors provided for in G.S. 28A-14-1.

(2) The date by which an action for recovery of a rejected claim must be commenced under G.S. 28A-19-6.

(b) Action by Clerk. - The affidavit or report shall be reviewed and recorded by the clerk of superior court. Following the review, the clerk of superior court shall take one of the following actions:

(1) Discharge the limited personal representative from office.

(2) Require the filing of any additional information or documents determined by the clerk to be necessary to the understanding of the affidavit or report.

(3) Order the full administration of the decedent's estate and appoint a personal representative. (2009-444, s. 2.)

§ 28A-21-6. Permissive notice of final accounts.

The personal representative or collector may, but is not required to, give written notice of a proposed final account pursuant to G.S. 1A-1, Rule 4, to all devisees of the estate in the case of testacy, and to all heirs of the estate in the case of intestacy, of the date and place of filing of such account. In giving written notice, the personal representative shall attach a copy of the proposed final accounting with exhibits made a part thereof, but is not required to include copies of vouchers, account statements, or other supporting evidence submitted to the clerk. If the personal representative or collector elects to provide this notice, the personal representative or collector shall file with the clerk of superior court a certificate indicating that this notice has been given to all devisees and heirs. Notwithstanding any right to appeal an order or judgment under G.S. 1-301.3, any payment, distribution, action, or other matter disclosed on such account or any annual account for the estate attached to the written notice must be objected to by a devisee or heir within 30 days after the receipt of the written notice or will be deemed to be accepted by the devisee or heir. (2011-344, s. 4; 2012-18, s. 3.8.)

Article 22.

Distribution.

§ 28A-22-1. Scheme of distribution; testate and intestate estates.

After the payment of costs of administration, taxes and other valid claims against the decedent's estate, the personal representative shall distribute the remaining assets of the estate in accordance with the terms of decedent's valid probated will or the provisions of Chapter 29 of the General Statutes or as otherwise lawfully authorized. (1973, c. 1329, s. 3.)

§ 28A-22-2. Shares of after-born and after-adopted children.

The share of an after-born or after-adopted child, as provided by G.S. 29-9 and 31-5.5, shall be allotted to the after-born or after-adopted child out of any undevised real or personal property, or out of both, if there is enough such undevised property for that purpose. If there is no undevised real or personal property, or if there is not enough, then the whole of the child's share, or the deficiency, shall be made up from the devised real or personal property, or from both. The portion contributed by a devisee shall bear the same ratio to the devisee's devise as the after-born or after-adopted child's share bears to the net estate. (1868-9, c. 113, ss. 108, 109; Code, ss. 1536, 1537; Rev., ss. 138, 139; C.S., ss. 141, 142; 1973, c. 1329, s. 3; 2011-344, s. 4.)

§ 28A-22-3. Special proceeding against unknown heirs of decedent before distribution of estate.

If there may be heirs, born or unborn, of the decedent, other than those known to the personal representative and whose names and residences are unknown, before distributing such estate the personal representative is authorized to institute a special proceeding before the clerk of superior court for the purpose of determining who are the heirs of the decedent. All unknown heirs of the decedent shall be made parties thereto and shall be served with summons by publication as provided by G.S. 1A-1, Rule 4. Upon such service being had, the court shall appoint some discreet person to act as guardian ad litem for said unknown heirs and summons shall issue as to such guardian ad litem. Said guardian ad litem shall file answer on behalf of said unknown heirs and the guardian ad litem may be paid for services of the guardian ad litem such sum as the court may fix, to be paid as other costs out of the estate. Upon the filing of the answer by said guardian ad litem all such unknown heirs shall be before the court for the purposes of the proceeding to the same extent as if each had been personally served with summons. Any judgment entered by the court in such proceeding shall be as binding upon said unknown heirs as if they were personally before the court and any payment or distribution made by the personal representative under orders of the court shall have the effect of fully discharging such personal representative and any sureties on the personal representative's official bond to the full extent of such payment or distribution as ordered. (1957, c. 1248; 1973, c. 1329, s. 3; 2011-344, s. 4.)

§ 28A-22-4. Distribution to nonresident trustee only upon appointment of process agent.

(a)   No assets of the estate of a decedent subject to administration in this State shall be delivered or transferred to a trustee of a testamentary trust or an inter vivos trust who is a nonresident of this State who has not appointed a resident agent for the service of civil process for actions or proceedings arising out of the administration of the trust with regard to such property.

(b)   If property is delivered or transferred to a trustee in violation of this section, process may be served outside this State or by publication, as provided by G.S. 1A-1, Rule 4, and the courts of this State shall have the same jurisdiction over the trustee as might have been obtained by service upon a properly appointed process agent. The provisions of this section with regard to jurisdiction shall be in addition to other means of obtaining jurisdiction permissible under the laws of this State. (1967, c. 947; 1973, c. 1329, s. 3.)

§ 28A-22-5. Distribution of assets in kind in satisfaction of devises and transfers in trust.

(a) Subject to the provisions of subsection (b) of this section, whenever under any will or trust indenture the executor, trustee or other fiduciary is required to, or has an option to, satisfy a devise or transfer in trust by a transfer of assets of the estate or trust in kind at the values as finally determined for federal estate tax purposes, the executor, trustee or other fiduciary shall, in the absence of contrary provisions in such will or trust indenture, be required to satisfy such devise or transfer by the distribution of assets fairly representative of the appreciation or depreciation in the value of all property available for distribution in satisfaction of such devise or transfer.

(b) The provisions of subsection (a) of this section shall not apply unless either:

(1) The decedent's surviving spouse is the beneficiary of the devise or trust transfer described in subsection (a) of this section or of the residue of the estate or trust; or

(2) Any "skip person", as that term is defined in Chapter 13 of the Internal Revenue Code of 1986, as amended, is or may be a current or future beneficiary of the devise or trust transfer described in subsection (a) of this section or of the residue of the estate or trust, and the value of the decedent's gross estate for federal tax purposes exceeds the value of the decedent's unused generation-skipping tax exemption available under Chapter 13 of the Internal Revenue Code of 1986, as amended. (1965, c. 764, s. 1; 1973, c. 1329, s. 3; 1995, c. 235, s. 5; 2011-284, s. 17.)

§ 28A-22-6. Agreements with taxing authorities to secure benefit of federal marital deduction.

The executor, trustee, or other fiduciary having discretionary powers under a will or trust indenture with respect to the selection of assets to be distributed in satisfaction of a devise or transfer in trust to or for the benefit of the surviving spouse of a decedent shall be authorized to enter into agreements with the Commissioner of Internal Revenue of the United States of America, and other taxing authorities, requiring the fiduciary to exercise the fiduciary's discretion so that cash and other properties distributed in satisfaction of such devise or transfer in trust will be fairly representative of the net appreciation or depreciation in value on the date, or dates, of distribution of all property then available for distribution in satisfaction of such devise or transfer in trust. Any such fiduciary shall be authorized to enter into any other agreement not in conflict with the express terms of the will or trust indenture that may be necessary or advisable in order to secure for federal estate tax purposes the appropriate marital deduction available under the Internal Revenue Laws of the United States of America and to do and perform all acts incident to such purpose. (1965, c. 744; 1973, c. 1329, s. 3; 2011-284, s. 18.)

§ 28A-22-7. Distribution to parent or guardian of a minor.

(a) If a devise of personal property to a person under the age of 18 has a total value of less than one thousand five hundred dollars ($1,500), and the devisee is residing in the same household with a parent or a guardian appointed prior to the decedent's death, the personal representative may distribute to the parent or guardian the devise. However, such distribution shall only be made with the prior approval of the clerk of court who issued the letters testamentary or of administration.

(b) If such distribution has been made the parent or guardian shall use the property solely for the education, maintenance and support of the devisee. However, the parent or guardian shall not be required to file an accounting with the clerk of court or to the personal representative, nor shall such distribution be cause for a delay in the filing of the personal representative's final account under the provisions of Article 21 of this Chapter.

(c) This section establishes a procedure that is separate from the provisions of G.S. 33-69.1 and it is not the intention of this section to repeal in whole or in part the provisions of G.S. 33-69.1.

(d) This section may also be applied to several devises of personal property to a single devisee having a combined total value of less than one thousand five hundred dollars ($1,500). (1975, c. 813, s. 1; 2011-284, s. 19.)

§ 28A-22-8. Executor or trustee; discretion over distributions.

Unless otherwise restricted by the terms of the will or trust, an executor or trustee shall have absolute discretion to make distributions in cash or in specific property, real or personal, or an undivided interest therein or partly in cash or partly in such property, and to do so without regard to the income tax basis for federal tax purposes of specific property allocated to any beneficiary. (1977, c. 740.)

§ 28A-22-9. Distribution to known but unlocated devisees or heirs.

(a)   If there are known but unlocated devisees or heirs of property held by the personal representative, the personal representative may deliver the share of such devisee or heir to the clerk of superior court immediately prior to filing of the final account. If the devisee or heir is located after the final account has been filed, the devisee or heir may present a claim for the share to the clerk. If the clerk determines that the claimant is entitled to the share, the clerk shall deliver the share to the devisee or claimant. If the clerk denies the claim, the claimant may take an appeal as in a special proceeding.

(b)   The clerk shall hold the share without liability for profit or interest. If no claim has been presented within a period of one year after the filing of the final account, the clerk shall deliver the share to the State Treasurer as abandoned property.

(c)   The clerk shall not be required to publish any notice to such devisee or heir and shall not be required to report such share to the State Treasurer. If the devisee or heir is located, the clerk shall inform the devisee or heir that the devisee or heir is entitled to file a claim with the State Treasurer for the share under the provisions of G.S. 116B-67. (1979, 2nd Sess., c. 1311, s. 2; 2002-62, s. 1; 2011-344, s. 4.)

§ 28A-22-10. Distribution of assets of inoperative trust.

When the facts at the time of distribution of property to a trust are such that the trust would be inoperative under the terms of the instrument creating the trust for any reason, including the death of a beneficiary, renunciation by a beneficiary, the exercise of a right to withdraw the property by a beneficiary, or the attainment of a stipulated age by a beneficiary, the personal representative or the trustee authorized or required to make the distribution of that property to the trust may distribute the property directly to the person or persons entitled to it under the terms of the instrument creating the trust without the interposition of the establishment of the trust. If only a portion of the trust would be inoperative, the property distributable to that portion of the trust may be distributed directly to the person or persons entitled to the property under the terms of the instrument creating the trust. (2001-413, s. 3.)

§ 28A-22-11. Agreements with heirs.

Any agreement by an heir, unknown or known but unlocated, the primary purpose of which is to locate or recover, or assist in the recovery of, a share in a decedent's estate shall be subject to the provisions of G.S. 116B-78. (2009-312, s. 3.)

Article 23.

Settlement.

§ 28A-23-1. Settlement after final account filed.

When the personal representative or collector has paid or otherwise satisfied or provided for all claims against the estate, has distributed the remainder of the estate pursuant to G.S. 28A-22-1 and has filed the personal representative's or collector's final account for settlement pursuant to G.S. 28A-21-2, if the clerk of superior court, after review of the personal representative's or collector's final account, approves the same, the clerk of superior court shall enter an order discharging the personal representative or collector from further duties and liabilities as personal representative or collector, including those set forth in Article 13 of this Chapter. However, that such an order shall not include a release or discharge of liability for any breach of duty set forth in G.S. 28A-13-10(c). (1973, c. 1329, s. 3; 1977, c. 446, s. 1; 2011-344, s. 4.)

§ 28A-23-2. Payment into court of fund due minor.

When any personal representative or collector holds property due a minor without a guardian and desires to file the personal representative's or collector's petition for settlement, the personal representative or collector may deliver the property to the clerk of superior court who shall invest upon interest or otherwise manage said property for the use of the minor or the clerk may proceed to appoint a guardian for the minor pursuant to the provisions of Chapter 35A of the General Statutes and then may deliver the property of the minor to the guardian. (1868-9, c. 113, s. 97; Code, s. 1526; 1893, c. 317; Rev., s. 151; C.S., s. 153; 1965, c. 815, s. 3; 1973, c. 1329, s. 3; 1987, c. 550, s. 17; 2011-344, s. 4.)

§ 28A-23-3. Commissions allowed personal representatives; representatives guilty of misconduct or default.

(a) Personal representatives, collectors or public administrators shall be entitled to commissions to be fixed in the discretion of the clerk of superior court not to exceed five percent (5%) upon the amounts of receipts, including the value of all personal property when received, and upon the expenditures made in accordance with law. In determining the maximum commissions allowable under this subsection, the clerk of superior court may take into consideration fees paid by the estate for professional services performed in the ordinary course of administering the estate, including services performed by attorneys and accountants. However, the clerk is not required to reduce the maximum commissions allowed by the aggregate fees paid to professionals on a dollar-for-dollar basis.

The commissions shall be charged as a part of the costs of administration and, upon allowance, may be retained out of the assets of the estate against creditors and all other persons claiming an interest in the estate. If the gross value of an estate is two thousand dollars ($2,000) or less, the clerk of superior court may fix the commission to be received by the personal representative, collector or public administrator in an amount the clerk of superior court, in the clerk's discretion, deems just and adequate.

(b) In determining the amount of the commissions, both upon personal property received and upon expenditures made, the clerk of superior court shall consider the time, responsibility, trouble and skill involved in the management of the estate. Where real property is sold to pay debts or devises, the commission shall be computed only on the proceeds actually applied in the payment of debts or devises.

(c) The clerk of superior court may allow commissions from time to time during the course of the administration, but the total commissions allowed shall be determined on final settlement of the estate and shall not exceed the limit fixed in this section.

(d) Nothing in this section shall be construed to:

(1) Prevent the clerk of superior court from allowing reasonable sums for necessary charges and disbursements incurred in the management of the estate.

(2) Allow commissions on distribution of the shares of heirs or on distribution of shares of devisees.

(3) Abridge the right of any party interested in the administration of a decedent's estate to appeal an order of the clerk of superior court to a judge of superior court.

(e) No personal representative, collector or public administrator, who has been guilty of default or misconduct in the due execution of the personal representative's, collector's, or public administrator's office resulting in the revocation of the appointment of the personal representative, collector, or public administrator under the provisions of G.S. 28A-9-1, shall be entitled to any commission under the provisions of this section.

(f) For the purpose of computing commissions whenever any portion of the dividends, interest, rents or other amounts payable to a personal representative, collector or public administrator is required by any law of the United States or other governmental unit to be withheld for income tax purposes by the person, corporation, organization or governmental unit paying the same, the amount withheld shall be deemed to have been received and expended.

(g) Subsection (a) of this section does not apply if the testator's will specifies a stipulated amount or method or standard for determining the compensation for the services rendered by the personal representative, including a provision in the will that the compensation of the personal representative is to be determined by applying the personal representative's regularly adopted schedule of compensation in effect at the time of performance of those services. Subsection (a) of this section also shall not apply if the testator's will provides that the personal representative is to receive "reasonable compensation" for those services or similar language to that effect if the personal representative and the beneficiaries whose shares would be charged with the payment of the personal representative's compensation consent in writing to the specific amount that constitutes reasonable compensation.

(h)   Subsection (a) of this section shall apply if the testator's will provides that compensation of the personal representative shall be the amount "as provided by law," the "maximum amount provided by law," or other similar language. (1868-9, c. 113, s. 95; 1869-70, c. 189; Code, s. 1524; Rev., s. 149; C.S., s. 157; 1941, c. 124; 1953, c. 855; 1959, c. 662; c. 879, s. 8; 1961, cc. 362, 575; 1973, c. 1329, s. 3; 1977, c. 814, s. 2; 2005-388, s. 1; 2011-284, s. 20; 2011-344, s. 4.)

§ 28A-23-4. Counsel fees allowable to attorneys serving as representatives.

The clerk of superior court, in the discretion of the clerk of superior court, is authorized and empowered to allow counsel fees to an attorney serving as a personal representative, collector or public administrator (in addition to the commissions allowed the attorney as such representative, collector or public administrator) where such attorney in behalf of the estate the attorney represents renders professional services, as an attorney, which are beyond the ordinary routine of administration and of a type which would reasonably justify the retention of legal counsel by any such representative, collector or public administrator not licensed to practice law. (1957, c. 375; 1973, c. 1329, s. 3; 1977, c. 814, s. 3; 2011-344, s. 4.)

§ 28A-23-5. Reopening administration.

If, after an estate has been settled and the personal representative discharged, other property of the estate shall be discovered, or if it shall appear that any necessary act remains unperformed on the part of the personal representative, or for any other proper cause, the clerk of superior court, upon the petition of any person interested in the estate and without notice or upon such notice as the clerk of superior court may direct, may order that said estate be reopened. The clerk of superior court may reappoint the personal representative or appoint another personal representative to administer such property or perform such acts as may be deemed necessary. Unless the clerk of superior court shall otherwise order, the provisions of this Chapter as to an original administration shall apply to the proceedings had in the reopened administration; but no claim which is already barred can be asserted in the reopened administration. (1973, c. 1329, s. 3; 2011-344, s. 4.)

Article 24.

120-Hour Survivorship Requirement; Revised Simultaneous Death Act.

§ 28A-24-1. Definitions.

In this Article:

(1) "Co-owners with right of survivorship" includes joint tenants in a joint tenancy with right of survivorship, tenants by the entireties, and other co-owners of property or accounts held under circumstances that entitle one or more to the whole of the property or account on the death of the other or others.

(2) "Governing instrument" means a deed, will, trust, insurance or annuity policy, account with a POD designation, pension, profit sharing, retirement, or similar benefit plan, instrument creating or exercising a power of appointment or a power of attorney, or a dispositive, appointive, or nominative instrument of any similar type.

(3) "Payor" means a trustee, insurer, business entity, employer, government, governmental agency or subdivision, or any other person authorized or obligated by law or a governing instrument to make payments. (1947, c. 1016, s. 1; 1973, c. 1329, s. 3; 2007-132, s. 1.)

§ 28A-24-2. Requirement of survival by 120 hours.

(a) Except as otherwise provided in this Article, where the title to property, the devolution of property, the right to elect an interest in property, or any other right or benefit depends upon an individual's survivorship of the death of another individual, an individual who is not established by clear and convincing evidence to have survived the other individual by at least 120 hours is deemed to have predeceased the other individual.

(b) If the language of the governing instrument disposes of property in such a way that two or more beneficiaries are designated to take alternatively by reason of surviving each other and it is not established by clear and convincing evidence that any such beneficiary has survived any other such beneficiary by at least 120 hours, the property shall be divided into as many equal shares as there are alternative beneficiaries, and these shares shall be distributed respectively to each such beneficiary's estate.

(c) If the language of the governing instrument disposes of property in such a way that it is to be distributed to the member or members of a class who survived an individual, each member of the class will be deemed to have survived that individual by at least 120 hours unless it is established by clear and convincing evidence that the individual survived the class member or members by at least 120 hours. (1947, c. 1016, s. 2; 1973, c. 1329, s. 3; 2007-132, s. 1.)

§ 28A-24-3. Co-owners with right of survivorship; requirement of survival by 120 hours.

Except as otherwise provided in this Article:

(1) If there are two or more co-owners with right of survivorship and it is not established by clear and convincing evidence that at least one of them survived the other or others by at least 120 hours, then, unless the governing instrument provides otherwise, each co-owner's pro rata interest in the property passes as if that co-owner had survived all other co-owners by at least 120 hours.

(2) If there are two or more co-owners with right of survivorship and it is established by clear and convincing evidence that at least one of them survived the other or others by at least 120 hours, then, unless the governing instrument provides otherwise, the pro rata interest or interests of the deceased owner or owners who are not established by clear and convincing evidence to have survived by at least 120 hours passes to (i) the remaining owner if only one or (ii) if more than one, then to those remaining owners according to the pro rata interest of each. (1947, c. 1016, s. 3; 1973, c. 1329, s. 3; 2007-132, s. 1; 2012-69, s. 1.)

§ 28A-24-4. Survival of an event; 120-hour period not applicable.

For purposes of a governing instrument that requires survival of an event, other than the death of another individual, the 120-hour survivorship requirement of this Article does not apply. (1947, c. 1016, s. 4; 1973, c. 1329, s. 3; 2007-132, s. 1.)

§ 28A-24-5. Victim deemed to survive slayer.

Notwithstanding any other provisions of this Article, solely for the purpose of determining whether the victim is entitled to any right or benefit that depends on surviving the death of a slayer under G.S. 31A-3, the slayer is deemed to have predeceased the victim and the victim is deemed to have survived the slayer by at least 120 hours (or any greater survival period required of the victim under the slayer's will or other governing instrument) unless it is established by clear and convincing evidence that the slayer survived the victim by at least 120 hours. (1947, c. 1016, s. 6; 1973, c. 1329, s. 3; 2007-132, s. 1.)

§ 28A-24-6. Exceptions to the 120-hour survival requirement.

Survival by 120 hours is not required if any of the following apply:

(1) The governing instrument contains language dealing explicitly with simultaneous deaths or deaths in a common disaster and the language is operable under the facts of the case.

(2) The governing instrument expressly indicates that an individual is not required to survive the death of another individual by any specified period or expressly requires the individual to survive another individual for a specified period; but survival must be established by clear and convincing evidence.

(3) The imposition of a 120-hour requirement of survival would cause a nonvested property interest or a power of appointment to fail to qualify for validity under G.S. 41-15; but survival must be established by clear and convincing evidence.

(4) The application of a 120-hour requirement of survival to multiple governing instruments would result in an unintended failure or duplication of a disposition; but survival must be established by clear and convincing evidence.

(5) The application of a 120-hour requirement of survival would deprive an individual or the estate of an individual of an otherwise available tax exemption, deduction or credit, expressly including the marital deduction, resulting in the imposition of a tax upon a donor or testator or other person (or their estate) as the transferor of any property. "Tax" includes any federal or State gift, estate or inheritance tax.

(6) The application of a 120-hour requirement of survival would result in an escheat. (1947, c. 1016, s. 7; 1973, c. 1329, s. 3; 2007-132, s. 1.)

§ 28A-24-7. Evidence of death or status.

For purposes of this Article, the following rules of evidence apply relating to the determination of death and status of a beneficiary subject to a requirement of survivorship and of the person the beneficiary must survive:

(1) Death occurs when an individual is determined to be dead pursuant to G.S. 90-323 or Chapter 28C of the General Statutes.

(2) A certified or authenticated copy of a death certificate purporting to be issued by an official or agency in the place where the death purportedly occurred is prima facie evidence of the fact, place, date, and time of death and the identity of the decedent. In the absence of evidence disputing the death certificate, that certificate shall be conclusive evidence of the fact, place, date, and time of death and the identity of the decedent.

(3) A certified or authenticated copy of any record or report of a governmental agency, domestic or foreign, that an individual is missing, detained, dead, or alive is prima facie evidence of the status and of the dates, circumstances, and places disclosed by the record or report. The record or report is conclusive evidence of the status and of the dates, circumstances, and places disclosed by the record or report unless there is evidence to the contrary.

(4) In the absence of prima facie evidence of death under subdivision (2) or (3) of this section, the fact of death may be established by clear and convincing

evidence, including circumstantial evidence. (1947, c. 1016, s. 8; 1973, c. 1329, s. 3; 2007-132, s. 1.)

§ 28A-24-8. Protection of payors, bona fide purchasers, and other third parties; personal liability of recipient.

(a)   A payor or other third party is not liable for having made a payment or transferred an item of property or any other benefit to a person designated in a governing instrument who, under this Article, is not entitled to the payment or item of property, or for having taken any other action in good faith reliance on the person's apparent entitlement under the terms of the governing instrument, before the payor or other third party received written notice of a claimed lack of entitlement under this Article. A payor or other third party is liable for a payment made or other action taken after the payor or other third party received written notice of a claimed lack of entitlement under this Article.

Written notice of a claimed lack of entitlement under this Article must be mailed to the payor's or other third party's main office or home by registered or certified mail, return receipt requested, or served upon the payor or other third party in the same manner as a summons in a civil action. Upon receipt of written notice of a claimed lack of entitlement under this Article, a payor or other third party may pay any amount owed or transfer or deposit any item of property other than tangible personal property held by it to or with the clerk of the superior court having jurisdiction of the probate proceedings relating to the decedent's estate, or if no proceedings have been commenced, to or with the clerk of the superior court having jurisdiction of probate proceedings relating to decedents' estates located in the county of the decedent's residence. The clerk shall hold the funds or item of property and, upon the clerk's determination under this Article, shall order disbursement in accordance with the determination. Payments, transfers, or deposits made to or with the clerk discharge the payor or other third party from all claims for the value of amounts paid to or items of property transferred to or deposited with the clerk.

(b)   A person who purchases property for value and without notice, or who received a payment or other item of property in partial or full satisfaction of a legally enforceable obligation, is neither obligated under this Article to return the payment, item of property, or benefit, nor liable under this Article for the amount of the payment or the value of the item of property or benefit. But a person who, not for value, receives a payment, item of property, or any other benefit to which the person is not entitled under this Article is obligated to return the payment, item of property, or benefit, or is personally liable for the amount of the payment or the value of the item of property or benefit, to the person who is entitled to it under this Article. (2007-132, s. 1.)

Article 25.

Small Estates.

§ 28A-25-1. Collection of property by affidavit when decedent dies intestate.

(a) When a decedent dies intestate leaving personal property, less liens and encumbrances thereon, not exceeding twenty thousand dollars ($20,000) in value, at any time after 30 days from the date of death, any person indebted to the decedent or having possession of tangible personal property or an instrument evidencing a debt, obligation, stock or chose in action belonging to the decedent shall make payment of the indebtedness or deliver the tangible personal property or an instrument evidencing a debt, obligation, stock or chose in action to a person claiming to be the public administrator appointed pursuant to G.S. 28A-12-1, or an heir or creditor of the decedent, not disqualified under G.S. 28A-4-2, upon being presented a certified copy of an affidavit filed in accordance with subsection (b) and made by or on behalf of the heir or creditor or the public administrator stating:

(1) The name and address of the affiant and the fact that the affiant is the public administrator or an heir or creditor of the decedent;

(2) The name of the decedent and the decedent's residence at time of death;

(3) The date and place of death of the decedent;

(4) That 30 days have elapsed since the death of the decedent;

(5) That the value of all the personal property owned by the estate of the decedent, less liens and encumbrances thereon, does not exceed twenty thousand dollars ($20,000);

(6) That no application or petition for appointment of a personal representative is pending or has been granted in any jurisdiction;

(7) The names and addresses of those persons who are entitled, under the provisions of the Intestate Succession Act, to the personal property of the decedent and their relationship, if any, to the decedent; and

(8) A description sufficient to identify each tract of real property owned by the decedent at the time of the decedent's death.

In those cases in which the affiant is the surviving spouse and sole heir of the decedent, not disqualified under G.S. 28A-4-2, the property described in this subsection that may be collected pursuant to this section may exceed twenty thousand dollars ($20,000) in value but shall not exceed thirty thousand dollars ($30,000) in value, after reduction for any spousal allowance paid to the surviving spouse pursuant to G.S. 30-15. In such cases, the affidavit shall state: (i) the name and address of the affiant and the fact that the affiant is the surviving spouse and is entitled, under the provisions of the Intestate Succession Act, to all of the property of the decedent; (ii) that the value of all of the personal property owned by the estate of the decedent, less liens and encumbrances thereon, does not exceed thirty thousand dollars ($30,000); and (iii) the information required under subdivisions (2), (3), (4), (6), and (8) of this subsection.

(b) Prior to the recovery of any assets of the decedent, a copy of the affidavit described in subsection (a) shall be filed in the office of the clerk of superior court of the county where the decedent was domiciled at the time of death. The affidavit shall be filed by the clerk upon payment of the fee provided in G.S. 7A-307, shall be indexed in the index to estates, and a copy thereof shall be mailed by the clerk to the persons shown in the affidavit as entitled to the personal property.

(c) The presentation of an affidavit as provided in subsection (a) shall be sufficient to require the transfer to the affiant or the affiant's designee of the title and license to a motor vehicle registered in the name of the decedent owner; the ownership rights of a savings account or checking account in a bank in the name of the decedent owner; the ownership rights of a savings account or share certificate in a credit union, building and loan association, or savings and loan association in the name of the decedent owner; the ownership rights in any stock or security registered on the books of a corporation in the name of a decedent owner; or any other property or contract right owned by decedent at the time of the decedent's death. (1973, c. 1329, s. 3; 1975, c. 300, s. 9; 1983, c. 65, s. 1; c. 713, s. 21; 1985, c. 651, s. 1; 1989, c. 407, s. 1; 1995, c. 262, s. 1; 2009-175, s. 1; 2011-344, s. 4.)

§ 28A-25-1.1. Collection of property by affidavit when decedent dies testate.

(a) When a decedent dies testate leaving personal property, less liens and encumbrances thereon, not exceeding twenty thousand dollars ($20,000) in value, at any time after 30 days from the date of death, any person indebted to the decedent or having possession of tangible personal property or an instrument evidencing a debt, obligation, stock or chose in action belonging to the decedent shall make payment of the indebtedness or deliver the tangible personal property or an instrument evidencing a debt, obligation, stock or chose in action to a person claiming to be the public administrator appointed pursuant to G.S. 28A-12-1, a person named or designated as executor in the will, devisee, heir or creditor, of the decedent, not disqualified under G.S. 28A-4-2, upon being presented a certified copy of an affidavit filed in accordance with subsection (b) and made by or on behalf of the heir, the person named or designated as executor in the will of the decedent, the creditor, the public administrator, or the devisee, stating:

(1) The name and address of the affiant and the fact that the affiant is the public administrator, a person named or designated as executor in the will, devisee, heir or creditor, of the decedent;

(2) The name of the decedent and the decedent's residence at time of death;

(3) The date and place of death of the decedent;

(4) That 30 days have elapsed since the death of the decedent;

(5) That the decedent died testate leaving personal property, less liens and encumbrances thereon, not exceeding twenty thousand dollars ($20,000) in value;

(6) That the decedent's will has been admitted to probate in the court of the proper county and a duly certified copy of the will has been recorded in each

county in which is located any real property owned by the decedent at the time of the decedent's death;

(7) That a certified copy of the decedent's will is attached to the affidavit;

(8) That no application or petition for appointment of a personal representative is pending or has been granted in any jurisdiction;

(9) The names and addresses of those persons who are entitled, under the provisions of the will, or if applicable, of the Intestate Succession Act, to the property of the decedent; and their relationship, if any, to the decedent; and

(10) A description sufficient to identify each tract of real property owned by the decedent at the time of the decedent's death.

In those cases in which the affiant is the surviving spouse, is entitled to all of the property of the decedent, and is not disqualified under G.S. 28A-4-2, the property described in this subsection that may be collected pursuant to this section may exceed twenty thousand dollars ($20,000) in value but shall not exceed thirty thousand dollars ($30,000) in value, after reduction for any spousal allowance paid to the surviving spouse pursuant to G.S. 30-15. In such cases, the affidavit shall state: (i) the name and address of the affiant and the fact that the affiant is the surviving spouse and is entitled, under the provisions of the decedent's will, or if applicable, of the Intestate Succession Act, to all of the property of the decedent; (ii) that the decedent died testate leaving personal property, less liens and encumbrances thereon, not exceeding thirty thousand dollars ($30,000); and (iii) the information required under subdivisions (2), (3), (4), (6), (7), (8), and (10) of this subsection.

(b) Prior to the recovery of any assets of the decedent, a copy of the affidavit described in subsection (a) shall be filed in the office of the clerk of superior court of the county where the decedent was domiciled at the time of death. The affidavit shall be filed by the clerk upon payment of the fee provided in G.S. 7A-307, shall be indexed in the index to estates, and a copy shall be mailed by the clerk to the persons shown in the affidavit as entitled to the property.

(c) The presentation of an affidavit as provided in subsection (a) shall be sufficient to require the transfer to the affiant or the affiant's designee of the title and license to a motor vehicle registered in the name of the decedent owner; the ownership rights of a savings account or checking account in a bank in the name of the decedent owner; the ownership rights of a savings account or share certificate in a credit union, building and loan association, or savings and loan association in the name of the decedent owner; the ownership rights in any stock or security registered on the books of a corporation in the name of a decedent owner; or any other property or contract right owned by decedent at the time of the decedent's death. (1985, c. 651, s. 2; 1987, c. 670, s. 1; 1989, c. 407, s. 2; 1995, c. 262, s. 2; 2009-175, s. 2; 2011-344, s. 4; 2012-18, s. 3.9.)

§ 28A-25-2. Effect of affidavit.

The person paying, delivering, transferring or issuing personal property or the evidence thereof pursuant to an affidavit meeting the requirements of G.S. 28A-25-1(a) or G.S. 28A-25-1.1(a) is discharged and released to the same extent as if the person dealt with a duly qualified personal representative of the decedent. The person is not required to see to the application of the personal property or evidence thereof or to inquire into the truth of any statement in the affidavit. If any person to whom an affidavit is delivered refuses to pay, deliver, transfer, or issue any personal property or evidence thereof, it may be recovered or its payment, delivery, transfer, or issuance compelled upon proof of their right in an action brought for that purpose by or on behalf of the persons entitled thereto. The court costs and attorney's fee incident to the action shall be taxed against the person whose refusal to comply with the provisions of G.S. 28A-25-1(a) or G.S. 28A-25-1.1(a) made the action necessary. The heir or creditor to whom payment, delivery, transfer or issuance is made is answerable and accountable therefor to any duly qualified personal representative or collector of the decedent's estate or to any other person having an interest in the estate. (1973, c. 1329, s. 3; 1985, c. 651, s. 3; 1987, c. 670, s. 2; 2011-344, s. 4.)

§ 28A-25-3. Disbursement and distribution of property collected by affidavit.

(a)   If there has been no personal representative or collector appointed by the clerk of superior court, the affiant who has collected personal property of the decedent by affidavit pursuant to G.S. 28A-25-1 or G.S. 28A-25-1.1 shall:

(1)   Disburse and distribute the same in the following order:

a. To the payment of the surviving spouse's year's allowance and the children's year's allowance assigned in accordance with G.S. 30-15 through G.S. 30-33;

b. To the payment of the debts and claims against the estate of the decedent in the order of priority set forth in G.S. 28A-19-6, or to the reimbursement of any person who has already made payment thereof;

c. To the distribution of the remainder of the personal property to the persons entitled thereto under the provisions of the will or of the Intestate Succession Act; and

(2) File an affidavit with the clerk of superior court that the affiant has collected the personal property of the decedent and the manner in which the affiant has disbursed and distributed the same. This final affidavit shall be filed within 90 days of the date of filing of the qualifying affidavit provided for in G.S. 28A-25-1 or G.S. 28A-25-1.1. If the affiant cannot file the final affidavit within 90 days, the affiant shall file a report with the clerk within that time period stating the affiant's reasons. Upon determining that the affiant has good reason not to file the final affidavit within 90 days, the clerk may extend the time for filing up to one year from the date of filing the qualifying affidavit.

(b) Nothing in this section shall be construed as changing the rule of G.S. 28A-15-1 and G.S. 28A-15-5 rendering both real and personal property, without preference or priority, available for the discharge of debts and other claims against the estate of the decedent. If it appears that it may be in the best interest of the estate to sell, lease, or mortgage any real property to obtain money for the payment of debts or other claims against the decedent's estate, the affiant shall petition the clerk of superior court for the appointment of a personal representative to conclude the administration of the decedent's estate pursuant to G.S. 28A-25-5. (1973, c. 1329, s. 3; 1983, c. 711, s. 1; 1985, c. 651, s. 4; 1987, c. 670, s. 3; 1989, c. 407, s. 3; 2011-344, s. 4.)

§ 28A-25-4. Clerk may compel compliance.

If any affiant who has collected personal property of the decedent by affidavit pursuant to G.S. 28A-25-1 or G.S. 28A-25-1.1 shall fail to make distribution or file affidavit as required by G.S. 28A-25-3, the clerk of superior court may, upon motion of the clerk of superior court or at the request of any interested person, issue an attachment against the affiant for a contempt and commit the affiant until the affiant makes proper distribution and files the affidavit. In addition to or in lieu of filing this attachment, the clerk may require the affiant to post a bond conditioned as provided in G.S. 28A-8-2. (1973, c. 1329, s. 3; 1983, c. 711, s. 2; 1985, c. 651, s. 5; 1987, c. 670, s. 4; 1989, c. 407, s. 4; 2011-344, s. 4.)

§ 28A-25-5. Subsequently appointed personal representative or collector.

Nothing in this Article shall preclude any interested person, including the affiant, from petitioning the clerk of superior court for the appointment of a personal representative or collector to conclude the administration of the decedent's estate. If such is done, the affiant who has been collecting personal property by affidavit shall cease to do so, shall deliver all assets in the affiant's possession to the personal representative, and shall render a proper accounting to the personal representative or collector. A copy of the accounting shall also be filed with the clerk having jurisdiction over the personal representative or collector. (1973, c. 1329, s. 3; 1975, c. 300, s. 10; 1985, c. 651, s. 6; 1987, c. 670, s. 5; 2011-344, s. 4.)

§ 28A-25-6. Payment to clerk of money owed decedent.

(a) As an alternative to the small estate settlement procedures of this Article, any person indebted to a decedent may satisfy such indebtedness by paying the amount of the debt to the clerk of the superior court of the county of the domicile of the decedent:

(1) If no administrator has been appointed, and

(2) If the amount owed by such person does not exceed five thousand dollars ($5,000), and

(3) If the sum tendered to the clerk would not make the aggregate sum which has come into the clerk's hands belonging to the decedent exceed five thousand dollars ($5,000).

(b) Such payments may not be made to the clerk if the total amount paid or tendered with respect to any one decedent would exceed five thousand dollars

($5,000), even though disbursements have been made so that the aggregate amount in the clerk's hands at any one time would not exceed five thousand dollars ($5,000).

(c) If the sum tendered pursuant to this section would make the aggregate sum coming into the clerk's hands with respect to any one decedent exceed five thousand dollars ($5,000) the clerk shall appoint an administrator, or the sum may be administered under the preceding sections of this Article.

(d) If it appears to the clerk after making a preliminary survey that disbursements pursuant to this section would not exhaust funds received pursuant to this section, the clerk may, in the clerk's discretion, appoint an administrator, or the funds may be administered under the preceding sections of this Article.

(e) The receipt from the clerk of the superior court of a payment purporting to be made pursuant to this section is a full release to the debtor for the payment so made.

(f) If no administrator has been appointed, the clerk of superior court shall disburse the money received under this section for the following purposes and in the following order:

(1) To pay the surviving spouse's year's allowance and children's year's allowance assigned in accordance with law;

(2), (3) Repealed by Session Laws 1981, c. 383, s. 3.

(4) All other claims shall be disbursed according to the order set out in G.S. 28A-19-6.

Notwithstanding the foregoing provisions of this subsection, the clerk shall pay, out of funds provided the deceased pursuant to G.S. 111-18 and Part 3 of Article 2 of Chapter 108A of the General Statutes of North Carolina, any lawful claims for care provided by an adult care home to the deceased, incurred not more than 90 days prior to the deceased's death. After the death of a spouse who died intestate and after the disbursements have been made in accordance with this subsection, the balance in the clerk's hands belonging to the estate of the decedent shall be paid to the surviving spouse, and if there is no surviving spouse, the clerk shall pay it to the heirs in proportion to their respective interests.

(g)   The clerk shall not be required to publish notice to creditors.

(h)   Whenever an administrator is appointed after a clerk of superior court has received any money pursuant to this section, the clerk shall pay to the administrator all funds which have not been disbursed. The clerk shall receive no commissions for payments made to the administrator, and the administrator shall receive no commissions for receiving such payments. (1921, c. 93; Ex. Sess. 1921, c. 65; C.S., s. 65(a); Ex. Sess. 1924, cc. 15, 58; 1927, c. 7; 1929, cc. 63, 71, 121; 1931, c. 21; 1933, cc. 16, 94; 1935, cc. 69, 96, 367; 1937, cc. 13, 31, 55, 121, 336, 377; 1939, cc. 383, 384; 1941, c. 176; 1943, cc. 24, 114, 138, 560; 1945, cc. 152, 178, 555; 1947, cc. 203, 237; 1949, cc. 17, 81, 691, 762; 1951, c. 380, s. 1; 1955, c. 1246, s. 103; 1957, c. 491; 1959, c. 795, ss. 1-4; 1965, c. 576, s. 1; 1973, c. 23; c. 1329, s. 1; 1975, c. 344; 1979, c. 163; c. 762, s. 1; 1981, c. 383, s. 3; 1983, c. 65, s. 2; 1987, c. 282, s. 6; 1989 (Reg. Sess., 1990), c. 1015, s. 1; 1995, c. 535, s. 2; 2011-344, s. 4.)

§ 28A-25-7. Removal of tangible personal property by landlord after death of residential tenant.

(a)   When a decedent who is the sole occupant of a dwelling unit dies leaving tangible personal property in the dwelling unit, the landlord may take possession of the property upon the filing of an affidavit that complies with the provisions of subsection (b) of this section if all of the following conditions have been met:

(1)   At least 10 days has elapsed from the date the paid rental period for the dwelling unit has expired.

(2)   No personal representative, collector, or receiver has been appointed for the decedent's estate under the provisions of this Chapter, Chapter 28B, or Chapter 28C of the General Statutes in the county in which the dwelling unit is located.

(3)   No affidavit related to the decedent's estate has been filed under the provisions of G.S. 28A-25-1 or G.S. 28A-25-1.1 in the county in which the dwelling unit is located.

(b) The affidavit required by subsection (a) of this section shall be on a form approved by the Administrative Office of the Courts and supplied by the clerk of court. The affidavit shall state all of the following:

(1) The name and address of the affiant and the fact that the affiant is the lessor of the dwelling unit.

(2) The name of the decedent and the fact that the decedent was the lessee and sole occupant of the dwelling unit and died leaving tangible personal property in the dwelling unit. The affiant shall attach to the affidavit a copy of the decedent's death certificate.

(3) The address of the dwelling unit.

(4) The date of the decedent's death.

(5) The date the paid rental period expired and the fact that at least 10 days has elapsed since that date.

(6) The affiant's good faith estimate of the value of the tangible personal property remaining in the dwelling unit. The affiant shall attach to the affidavit an inventory of the property which shall include, at a minimum, the categories of furniture, clothing and accessories, and miscellaneous items.

(7) That no personal representative, collector, or receiver has been appointed for the decedent's estate under the provisions of this Chapter, Chapter 28B, or Chapter 28C of the General Statutes in the county in which the dwelling unit is located and that no affidavit has been filed in the county under the provisions of G.S. 28A-25-1 or G.S. 28A-25-1.1.

(8) The name of the person identified in the rental application, lease agreement, or other landlord document as the authorized person to contact in the event of the death or emergency of the tenant; that the affiant has made a good faith attempt to contact that person to urge that action be taken to administer the decedent's estate; and that either the affiant was unsuccessful in contacting the person or, if contacted, the person has not taken action to administer the decedent's estate. The affiant shall state the efforts made to contact the person identified in the rental application, lease agreement, or other landlord document.

(c) The affidavit shall be filed in the office of the clerk of court in the county in which the dwelling unit is located. The affidavit shall be filed by the clerk upon the landlord's payment of the fee of thirty dollars ($30.00) and shall be indexed in the index to estates. The landlord shall mail a copy of the affidavit to the person identified in the rental application, lease agreement, or other landlord document as the authorized person to contact in the event of the death or emergency of the tenant. If no contact person is identified in the rental application, lease agreement, or other landlord document, the landlord shall cause notice of the filing of the affidavit to be posted at the door of the landlord's primary rental office or the place where the landlord conducts business and at the county courthouse in the area designated by the clerk for the posting of notices.

(d) The filing of an affidavit that complies with the provisions of subsection (b) of this section shall be sufficient to require the transfer of the property remaining in the decedent's dwelling unit to the landlord. Upon the transfer, the landlord may remove the property from the dwelling unit and deliver it for storage to any storage warehouse in the county in which the dwelling unit is located or in an adjoining county if no storage warehouse is located in that county. The landlord may also store the property in the landlord's own storage facility. Notwithstanding any provision of Chapter 42 of the General Statutes, after removing the property from the dwelling unit as provided in this subsection, the landlord shall be in possession of the dwelling unit and may let the unit as the landlord deems fit.

(e) If, at least 90 days after the landlord filed the affidavit required by subsection (a) of this section, no personal representative, collector, or receiver has been appointed under the provisions of this Chapter, Chapter 28B, or Chapter 28C of the General Statutes in the county in which the dwelling unit is located and no affidavit has been filed in the county under the provisions of G.S. 28A-25-1 or G.S. 28A-25-1.1, the landlord may take any of the following actions related to the decedent's property:

(1) Sell the property as provided in subsection (f) of this section.

(2) Deliver the property into the custody of a nonprofit organization regularly providing free, or at a nominal price, clothing and household furnishings to people in need for disposition in the normal course of the organization's operations. The organization shall not be liable to anyone for the disposition of the property.

(f) If the landlord delivers the property to a nonprofit organization as authorized in subdivision (2) of subsection (e) of this section, the landlord shall provide an accounting to the clerk stating the nature of the action and the date on which the action was taken. A landlord who elects to sell the property as authorized in subdivision (1) of subsection (e) of this section may do so at a public or private sale. Whether the sale is public or private, the landlord shall, at least seven days prior to the day of sale, give written notice to the clerk and post written notice of the sale in the area designated by the clerk for the posting of notices and at the door of the landlord's primary rental office or the place where the landlord conducts business stating the date, time, and place of the sale, and that any surplus of proceeds from the sale, after payment of unpaid rents, damages, packing and storage fees, filing fees, and sale costs shall be delivered to the clerk. The landlord may apply the proceeds of the sale to the unpaid rents, damages, packing and storage fees, filing fees, and sale costs. Any surplus from the sale shall be paid to the clerk, and the landlord shall provide an accounting to the clerk showing the manner in which the proceeds of the sale were applied. The clerk shall administer the funds in the same manner as provided in G.S. 28A-25-6.

(g) If, at any time after the landlord files the affidavit required by subsection (a) of this section but before the landlord takes any of the actions authorized in subsection (e) of this section, the landlord is presented with letters of appointment or another document issued by a court indicating that a personal representative, collector, or receiver has been appointed for the decedent's estate or an affidavit filed under the provisions of G.S. 28A-25-1 or G.S. 28A-25-1.1, the landlord shall deliver the decedent's property to the personal representative, collector, or receiver appointed or to the person who filed the affidavit.

(h) Notwithstanding the provisions of subsections (a) through (g) of this section, if the decedent dies leaving tangible personal property of five hundred dollar ($500.00) value or less in the dwelling unit, the landlord may, without filing an affidavit, deliver the property into the custody of a nonprofit organization regularly providing free, or at a nominal price, clothing and household furnishings to people in need upon that organization agreeing to identify and separately store the property for 30 days and to release the property to a person authorized by law to act on behalf of the decedent at no charge within the 30-day period. Prior to delivering the property to the nonprofit organization, the landlord shall prepare an inventory of the property which shall include, at a minimum, the categories of furniture, clothing and accessories, and miscellaneous items. A landlord electing to act under this subsection shall immediately send a notice by first-class mail containing the name and address of the property recipient and a copy of the inventory to the person identified in the rental application, lease agreement, or other landlord document as the authorized person to contact in the event of the death or emergency of the tenant and shall post the same notice for 30 days or more at the door of the landlord's primary rental office or the place where the landlord conducts business. The notice posted shall not include an inventory of the property. Any nonprofit organization agreeing to receive personal property under this subsection shall not be liable to the decedent's estate for the disposition of the property, provided that the property has been separately identified and stored for release to a person authorized by law to act on behalf of the decedent for a period of 30 days.

(i) If any lessor, landlord, or agent seizes possession of the decedent's tangible personal property in any manner not in accordance with the provisions of this section, any person authorized by law to act on behalf of the decedent shall be entitled to recover possession of the property or compensation for the value of the property and, in any action brought by any person authorized by law to act on behalf of the decedent, the landlord shall be liable to the decedent's estate for actual damages, but not including punitive damages, treble damages, or damages for emotional distress.

(j) The procedure authorized in this section may be used as an alternative to a summary ejectment action under Chapter 42 of the General Statutes. A landlord shall, in his or her discretion, determine whether to proceed under the provisions of this section or under Chapter 42 of the General Statutes. (2012-17, s. 7.)

Article 26.

Foreign Personal Representatives and Ancillary Administration.

§ 28A-26-1. Domiciliary and ancillary probate and administration.

The domiciliary, or original, administration of the estates of all decedents domiciled in North Carolina at the time of death shall be under the jurisdiction of this State and of a proper clerk of superior court in this State, and the original probate of all wills of such persons shall be in this State. Any administration of the estate and any probate of a will of such decedents outside North Carolina shall be ancillary only. All assets, except real estate (but including proceeds from the sale of real estate), subject to ancillary administration in a jurisdiction outside North Carolina shall, to the extent such assets are not necessary for the requirements of such ancillary administration, be transferred and delivered by the ancillary personal representative to the duly qualified personal representative in this State for administration and distribution by the domiciliary personal representative, and the domiciliary personal representative in this State shall have the duty of collecting all such assets from the ancillary personal representative. The receipt of the domiciliary personal representative shall fully acquit the ancillary personal representative with respect to the assets covered thereby. The domiciliary personal representative in North Carolina shall have the exclusive right and duty to pay all federal and North Carolina taxes owed by the estate of such decedent and to make proper distribution of all assets including those collected from the ancillary personal representative. (1963, c. 634; 1973, c. 1329, s. 3.)

§ 28A-26-2. Payment of debt and delivery of property to domiciliary personal representative of a nonresident decedent without ancillary administration in this State.

(a) At any time after the expiration of 60 days from the death of a nonresident decedent, any resident of this State indebted to the estate of the nonresident decedent or having possession or control of personal property, or of an instrument evidencing a debt, obligation, stock or chose in action belonging to the estate of the nonresident decedent may pay the debt or deliver the personal property, or the instrument evidencing the debt, obligation, stock or chose in action, to the domiciliary personal representative of the nonresident decedent upon being presented with a certified or exemplified copy of the domiciliary personal representative's letters of appointment and an affidavit made by or on behalf of the domiciliary personal representative stating:

(1) The date of the death of the nonresident decedent;

(2) That to the best of the domiciliary personal representative's knowledge no administration, or application or petition therefor, is pending in this State;

(3) That the domiciliary personal representative is entitled to payment or delivery.

(b) Payment or delivery made in good faith on the basis of the proof of appointment as domiciliary personal representative of a nonresident decedent and an affidavit meeting the requirements of subsection (a) constitutes a release to the same extent as if payment or delivery had been made to an ancillary personal representative.

(c) Payment or delivery under this section shall not be made if a resident creditor of the nonresident decedent has, by registered or certified mail, notified the resident debtor of the nonresident decedent or the resident having possession of the personal property belonging to the nonresident decedent that the debt should not be paid nor the property delivered to the domiciliary personal representative of the nonresident decedent. If no ancillary administrator qualifies within 90 days from the date of the notice, however, the resident debtor may pay the debt or deliver the property directly to the nonresident domiciliary personal representative as set forth in subsection (a) of this section. (1973, c. 1329, s. 3; 1975, c. 300, s. 11; 2011-344, s. 4.)

§ 28A-26-3. Ancillary administration.

(a) Any domiciliary personal representative of a nonresident decedent upon the filing of a certified or exemplified copy of letters of appointment with the clerk of superior court who has venue under G.S. 28A-3-1 may be granted ancillary letters in this State notwithstanding that the domiciliary personal representative is a nonresident of this State or is a foreign corporation. If the domiciliary personal representative is a foreign corporation, it need not qualify under any other law of this State to authorize it to act as ancillary personal representative in the particular estate. If application is made for the issuance of ancillary letters to the domiciliary personal representative, the clerk of superior court shall give preference in appointment to the domiciliary personal representative unless the decedent shall have otherwise directed in a will.

(b) If, within 90 days after the death of the nonresident, or within 60 days after issue of domiciliary letters, should that be a shorter period, no application for ancillary letters has been made by a domiciliary personal representative, any person who could apply for issue of letters had the decedent been a resident may apply for issue of ancillary letters.

If it is known that there is a duly qualified domiciliary personal representative, the clerk of superior court shall send notice of such application, by registered mail, to that personal representative and to the appointing court. Such notice shall include a statement that, within 14 days after its mailing, the domiciliary personal representative may apply for the issue of ancillary letters with the preference specified in subsection (a) of this section; and that failure of the domiciliary personal representative to do so will be deemed a waiver, with the result that letters will be issued to another. Upon such failure, the clerk of superior court may issue ancillary letters in accordance with the provisions of Article 4 of this Chapter.

If the applicant and the clerk of superior court have no knowledge of the existence of a domiciliary personal representative, the clerk of superior court may proceed to issue ancillary letters. Subsequently, upon it becoming known that a domiciliary personal representative has been appointed, whether such appointment occurred before or after the issue of ancillary letters, the clerk of superior court shall notify the domiciliary personal representative, by registered mail, of the action taken by the clerk of superior court and the state of the ancillary administration. Such notice shall include a statement that at any time prior to approval of the ancillary personal representative's final account the domiciliary personal representative may appear in the proceedings for any purpose the domiciliary personal representative may deem advisable; and that the domiciliary personal representative may apply to be substituted as ancillary personal representative, but that such request will not be granted unless the clerk of superior court finds that such action will be for the best interests of North Carolina administration of the estate. (1973, c. 1329, s. 3; 2011-344, s. 4.)

§ 28A-26-4. Bonds.

(a) Subject to the exception in subsection (b), any personal representative, including a domiciliary personal representative, who is granted ancillary letters of administration in this State must satisfy the bond requirements prescribed in Article 8 of this Chapter.

(b) Where a citizen or subject of a foreign country, or of any other state or territory of the United States, by will sufficient according to the laws of this State, and duly probated and recorded in the proper county, devises to that person's executor, with power to sell and convey, real property situated in this State in trust for a person named in the will, the power being vested in the executor as such trustee, the executor may execute the power without giving bond in this State. (1911, c. 176; C.S., s. 37; Ex. Sess. 1920, c. 86; 1945, c. 652; 1957, c. 320; 1969, c. 1067, ss. 1, 2; 1973, c. 1329, s. 3; 2011-344, s. 4.)

§ 28A-26-5. Authority of domiciliary personal representative of a nonresident decedent.

The domiciliary personal representative of the nonresident decedent after qualifying as ancillary personal representative in this State is authorized to administer the North Carolina estate of the nonresident decedent in accordance with the provisions of this Chapter. (1973, c. 1329, s. 3.)

§ 28A-26-6. Jurisdiction.

(a) A domiciliary personal representative of a nonresident decedent may invoke the jurisdiction of the courts of this State after qualifying as ancillary personal representative in this State except that the domiciliary personal representative may invoke such jurisdiction prior to qualification for the purpose of appealing from a decision of the clerk of superior court regarding a question of qualification.

(b) A domiciliary personal representative of a nonresident decedent submits to the jurisdiction of the courts of this State:

(1) As provided in G.S. 1-75.4, or

(2) By receiving payment of money or taking delivery of personal property under G.S. 28A-26-2; or

(3) By acceptance of ancillary letters of administration in this State under G.S. 28A-26-3; or

(4) By doing any act as personal representative in this State which if done as an individual would have given the State jurisdiction over the personal representative as an individual. (1973, c. 1329, s. 3; 2011-344, s. 4.)

§ 28A-26-7. Service on personal representative of a nonresident decedent.

A court of this State having jurisdiction of the subject matter and grounds for personal jurisdiction as provided in G.S. 28A-26-6 may exercise personal jurisdiction over a defendant by service of process in accordance with the provisions of G.S. 1A-1, Rule 4(j). (1973, c. 1329, s. 3.)

§ 28A-26-8. Duties of personal representative in an ancillary administration.

(a) All assets of estates of nonresident decedents being administered in this State are subject to all claims, allowances and charges existing or established against the estate of the decedent wherever existing or established.

(b) An adjudication of a claim rendered in any jurisdiction in favor of or against any personal representative of the estate of a nonresident decedent is binding on the ancillary personal representative in this State and on all parties to the litigation.

(c) Limitations on presentation of claims shall be governed by the provisions of this Chapter except that creditors residing in the domiciliary state barred by the statutes of that state may not file claims in an ancillary administration in this State.

(d) In the payment of claims by the ancillary administrator, the following rules shall apply:

(1) If the value of the entire estate, wherever administered, equals or exceeds family exemptions and allowances, prior charges and claims against the entire estate, the claims allowed in this State shall be paid in full from assets in this State, if such assets are sufficient for the purpose.

(2) If such total exemptions, allowances, charges and claims exceed the value of the entire estate, the claims allowed in this State shall be paid their proper percentage pro rata by class, if assets in this State are sufficient for the purpose.

(3) If assets in this State are inadequate for either of the purposes stated in subdivisions (1) or (2) above, the claims allowed in this State shall be paid, pro rata by class, to the extent the local assets will permit.

(4) If the value of the entire estate, wherever administered, is insufficient to pay all exemptions and allowances, prior charges and claims against the entire estate, the priority for order of payment established by the law of the domicile will prevail. (1973, c. 1329, s. 3; 1975, c. 19, ss. 10, 11.)

§ 28A-26-9. Remission of surplus assets by ancillary personal representative to domiciliary personal representative.

Unless a testator in a will otherwise directs, any assets (including proceeds from the sale of real estate) remaining after payment of claims against the estate of a nonresident decedent being administered by an ancillary personal representative other than the domiciliary personal representative shall be transferred and delivered to the domiciliary personal representative or, if none, to the court in the domicile of the decedent which has jurisdiction to administer the estate. (1973, c. 1329, s. 3.)

Article 27.

Apportionment of Federal Estate Tax.

§ 28A-27-1. Definitions.

For the purposes of this Article:

(1) "Estate" means the gross estate of a decedent as determined for the purpose of the federal estate tax.

(2) "Fiduciary" includes a personal representative and a trustee.

(3) "Person" means any individual, partnership, association, joint stock company, corporation, governmental agency, including any multiples or combinations of the foregoing as, for example, individuals as joint tenants.

(4) "Person interested in the estate" means any person, including a personal representative, guardian, or trustee, entitled to receive, or who has received, from a decedent while alive or by reason of the death of a decedent any property or interest therein included in the decedent's taxable estate.

(5) "State" means any state, territory, or possession of the United States, the District of Columbia, or the Commonwealth of Puerto Rico.

(6) "Tax" means the net Federal Estate Tax due, after application of any available unified transfer tax credit, and interest and penalties imposed in addition to the tax. (1985 (Reg. Sess., 1986), c. 878, s. 1.)

§ 28A-27-2. Apportionment.

(a) Except as otherwise provided in subsection (b) of this section, or in G.S. 28A-27-5, G.S. 28A-27-6, or G.S. 28A-27-8, the tax shall be apportioned among all persons interested in the estate in the proportion that the value of the interest of each person interested in the estate bears to the total value of the interests of all persons interested in the estate. The values as finally determined for federal estate tax purposes shall be used for the purposes of this computation.

(b) In the event the decedent's will provides a method of apportionment of the tax different from the method provided in subsection (a) above, the method described in the will shall control. However, in the case of any will executed on or after October 1, 1986, a general direction in the will that taxes shall not be apportioned, whether or not referring to this Article, but shall be paid from the residuary portion of the estate shall not, unless specifically stated otherwise, apply to taxes imposed on assets which are includible in the valuation of the decedent's gross estate for federal estate tax purposes only by reason of Sections 2041, 2042 or 2044 of the Internal Revenue Code of 1954 or corresponding provisions of any subsequent tax law. In the case of an estate administered under any will executed on or after October 1, 1986, in the event that the estate tax computation involves assets described in the preceding sentence, unless specifically stated otherwise, apportionment shall be made against such assets and the tax so apportioned shall be recovered from the persons receiving such assets as provided in Sections 2206, 2207 or 2207A of the Internal Revenue Code of 1954 or corresponding provisions of any subsequent tax law. (1985 (Reg. Sess., 1986), c. 878, s. 1; 1987, c. 694, s. 1.)

§ 28A-27-3. Procedure for determining apportionment.

(a) The personal representative of a decedent shall determine the apportionment of the tax.

(b) If the personal representative finds that it is inequitable to apportion interest and penalties in the manner provided in this Article because such interest or penalties were imposed due to the fault of one or more persons interested in the estate, the personal representative may direct apportionment thereon in the manner the personal representative finds equitable.

(c) The expenses reasonably incurred by the personal representative in connection with the apportionment of the tax shall be apportioned as provided for taxes under this Article. If the personal representative finds that it is inequitable to apportion the expenses because such expenses were incurred because of the fault of one or more persons interested in the estate, the personal representative may direct other more equitable apportionment. (1985 (Reg. Sess., 1986), c. 878, s. 1; 2011-344, s. 4.)

§ 28A-27-4. Uncollected tax.

The personal representative shall not be under any duty to institute any suit or proceeding to recover from any person interested in the estate the amount of the tax apportioned to the person until the expiration of the six months next following final determination of the tax. A personal representative who institutes the suit or proceeding within a reasonable time after the six months' period shall not be subject to any liability or surcharge because any portion of the tax apportioned to any person interested in the estate was collectable at a time following the death of the decedent but thereafter became uncollectable. If the personal representative cannot collect from any person interested in the estate the amount of the tax apportioned to the person, the amount not recoverable shall be apportioned among the other persons interested in the estate who are subject to apportionment. The apportionment shall be made in the proportion that the value of the interest of each remaining person interested in the estate bears to the total value of the interests of all remaining persons interested in the estate. (1985 (Reg. Sess., 1986), c. 878, s. 1.)

§ 28A-27-5. Exemptions, deductions, and credits.

(a) Any interest for which a deduction or exemption is allowed under the federal revenue laws in determining the value of the decedent's net taxable estate, such as property passing to or in trust for a surviving spouse and gifts or devises for charitable, public, or similar purposes, shall not be included in the computation provided for in G.S. 28A-27-2 to the extent of the allowable deduction or exemption. When such an interest is subject to a prior present interest which is not allowable as a deduction or exemption, such present interest shall not be included in the computation provided for in this Article and no tax shall be apportioned to or paid from principal.

(b) Any credit for property previously taxed and any credit for gift taxes or death taxes of a foreign country paid by the decedent or the decedent's estate shall inure to the proportionate benefit of all persons liable to apportionment; provided, however, that if the tax which gives rise to such a credit has in fact been paid by a person interested in the estate, the benefit of such credit shall inure to that person paying the tax.

(c) Any credit for inheritance, succession, or estate taxes or taxes in the nature thereof in respect to property or interests includible in the estate shall inure to the benefit of the persons or interests chargeable with the payment thereof to the extent that, or in the proportion that, the credit reduces the tax.

(d) To the extent that property passing to or in trust for a surviving spouse or any charitable, public, or similar gift or devise does not constitute an allowed deduction for purposes of the tax solely by reason of an inheritance tax or other death tax imposed upon and deductible from the property, the property shall not be included in the computation provided for in this Article, and to that extent no apportionment shall be made against the property. This section does not apply in any instance where the result will be to deprive the estate of a deduction otherwise allowable under Section 2053(d) of the Internal Revenue Code of 1954 of the United States or corresponding provisions of any subsequent tax law, relating to deduction for State death taxes on transfers for public, charitable, or religious uses. (1985 (Reg. Sess., 1986), c. 878, s. 1; 1987, c. 694, ss. 2, 3; 2011-284, s. 21(a), (b); 2011-344, s. 4.)

§ 28A-27-6. No apportionment between temporary and remainder interests.

No interest in income and no estate for years or for life or other temporary interest in any property or fund is subject to apportionment as between the temporary interest and the remainder. The tax on the temporary interest and the tax, if any, on the remainder is chargeable against the corpus of the property or funds subject to the temporary interest and remainder. (1985 (Reg. Sess., 1986), c. 878, s. 1.)

§ 28A-27-7. Fiduciary's rights and duties.

(a)   The personal representative may withhold from any property of the decedent in the personal representative's possession, distributable to any person interested in the estate, the amount of the tax apportioned to the person's interest. If the property in possession of the personal representative and distributable to any person interested in the estate tax is insufficient to satisfy the proportionate amount of the tax determined to be due from the person, the personal representative may recover the deficiency from the person interested in the estate. If the property is not in the possession of the personal representative, the personal representative may recover from any person interested in the estate the amount of the tax apportioned to the person in accordance with this Article.

(b)   If property held by the fiduciary or other person is distributed prior to final apportionment of the tax, the personal representative may require the distributee to provide a bond or other security for the apportionment liability in the form and amount prescribed by the fiduciary, with the approval of the clerk of superior court having jurisdiction of the administration of the estate. (1985 (Reg. Sess., 1986), c. 878, s. 1; 2011-344, s. 4.)

§ 28A-27-8. Difference with Federal Estate Tax Law.

If the liabilities of persons interested in the estate as prescribed by this Article differ from those which result under the Federal Estate Tax Law, the liabilities imposed by the federal law will control and the balance of this Article shall apply as if the resulting liabilities had been prescribed herein. (1985 (Reg. Sess., 1986), c. 878, s. 1.)

§ 28A-27-9. Effective date.

The provisions of this Article shall not apply to taxes due on account of the death of decedents dying prior to October 1, 1986. (1985 (Reg. Sess., 1986), c. 878, s. 1.)

Article 28.

Summary Administration.

§ 28A-28-1. Summary administration where spouse is sole beneficiary.

When a decedent dies testate or intestate leaving a surviving spouse as the sole devisee or heir, the surviving spouse may file a petition for summary administration with the clerk of superior court of the county where the decedent was domiciled at the time of death. This procedure is available if the decedent died partially testate, provided that the surviving spouse is the sole devisee under the will and the sole heir of the decedent's intestate property. This procedure is not available if the decedent's will provides that it is not available or if the devise to the surviving spouse is in trust rather than outright. (1995, c. 294, s. 1.)

§ 28A-28-2. Petition.

(a) The petition shall be signed by the surviving spouse and verified to be accurate and complete to the best of the spouse's knowledge and belief and shall state as follows:

(1) The name and address of the spouse and the fact that the spouse is the surviving spouse of the decedent;

(2) The name and domicile of the decedent at the time of death;

(3) The date and place of death of the decedent;

(4) The date and place of marriage of the spouse and the decedent;

(5) A description sufficient to identify each tract of real property owned in whole or in part by the decedent at the time of death;

(6) A description of the nature of the decedent's personal property and the location of such property, as far as these facts are known or can with reasonable diligence be ascertained;

(7) The probable value of the decedent's personal property, so far as the value is known or can with reasonable diligence be ascertained;

(8) That no application or petition for appointment of a personal representative is pending or has been granted in this State;

(9) That the spouse is the sole devisee or sole heir, or both, of the decedent, and that there is no other devisee or heir; that the decedent's will, if any, does not prohibit summary administration; and that any property passing to the spouse under the will is not in trust;

(10) The name and address of any executor or coexecutor named by the will and that, if the decedent died testate, a copy of the petition has been personally delivered or sent by first-class mail by the spouse to the last-known address of any executor or coexecutor named by the will, if different from the spouse;

(11) That, to the extent of the value of the property received by the spouse under the will of the decedent or by intestate succession, the spouse assumes all liabilities of the decedent that were not discharged by reason of death and assumes liability for all taxes and valid claims against the decedent or the estate, as provided in G.S. 28A-28-6; and

(12) If the decedent died testate, that the decedent's will has been admitted to probate in the court of the proper county; that a duly certified copy of the will has been recorded in each county in which is located any real property owned by the decedent at the time of death; and that a certified copy of the decedent's will is attached to the petition.

(b) The petition shall be filed by the clerk upon payment of the fee provided in G.S. 7A-307 and shall be indexed in the index to estates. (1995, c. 294, s. 1; c. 509, s. 135.2(a); 2011-344, s. 4.)

§ 28A-28-3. Clerk's order.

If it appears to the clerk that the petition and supporting evidence, if any, comply with the requirements of G.S. 28A-28-2 and on the basis thereof the spouse is entitled to summary administration, the clerk shall enter an order to that effect and no further administration of the estate is necessary. Nothing in this section shall preclude a petition under the provisions of G.S. 28A-28-7(a) or the appointment of a personal representative or a collector under the provisions of Article 6 or Article 11 of this Chapter. (1995, c. 294, s. 1.)

§ 28A-28-4. Effect of order.

(a) The presentation of a certified copy of the order described in G.S. 28A-28-3 shall be sufficient to require the transfer to the spouse of any property or contract right owned by the decedent at the time of death, including but not limited to: (i) wages and salary; (ii) the title and license to a motor vehicle registered in the name of the decedent owner; (iii) the ownership rights of a savings account, checking account, or certificate of deposit in a bank in the name of the decedent owner; (iv) the ownership rights of a savings account, share certificate, or certificate of deposit in a credit union, building and loan association, or savings and loan association in the name of the decedent owner; and (v) the ownership rights in any stock or security registered on the books of a corporation in the name of the decedent owner.

(b) After the entry of the order described in G.S. 28A-28-3, the spouse may convey, lease, sell, or mortgage any real property devised to or inherited by the spouse from the decedent, at public or private sale, upon such terms as the spouse may determine. This section shall not limit any other powers the spouse may have over property devised to or inherited by the spouse from the decedent. The provisions of G.S. 28A-17-12 are not applicable to a conveyance, sale, lease, or mortgage under this subsection. (1995, c. 294, s. 1.)

§ 28A-28-5. Effect of payment.

The person paying, delivering, transferring, or issuing property or the evidence thereof pursuant to the order described in G.S. 28A-28-3 is discharged and released to the same extent as if the person dealt with a duly qualified personal representative of the decedent. The person is not required to see to the application of the property or evidence thereof or to inquire into the truth of any statement in the petition or order.

If any person to whom the order is presented refuses to pay, deliver, transfer, or issue any property or evidence thereof, the property may be recovered or its payment, delivery, transfer, or issuance may be compelled in an action brought for that purpose by the surviving spouse. The court costs and attorney's fee incident to the action shall be taxed against the person whose refusal to comply with the provisions of G.S. 28A-28-4 made the action necessary. (1995, c. 294, s. 1.)

§ 28A-28-6. Spouse's assumption of liabilities.

If the clerk grants the order for summary administration, the spouse shall be deemed to have assumed, to the extent of the value of the property received by the spouse under the will of the decedent or by intestate succession, all liabilities of the decedent that were not discharged by reason of death and liability for all taxes and valid claims against the decedent or the estate. The value of the property is the fair market value of the property on the date of death of the decedent less any liens or encumbrances on the property so received. The spouse may assert any defense, counterclaim, cross-claim, or setoff which would have been available to the decedent if the decedent had not died except for actions listed in G.S. 28A-18-1(b). A spouse shall not be deemed to have assumed any liabilities of the decedent that were discharged by reason of death. (1995, c. 294, s. 1.)

§ 28A-28-7. Right to petition for appointment of personal representative; discharge of spouse's liability.

(a) Nothing in this Article shall preclude any person qualified to serve as personal representative pursuant to G.S. 28A-4-1, including the surviving spouse, from petitioning the clerk of superior court for the appointment of a personal representative or collector to administer the decedent's estate. If a personal representative or collector is appointed, the spouse shall render a proper accounting to the personal representative or collector and file a copy of the accounting with the clerk. The spouse shall deliver assets of the decedent's estate, cash, or other property and shall be discharged of liability in accordance with the provisions of subsection (b) of this section.

(b) In the event that a personal representative or collector is appointed, the spouse shall be discharged of liability for the debts of the decedent as follows:

(1) If the spouse delivers to the personal representative or collector all of the property received by the spouse in the identical form that it was received by the spouse, then the spouse will be discharged of all liability.

(2) If the spouse does not deliver to the personal representative or collector all of the property in the identical form that it was received by the spouse, then the spouse shall be discharged of liability as follows:

a. For property delivered to the personal representative or collector that is in the identical form that it was received by the spouse, the spouse is discharged to the extent of the fair market value of the property at the time of the decedent's death or the fair market value at the time the property was received by the personal representative or collector, whichever is greater.

b. For property delivered to the personal representative or collector that is not in the identical form that it was received by the spouse, the spouse is discharged to the extent of the fair market value of such property at the time it was delivered to the personal representative or collector. (1995, c. 294, s. 1.)

Article 29.

Notice to Creditors Without Estate Administration.

§ 28A-29-1. Notice to creditors without estate administration.

When (i) a decedent dies testate or intestate leaving no personal property subject to probate and no real property devised to the personal representative; (ii) a decedent's estate is being administered by collection by affidavit pursuant to Article 25 of this Chapter; (iii) a decedent's estate is being administered under the summary administration provisions of Article 28 of this Chapter; (iv) a decedent's estate consists solely of a motor vehicle that can be transferred by the procedure authorized by G.S. 20-77(b); or (v) a decedent has left assets that may be treated as assets of an estate for limited purposes as described in G.S. 28A-15-10, and no application or petition for appointment of a personal representative is pending or has been granted in this State, any person otherwise qualified to serve as personal representative of the estate pursuant to Article 4 of this Chapter or the trustee then serving under the terms of a revocable trust created by the decedent may file a petition to be appointed as a limited personal representative to provide notice to creditors without administration of an estate before the clerk of superior court of the county where the decedent was domiciled at the time of death. This procedure is not available if the decedent's will provides that it is not available. A limited personal representative shall have the rights and obligations provided for in this Article. (2009-444, s. 1; 2013-91, s. 1(b).)

§ 28A-29-2. Petition.

(a) The application for appointment as limited personal representative shall be in the form of an affidavit sworn to before an officer authorized to administer oaths, signed by the applicant or the applicant's attorney, which may be supported by other proof under oath in writing, all of which shall be recorded and filed by the clerk of superior court, and shall allege all of the following facts:

(1) The name and domicile of the decedent at the time of death.

(2) The date and place of death of the decedent.

(3) That, so far as is known or can with reasonable diligence be ascertained, (i) the decedent left no personal property subject to probate and no real property devised to the personal representative; (ii) the decedent's estate is being administered by collection by affidavit pursuant to Article 25 of this Chapter; (iii) the decedent's estate is being administered under the summary administration provisions of Article 28 of this Chapter; (iv) the decedent's estate consists solely of a motor vehicle that can be transferred by the procedure

authorized by G.S. 20-77(b); or (v) the decedent left assets that may be treated as assets of an estate for limited purposes as described in G.S. 28A-15-10.

(4)   That no application or petition for appointment of a personal representative is pending or has been granted in this State.

(b)   If it appears to the clerk of superior court that the application and supporting evidence comply with the requirements of subsection (a) of this section and on the basis thereof the clerk finds that the applicant is entitled to appointment, the clerk shall issue letters of limited administration.

(c)   The petition shall be filed by the clerk upon payment of the fee provided in G.S. 7A-307(a) and shall be indexed in the index to estates. (2009-444, s. 1; 2013-91, s. 1(c).)

§ 28A-29-3. Effect of appointment.

A limited personal representative appointed under this Article shall provide notice to all persons, firms, and corporations having claims against the decedent, and proof of such notice shall be in accordance with the provisions of Article 14 of this Chapter. (2009-444, s. 1.)

§ 28A-29-4. Presentation, payment, and limitation of claims.

Upon compliance with G.S. 28A-29-3, creditors of the decedent and the decedent's property shall present claims in accordance with the provisions of Article 19 of this Chapter, and creditors failing to file such claims shall be barred as provided in G.S. 28A-19-3. The limited personal representative shall administer claims so presented in accordance with the procedures and priorities provided pursuant to Article 19 of this Chapter. At any time after a claim is presented in accordance with the provisions of this section, the clerk may appoint a personal representative to administer the decedent's estate. (2009-444, s. 1.)

§ 28A-29-5. Right to petition for appointment of personal representative.

Nothing in this Article shall preclude any person qualified to serve as personal representative pursuant to G.S. 28A-4-1, including the limited personal representative, from petitioning the clerk of superior court for the appointment of a personal representative to administer the decedent's estate. (2009-444, s. 1.)

Chapter 28B.

Estates of Absentees in Military Service.

§ 28B-1. Absentee in military service; definition.

Any person serving in or with the Armed Forces of the United States, in or with the Red Cross, in or with the United States Merchant Marine, during any time when a state of hostilities exists between the United States and any other power, who has been reported or listed by the appropriate federal agency as missing in action or as a prisoner of war for a period of one year, shall be an "absentee in military service" within the meaning of this Chapter. (1973, c. 522, s. 1; 2011-183, s. 25.)

§ 28B-2. Action for receiver; jurisdiction; contents of complaint.

(a) Whenever any absentee in military action as defined in this Chapter has an interest in any form of property in this State and has not provided an adequate power of attorney authorizing another to act in his behalf in regard to such property or interest, any person who would have an interest in the property or estate of the absentee in military service were such absentee in military service deceased, or any person who is dependent on such absentee in military service for his maintenance or support, may commence an action for the appointment of a receiver to care for the estate of the absentee in military service by filing a verified complaint in the superior court in the county of domicile of the absentee in military service or in any county where his property is situated.

(b) The complaint shall show the following:

(1) The name, age, address, relationship of the person filing the complaint to the alleged absentee, and the interest of that person in the property of the

absentee in military service or his dependency upon the absentee in military service for his maintenance and support.

(2)   The name, age, and address of all persons who would have an interest in the estate of the absentee in military service were he deceased and the name, age, and address of all persons dependent upon him for their maintenance and support.

(3)   The name, age, and last known address of the absentee in military service.

(4)   The date on which the absentee in military service was first reported as missing or captured by the appropriate federal agency, and, as far as is known, the circumstances surrounding his absence.

(5)   The necessity for and the reasons why a receiver should be appointed.

(6)   Whether or not the person alleged to be an absentee in military service has a will and the whereabouts of said will.

(7)   So far as known, a schedule of all his property within this State, including property in which he is co-owner with or without the right of survivorship. (1973, c. 522, s. 2.)

§ 28B-3. Notice; hearing; guardian ad litem.

(a)   Notice of the hearing on the complaint to appoint a receiver shall be given to all persons named in the petition by registered mail or certified mail with return receipt requested.

(b)   The judge shall hear evidence on the questions of whether the person alleged to be missing or captured is an absentee in military service as defined by G.S. 28B-1, on the question of the necessity for the appointment of a receiver, and on the question of who is entitled to appointment as the receiver.

(c)   The court may in its discretion appoint a guardian ad litem to represent the alleged absentee in military service at the hearing. (1973, c. 522, s. 3.)

§ 28B-4. Order of appointment.

(a) If after the hearing, the court is satisfied that said person is, in fact, an absentee in military service as defined in G.S. 28B-1 and that it is necessary that a receiver be appointed, he shall appoint a receiver of the estate and property of said absentee in military service under the supervision and subject to the further orders of the court.

(b) In the appointment of a receiver, the court shall give due consideration to the appointment of the spouse or one of the next of kin of the absentee in military service if such spouse or next of kin is a fit and proper person and is qualified to act. (1973, c. 522, s. 4.)

§ 28B-5. Bond; inventory; accounting.

(a) Before receiving any property the judge shall require the receiver to qualify by giving bond in an amount and with surety approved by him.

(b) Within 30 days after the date of his appointment, the receiver shall file an inventory of all of the property of the absentee in military service taken in charge. Every year thereafter, within 30 days of the anniversary date of his appointment the receiver shall file a full and complete inventory and accounting with the clerk of superior court under oath, of the amount of property received by him, or invested by him, and the manner and nature of such investment, and his receipts and disbursements for the past year in the form of debit and credit. The clerk shall inspect and audit the inventory and accounting and if he approves the same he shall endorse his approval thereon, which shall be deemed prima facie evidence of correctness. If the clerk finds evidence of misconduct or default on the part of the receiver he shall report the same to the court. In such event, the procedures found in G.S. 28B-7(b) shall be followed. (1973, c. 522, s. 5.)

§ 28B-6. Powers and duties of receiver.

(a) Under the direction of a judge, the receiver shall administer the property of the absentee in military service as an equity receivership with the following powers:

(1) To take custody and control of all property of the absentee in military service wherever situated.

(2) To collect all debts due to the absentee in military service and pay all debts owed by him.

(3) To bring and defend suits.

(4) To pay insurance premiums.

(5) With the approval of the judge in each instance, to continue to operate and manage any business enterprise, farm or farming operations, and to make necessary contracts with reference thereto.

(6) With the approval of the judge in each instance, to renew notes and other obligations, obtain loans on life insurance policies, and pledge or mortgage property for loans necessary in carrying on or liquidating the affairs of such absentee in military service.

(7) With the approval of the judge in each instance, to institute proceedings to partition property owned by the absentee and another as joint tenants or tenants in common, with or without the right of survivorship; provided, in the case of property owned by the absentee in military service and spouse as tenants by the entirety, such proceedings may be instituted only if the spouse of the absentee in military service consents in writing to the partitioning, and, in the event of partitioning, one half of the property or proceeds shall belong to the spouse and one half shall belong to the receiver as property of the absentee in military service.

(8) With the approval of the judge in each instance, to sell, lease, invest, and reinvest any or all property, its income, or its proceeds.

(9) To pay over or apply the proceeds of mortgage and sales of such portion, or all of the property or the income thereof, as may be necessary for the maintenance and support of the dependents of the absentee in military service. If the income from the property of the absentee in military service is not sufficient to pay all of his debts and to provide for the maintenance and support

of his dependents, the receiver may apply to the judge for an order to sell or mortgage so much of the real or personal property as may be necessary therefor. Such sale or mortgage shall be reported to the judge, and if approved and confirmed by the judge, the receiver shall execute the required conveyances or mortgages of such property to the purchaser or lender upon his complying with the terms of sale or mortgage.

(b)   The judge may, in his discretion, by written order, modify, add to, or subtract from the statutory powers granted in this section. (1973, c. 522, s. 6.)

§ 28B-7. Resignation and removal.

(a)   A receiver appointed under authority of this Chapter may resign and his successor be appointed by complying with the provisions set forth in G.S. 36-9 through 36-18.2.

(b)   If, after a receiver has been appointed, it is made to appear to the court upon the filing of a complaint or upon information received that the person appointed as receiver of the estate and property of the absentee in military service is legally incompetent, or that such person has been guilty of default or misconduct in due execution of his office, or that his appointment was obtained by false representation, or that such person has removed himself from this State, the court shall issue an order requiring such person to show cause why his appointment as a receiver should not be revoked. Upon the removal of a receiver of the estate or property of an absentee in military service, the court shall immediately appoint his successor. Pending any suit or proceeding between parties respecting such revocation, the clerk of superior court is authorized to make such interlocutory orders as may tend to better secure the estate and property of the absentee in military service. (1973, c. 522, s. 7.)

§ 28B-8. Termination of receivership.

(a)   At any time upon petition signed by the absentee in military service, or on petition of an attorney-in-fact acting under an adequate power of attorney granted by the absentee in military service, the court shall direct the termination of the receivership and the transfer of all property held thereunder to the absentee in military service or to the designated attorney-in-fact.

(b) If at any time subsequent to the appointment of a receiver it shall appear that the absentee in military service has died and an executor or administrator has been appointed for his estate, the court shall terminate the receivership, certify all proceedings under the receivership to the clerk of superior court, and transfer all property of the deceased absentee in military service held thereunder to such executor or administrator.

(c) When the need for a receivership terminates, the receiver shall promptly file a final inventory and accounting and his application for discharge with the court. If it appears to the court that the inventory and accounting are correct and that the receiver has made full and complete transfer of the assets of the absentee in military service as directed, the court may approve the inventory and accounting and discharge the receiver. If objections to the final inventory and accounting are filed, the court shall conduct a hearing under the same conditions for a hearing on objections to the annual accounting and inventory.

(d) Such discharge shall operate as a release from the duties of the receivership and as a bar to any suit against said receiver or his surety, unless such suit is commenced within one year from the date of discharge. (1973, c. 522, s. 8.)

§ 28B-9. Specific property valued at less than $5,000; summary procedure.

(a) If the spouse of any person defined as an absentee in military service by this Chapter, or his next of kin, if said absentee in military service has no spouse, shall wish to sell or transfer any property of the absentee in military service which has a gross value of less than five thousand dollars ($5,000), or shall require the consent of the absentee in military service in any matter regarding the children of the absentee in military service, or in any other matter in which the gross value of the subject matter is less than five thousand dollars ($5,000), such spouse may apply to the superior court for an order authorizing said sale, transfer, or consent without opening a full receivership proceeding as provided by this Chapter. Said application shall be made by petition on the following form, which form shall be made available to the applicant by the clerk of the superior court:

STATE OF NORTH CAROLINA

_____COUNTY

IN THE GENERAL COURT OF JUSTICE

SUPERIOR COURT DIVISION

In re: (absentee), PETITION FOR SUMMARY APPOINTMENT OF RECEIVER
NOW COMES, (name of petitioner), petitioner in this action, pursuant to G.S._____, and requests the Court that he be appointed a receiver to sell/transfer (describe property) of the value of (value) because (give reasons). Petitioner is_____ years of age, resides at (address) in _____ County, North Carolina, and is the (relation) of (name of absentee) who has been (pow or mia) since (date of notification). The terms of the sale/transfer are (terms). Petitioner requires the consent of the absentee for the purpose of (give reasons).

(Signature)

_____

The above named, _____, being by me duly sworn, says the foregoing petition is true and correct to the best of his knowledge.

_____

Notary Public

My commission expires _____

(b) The court shall, without hearing or notice, enter an order on said petition if it deems the relief requested in said petition necessary to protect the best interest of the absentee in military service or his dependents.

(c) Such order shall be prima facie evidence of the validity of the proceedings and the authority of the petitioner to make a conveyance or transfer property or to give the consent of the absentee in military service in any matter prescribed by subsection (a). (1973, c. 522, s. 9.)

§ 28B-10. Specific property valued at more than $5,000; summary procedure.

(a) If the spouse, or the next of kin if there is no spouse, of any person defined as an absentee in military service under this Chapter shall wish to sell, lease, or mortgage specific property having a gross value of five thousand dollars ($5,000) or more owned by the absentee in military service or in which the absentee has an interest, or take specific action with respect to any interest of the absentee in military service having a gross value of five thousand dollars ($5,000) or more, such spouse may file a complaint with the superior court for an order authorizing the action with respect to such property or interest.

(b) The complaint shall contain all of the information called for by G.S. 28B-2(b) and, in addition, shall contain a description of the specific property or interest and the disposition to be made of it.

(c) The court shall hear evidence on the question of whether the person alleged to be missing or captured is an absentee in military service as defined by G.S. 28B-1 and on the question of whether the action in question should be authorized. Any person interested in such proceedings may intervene with leave of the court.

(d) The court may in its discretion appoint a guardian ad litem to represent the alleged absentee in military service at the hearing.

(e) If, after hearing, the court is satisfied that the person alleged to be an absentee in military service is, in fact, an absentee in military service as defined in G.S. 28B-1, and that the action is in the best interest of the absentee in military service and his dependents, the court shall enter an order appointing the petitioner as receiver for the purposes of the specific action which is the subject of the complaint and authorizing the receiver to take the specific action requested in the complaint. The court shall require the receiver to account for the proceeds of the specific sale, the specific lease, or other specific action. The court may retain jurisdiction of the proceeding to make such further orders as it deems proper.

(f) Such order shall be prima facie evidence of the validity of the proceedings and the authority of the petitioner to take the specific action requested.

(g) Other property of the absentee in military service not the specific subject of the complaint is not affected in any manner by the filing of such complaint as provided for in this section. (1973, c. 522, s. 10.)

Chapter 28C.

Estates of Missing Persons.

§ 28C-1. Death not presumed from seven years' absence; exposure to peril to be considered.

(a) Death Not to Be Presumed from Mere Absence. - In any action under this Chapter, where the death of a person and the date thereof, or either, is in issue the fact that he has been absent from his place of residence, unheard of for seven years, or for any other period, creates no presumption requiring the judge or the jury to find that he is now deceased. The issue shall be decided by the judge as one of fact upon the evidence.

(b) Exposure to Specific Peril to Be Considered. - If during such absence the person has been exposed to a specific peril of death, this fact shall be considered by the judge; or if there be a jury, shall be sufficient evidence to be submitted to the jury. (1965, c. 815, s. 1; 1973, c. 1329, s. 2.)

§ 28C-2. Action for receiver; contents of complaint; parties.

(a) Action for Receiver to Be Instituted in the Superior Court. - If any person having an interest in any property in this State disappears and is absent from his place of residence and after diligent inquiry his whereabouts remains unknown to those persons most likely to know the same, for a period of 30 days or more, anyone who would be entitled to administer the estate of such absentee if he were deceased, or any interested person, may commence a civil action and file a duly verified complaint in the superior court of either the county of such absentee's domicile, or the county where any of his property is situated.

(b) Contents of the Complaint. - The complaint shall contain the following:

(1) The name, age, occupation, and last known residence or address of such absentee;

(2) The date and circumstances of his disappearance;

(3) So far as known, a schedule of all his property within this State, including property in which he has an interest as tenant by the entirety, and other property in which he is co-owner with or without the right of survivorship;

(4) The names and addresses of the person who would have an interest in the estate of such absentee if he were deceased;

(5) The names and addresses of all persons known to the complainant to claim an interest in the absentee's property; and

(6) A prayer, that ancillary to the principal action, a receiver be appointed by virtue of the provisions of this Chapter to take custody and control of such property of the absentee and to preserve and manage the same pending final disposition of the action as provided in G.S. 28C-11.

(c) Parties to the Action. - The absentee, all persons who would have an interest in the estate of such absentee if he were deceased, all persons known to claim an interest in the absentee's property, and all known insurers of the life of the absentee shall be made parties to the action. A guardian ad litem shall be appointed for the absentee, and shall file an answer in his behalf. (1965, c. 815, s. 1; 1973, c. 522, s. 11; c. 1329, s. 2.)

§ 28C-3. Procedure on complaint.

Upon the filing of the complaint referred to in G.S. 28C-2, the judge may for cause shown appoint a temporary receiver to take charge of the property of the absentee to conserve it pending hearing on the complaint. Such temporary receiver shall qualify by giving bond in an amount and with surety approved by the judge and shall exercise only the powers specified by the judge. Within 30 days after the date of his appointment, he shall file an inventory of the property taken in charge. If a permanent receiver is appointed, the temporary receiver shall transfer and deliver to the permanent receiver all property in his custody and control, less such only as may be necessary to cover his expenses and compensation as allowed by the judge, and shall file his final account, and upon its approval be discharged. If the prayer for a permanent receiver is denied, the temporary receiver shall transfer and deliver to those entitled thereto all property in his custody and control less such only as may be necessary to cover his expenses and compensation as allowed by the judge, and shall file his final account, and upon its approval be discharged. If the prayer for a permanent receiver is denied the expenses and compensation of the temporary receiver may in the discretion of the judge be taxed as costs of the action to be paid by the complainant, but if the judge finds that the complaint was brought in good faith and upon reasonable grounds, he may charge such costs against the property of the absentee. (1965, c. 815, s. 1; 1973, c. 1329, s. 2.)

§ 28C-4. Notice to interested persons.

Upon the filing of the inventory by the temporary receiver, the judge shall issue a notice reciting the substance of the complaint and the appointment and action of the temporary receiver. This notice shall be addressed to such absentee, to all persons who would have an interest in the estate of such absentee if he were deceased, to all persons alleged in the complaint to claim an interest in the absentee's property, and to all whom it may concern. It shall direct them to file in the court within a time fixed by the judge a written statement of the nature and extent of the interest claimed in the property, and to appear at a time and place named and show cause why a permanent receiver of the absentee's property should not be appointed to hold and dispose of the property under the provisions of this Chapter. The return day of the notice shall be not less than 30 nor more than 60 days after its date unless otherwise ordered by the judge. (1965, c. 815, s. 1; 1973, c. 1329, s. 2.)

§ 28C-5. Service of notices.

All notices required under this Chapter shall be served on all parties to the action and on all other persons entitled to such notice in the manner now prescribed by Rules of Civil Procedure, and in addition thereto the absentee shall be served by publication once in each of four successive weeks in one or more newspapers in the county where the proceeding is pending, and one copy shall be posted in a conspicuous place upon each parcel of land shown in the temporary receiver's inventory, and one copy shall be sent by registered or certified mail with return receipt requested to the last known address of such absentee. The judge may in his discretion cause other and further notice to be given within or without the county. (1965, c. 815, s. 1; 1973, c. 1329, s. 2; 1981, c. 682, s. 8.)

§ 28C-6. Procedure after notice.

The absentee or any person entitled to notice as provided in G.S. 28C-4 may appear and show cause why a permanent receiver of the absentee's property should not be appointed to hold and dispose of the property under the provisions of this Chapter. The judge may, after the hearing, either dismiss the complaint and order that the property in the custody and control of the temporary receiver be returned to the persons entitled thereto or he may make a finding that the absentee disappeared as of a stated date and appoint a permanent receiver of the absentee's property. (1965, c. 815, s. 1; 1973, c. 1329, s. 2.)

§ 28C-7. Property transferred to permanent receiver by order of judge; filing of inventory; recordation of order of transfer.

Upon the permanent receiver giving bond as required by G.S. 28C-16 and its approval by the judge, the judge shall order the temporary receiver to transfer and deliver to the permanent receiver custody and control of the absentee's property, and the permanent receiver shall file with the court an inventory of the property received by him. A copy of this order as it affects any real property shall be issued by the judge and delivered to the permanent receiver who shall cause the same to be recorded in the office of the register of deeds of each county wherein such real property is situated. (1965, c. 815, s. 1; 1973, c. 1329, s. 2.)

§ 28C-8. Powers and duties of permanent receiver.

The permanent receiver shall under the direction of the judge administer the absentee's property as an equity receivership with the following powers:

(1) To take custody and control of all property of the absentee wherever situated,

(2) To collect all debts due to the absentee and to pay all debts owed by him,

(3) To bring and defend suits,

(4) To pay insurance premiums,

(5) With the approval of the judge in each instance, to continue to operate and manage any business enterprise, farm or farming operations, and to make necessary contracts with reference thereto,

(6) With the approval of the judge in each instance, to renew notes and other obligations, obtain loans on life insurance policies, and pledge or mortgage property for loans necessary in carrying on or liquidating the affairs of such absentee,

(7) With the approval of the judge in each instance, to partition property owned by the absentee and another as joint tenants or tenants in common, with or without the right of survivorship; provided, in the case of property owned by the absentee and spouse as tenants by the entirety, such property may be partitioned only if the absentee's spouse consents in writing to the partitioning, and, in the event of partitioning, one half of the property or proceeds shall belong to the spouse and one half shall belong to the receiver as property of the absentee,

(8) With the approval of the judge in each instance to sell, lease, invest and reinvest any or all property, its income, or its proceeds,

(9) To pay over or apply the proceeds of loans and sales of such portion, or all of the property or the income thereof as may be necessary for the maintenance and support of the absentee's dependents; and if the income from the property of the absentee is not sufficient to pay all his debts and to provide for the maintenance and support of his dependents, the permanent receiver may apply to the judge for an order to sell or mortgage so much of the real or personal property as may be necessary therefor; each such sale or mortgage shall be reported to the judge, and if approved and confirmed by the judge, the receiver shall execute the required conveyances or mortgages of such property to the purchaser or lender upon his complying with the terms of sale or mortgage.

The judge may, in his discretion, by written order modify, add to or subtract from the statutory powers granted in this section. (1965, c. 815, s. 1; 1973, c. 1329, s. 2.)

§ 28C-9. Search for absentee.

The judge shall by order direct the receiver to make a search for the absentee. The order shall specify the manner in which the search is to be conducted in order to insure that, in the light of the circumstances of the particular case, a diligent and reasonable effort be made to locate the absentee. The order may prescribe any methods of search deemed advisable by the judge, but must require, as a minimum, the following:

(1) Inquiry of persons at the absentee's home, his last known residence, the place where he was last known to have been, and other places where information would likely be obtained or where the absentee would likely have gone;

(2) Inquiry of relatives, friends and associates of the absentee, or other persons who should be most likely to hear from or of him;

(3) Insertion of a notice in one or more appropriate papers, periodicals or other news media, requesting information from any person having knowledge of the absentee's whereabouts; and

(4) Notification of local, state and national offices which should be most likely to know or learn of the absentee's whereabouts. (1965, c. 815, s. 1; 1973, c. 1329, s. 2.)

§ 28C-10. Claims against absentee.

Immediately upon the appointment of a permanent receiver under this Chapter, the permanent receiver shall publish a notice addressed to all persons having claims against the absentee informing them of the action taken and requiring them to file their claims under oath with the permanent receiver. If any claimant fails to file his sworn claim within six months from the date of the first publication of such notice, the receiver may plead this fact in bar of his claim. Such notice shall be published in the same manner as that now prescribed by statute (G.S. 28-47) for claims against the estate of a decedent. Any party in interest may contest the validity of any claim before the judge, on due notice given to the permanent receiver and the person whose claim is contested. (1965, c. 815, s. 1; 1973, c. 1329, s. 2.)

§ 28C-11. Final finding and decree.

(a) At any time, during the receivership proceedings, upon application to the judge by any party in interest and presentation of satisfactory evidence of the absentee's death, the judge may make a final finding and decree that the absentee is dead; in which event the decree and transcript of all of the receivership proceedings shall be certified to the clerk of the superior court for any administration as may be required by law upon the estate of a decedent, and the judge shall proceed no further except for the purposes hereinafter set forth in G.S. 28C-12, subdivisions (1) and (4); or

(b) At any time during the receivership proceedings, upon application to the judge by any party in interest and presentation of satisfactory evidence of the absentee's existence and whereabouts, except as provided in G.S. 28C-20, the judge may be decree revoke his finding that he is an absentee, and the judge shall proceed no further except for the purposes hereinafter set forth in G.S. 28C-12, subdivisions (2) and (4); or

(c) After the lapse of five years from the date of the finding of disappearance provided for in G.S. 28C-6, if the absentee has not appeared and no finding and decree have been made in accordance with the provisions of either subsections (a) or (b) above, and subject to the provisions of G.S. 28C-14, the judge may proceed to take further evidence and thereafter make a final finding of such absence and enter a decree declaring that all interest of the absentee in his property, including property in which he has an interest as tenant by the entirety and other property in which he is co-owner with or without the right of survivorship, subject to the provisions of G.S. 28C-8(7), has ceased and devolved upon others by reason of his failure to appear and make claim. (1965, c. 815, s. 1; 1973, c. 1329, s. 2.)

§ 28C-12. Termination of receivership.

Upon the entry of any final finding and decree as provided in G.S. 28C-11, the judge shall proceed to wind up the receivership and terminate the proceedings:

(1) In the case of a decree under G.S. 28C-11, subsection (a), that the absentee is dead:

a. By satisfying all outstanding expenses and costs of the receivership, and

b. By then deducting for the insurance fund provided in G.S. 28C-19 a sum equal to five percent (5%) of the total value of the property remaining for distribution upon settlement of the absentee's estate, including amounts paid to the estate from policies of insurance on the absentee's life, and

c. By then certifying the proceedings to the clerk of the superior court subject to an order by the judge administering the receivership, or

(2) In the case of a decree under G.S. 28C-11, subsection (b), revoking the finding that the missing person is an absentee:

a. By satisfying all outstanding expenses and costs of the receivership, and

b. By then returning his remaining property to him and rendering an accounting for that property not returned; or

(3) In the case of a decree under G.S. 28C-11, subsection (c), declaring that all interest of the absentee in his property has ceased:

a. By satisfying all outstanding expenses and costs of the receivership, and

b. By then satisfying all outstanding taxes, other debts and charges, and

c. By then deducting for the insurance fund provided in G.S. 28C-19 a sum equal to five percent (5%) of the total value of the property remaining, including amounts paid to the receivership estate from policies of insurance on the absentee's life, and

d. By transferring or distributing the remaining property as provided in G.S. 28C-13; and

(4) In all three cases by requiring the receiver's account, and upon its approval, discharging him and his bondsmen and entering a final decree terminating the receivership. (1965, c. 815, s. 1; 1973, c. 1329, s. 2.)

§ 28C-13. Distribution of property of absentee.

The property remaining for distribution in accordance with the provisions of G.S. 28C-12, subdivision (3)d shall be transferred or distributed by the receiver and in accordance with the judge's decree to those persons who would be entitled thereto under the applicable laws of intestate succession as though the absentee died intestate on the day five years after the date of his disappearance as determined by the judge in his final finding and decree; or, if the absentee leaves a document which, had he died, might have been admissible to probate as his will, the judge administering the receivership shall cause citations to issue to all persons entitled to notice upon the probate of wills in solemn form and determine whether the will would have been admitted to probate, and, if it shall be so determined, the transfer and distribution shall be according to the provisions of the document as of the date of the decree under G.S. 28C-12, subdivision (3)d, subject, however, to the right of the spouse of such absentee, or others, to claim whatever property they would have been entitled by law to claim in derogation of the terms of the will as if the absentee had actually died testate on the date five years after the date of his disappearance as determined by the judge in his final finding and decree. (1965, c. 815, s. 1; 1973, c. 1329, s. 2.)

§ 28C-14. Additional limitations on accounting, distribution or making claim by absentee.

If, at the time of the hearing in G.S. 28C-6 wherein a permanent receiver is appointed by the judge after a finding of disappearance as of a stated date, the date of disappearance so found is more than four years prior to the date of such hearing, the time limited for accounting for or fixed for transferring or distributing the property or its proceeds, or for barring actions by or on behalf of the absentee relative thereto, shall be not less than two years after the date of the appointment of the permanent receiver instead of the five years provided in G.S. 28C-11(c).

Provided, however, that the time limited for accounting for or fixed for transferring and distributing any additional property or its proceeds within the State coming into the custody and control of the permanent receiver during such two-year period, or for barring actions by or on behalf of the absentee relative thereto, shall be not more than one year after the expiration of said two-year period. (1965, c. 815, s. 1; 1973, c. 1329, s. 2.)

§ 28C-15. When claim of absentee barred.

No action shall be brought by an absentee to recover any portion of the property which is the subject of this proceeding after a final finding and decree as provided for in G.S. 28C-11(a) or 28C-11(c). (1965, c. 815, s. 1; 1973, c. 1329, s. 2.)

§ 28C-16. Laws of administration of estates applicable.

Except as otherwise provided in this Chapter, the laws of this State applicable to administration of decedents' estates as to the amount and type of bond, inventories, reports, priority of creditors, compensation and court costs shall govern receivers appointed under this Chapter. (1965, c. 815, s. 1; 1973, c. 1329, s. 2.)

§ 28C-17. Appointment of public administrator as receiver for estate of less than $1,000.

Whenever a receiver is to be appointed under this Chapter, and it is found by the judge that the fair value of the estate involved is less than one thousand dollars ($1,000), the judge shall appoint the public administrator as such receiver, if there be one for the county. In case such public administrator is appointed, he shall act as receiver under his official bond as public administrator which shall be liable for any default, and no other bond shall be required. (1965, c. 815, s. 1; 1973, c. 1329, s. 2.)

§ 28C-18. Payment of insurance policies.

(a) At the time of the distribution under G.S. 28C-13 the judge may direct the payment of any sums as they become due on any policies of insurance upon the life of the absentee, to the proper parties as their interest may appear.

(b) If the insurer refuses payment, the judge, upon the finding of appropriate supplemental pleadings in the pending action, shall determine all issues arising upon the pleadings, provided that all issues of fact shall be tried by a jury, unless trial by jury is waived.

(c) Where the required survival of a beneficiary is not established the provisions of this Chapter shall apply as if the proceeds of the insurance were a part of the estate of the absentee, unless the absentee retained no interest in the policy.

(d) If in any proceeding under subsection (b) it is determined that the absentee is not dead and the policy provides for a surrender value, the receiver or an otherwise entitled beneficiary acting through the receiver, may demand the payment of the surrender value or obtain a policy loan. The receiver's receipt for such payment of surrender value shall be a release to the insurer of all claims under the policy. The receiver shall pay over to such beneficiary any money so received, first reserving only an amount allowed by the judge as costs of the proceedings under this section and that amount required by G.S. 28C-12(3)b. (1965, c. 815, s. 1; 1973, c. 1329, s. 2.)

§ 28C-19. Absentee Insurance Fund.

(a) In each case of termination of the receivership, as provided in G.S. 28C-12, subdivisions (1) and (3), the judge shall set aside the sum therein named for the Absentee Insurance Fund and direct its payment by the receiver to the Treasurer of the State, who shall be liable therefor upon his official bond as for other moneys received by him in his official capacity.

(b) The Treasurer shall retain, invest and reinvest all funds thus paid in a separate account entitled the "Absentee Insurance Fund," and add thereto as received the interest or other earnings.

(c) If at any time thereafter, a person declared an absentee whose estate has been distributed under a final finding and decree made as provided in G.S. 28C-13 shall personally appear before the Treasurer and make claim for reimbursement from such fund, the superior court may in an action commenced in the Superior Court of Wake County by such person against the Treasurer, enter a judgment ordering payment to the claimant of such part of the accumulated fund from all sources as in its opinion is found to be fair, adequate and reasonable under the circumstances, taking into account the disposition made of his property, the reasons for his absence, and any other relevant matters.

(d) An action for compensation from the Absentee Insurance Fund shall be begun within three years from the time of the absentee's return. In cases of infancy or other disability recognized by law, persons under such disability shall have one year after the removal of such disability within which to begin the action.

(e) The Treasurer of the State shall from time to time prescribe the rate to be charged for the "Absentee Insurance Fund" under G.S. 28C-12, subdivisions (1) and (3) on the basis of actuarial experience. (1965, c. 815, s. 1; 1973, c. 1329, s. 2.)

§ 28C-20. Provisions applicable to person held incommunicado in foreign country.

As to a person who is known to be held incommunicado in a foreign country, G.S. 28C-1 through 28C-8 and G.S. 28C-10 may be applied as though the person were an absentee within the meaning of this Chapter, and if the person's whereabouts becomes unknown, the other provisions of this Chapter may be applied by such amendments to the pending proceeding as may be required. This section shall not apply to personnel serving in or with the Armed Forces of the United States, the United States Merchant Marine, or the Red Cross during a period of hostilities between the United States and some other power who are listed by the appropriate federal agency as prisoners of war or as missing in action. (1965, c. 815, s. 1; 1973, c. 522, s. 12; c. 1329, s. 2; 2011-183, s. 26.)

§ 28C-21. When agents' acts binding on estate of absentee.

Acts of an agent of an absentee, carried out in good faith, prior to the appointment of a receiver under this Chapter, shall be binding on the estate of such absentee if said acts were within the scope of the agent's real or apparent authority. (1965, c. 815, s. 1; 1973, c. 1329, s. 2.)

§ 28C-22. Provisions of Chapter severable.

If any provisions of this Chapter or the application thereof to any person or circumstances is held invalid, such invalidity shall not affect other provisions or applications of this Chapter which can be given effect without the invalid provision or application, and to this end the provisions of this Chapter are declared to be severable. (1965, c. 815, s. 1; 1973, c. 1329, s. 2.)

Vision Books Order Form

Fax Orders:	1-980-299-5965
Phone Orders:	1-704-898-0770
E-mail Orders:	www.visionbooks.org
Mail Orders:	Vision Books, LLC P.O. Box 42406 Charlotte, NC 28215

Shipp To:
Name_____
Address_____
City_____State_____Zip_____
Phone_____Fax_____
Email_____@_____

Bill To: We can bill a third party on your behalf.
Name_____
Address_____
City_____State_____Zip_____
Phone____(_____)_____Fax_____
Email_____@_____

Pamphlet Number ($15.00 Each)	Qty	Total Cost
_____	_____	_____
_____	_____	_____
_____	_____	_____
_____	_____	_____
_____	_____	_____
_____	_____	_____
_____	_____	_____
_____	_____	_____
<u>Full Volume Set 1-92</u>	<u>92 Pamphlets</u>	<u>1,380.00</u>

Free Shipping Shipping & Handling on Full Volume Orders
Add $1.00 Shipping & Handling per pamphlet $_____

Total Cost $_____

<u>Thank You for Your Support. Management!</u>

DID YOU ENJOY THIS BOOK?

Vision Books would like to hear from you! If you or someone you know has been falsely imprisoned, we would like to hear your story. If the 'North Carolina Criminal Law and Procedure' has had an effect in your life or if you have suggestions, we would like to hear from you. Send your letters to:

Vision Books, LLC
Attn: Staff Writers
P.O. Box 42406
Charlotte, NC 28215
Email: staff@visionbooks.org

Order Additional Copies:

Fax Orders:	1-980-299-5965
Phone Orders:	1-704-898-0770
E-mail Orders:	www.visionbooks.org
Mail Orders:	Vision Books, LLC P.O. Box 42406 Charlotte, NC 28215

www.ingramcontent.com/pod-product-compliance
Lightning Source LLC
Chambersburg PA
CBHW071756200526
45167CB00017B/293